The
Greatest Gift
A Guide to Parenting
from an Islamic Perspective

Muhammad Abdul Bari

Ta-Ha Publishers Ltd.
Unit 4, The Windsor Centre,
Windsor Grove,
West Norwood,
London SE27 9NT
UK

Published Sha'ban 1423/October 2002 by:
Ta-Ha Publishers Ltd.
Unit 4, The Windsor Centre,
Windsor Grove,
West Norwood,
London
SE27 9NT
Tel: +44 208 670 1888
Fax: +44 208 670 1998
E-mail: info@taha.co.uk
Web-site: www.taha.co.uk

By: Muhammad Abdul Bari
General Editor: Afsar Siddiqui
Edited by: Abdassamad Clarke

British Library Cataloguing in Publication Data
Abdul Bari, Muhammad
    Greatest Gift: A Guide to Parenting from an Islamic Perspective, The
I. Title

ISBN   1-84200-044-6 (10-digit).
            978-1-84200-044-1 (13-digit)

Typeset by: Bookwright
Website: http://www.bogvaerker.dk/Bookwright
Email: bookwright@bogvaerker.dk

Printed and bound by: Mega Printing, Turkey
E-mail: msu@mega.com.tr
Web-site: http://www.mega.com.tr

Contents

Contents

Contents

Preface

"If you are planning for a year, plant grain. If you are planning for a decade, plant trees. But if you are planning for a millennium, then plant human beings".

This old saying is extremely relevant to parenting, as young people are the future of any community.

Parenting is an ever-demanding task. With the increasing complexity of modern life this is becoming more challenging. For Muslims living in the West raising children in Islam can be a daunting experience. Although there are exemplary features in the Muslim community regarding child-rearing, unfortunately, Muslim parents in general do not seem to be well-equipped in this respect. Many Muslim parents are either unaware of the depth of the problem or are too simplistic in dealing with their young ones. There was a time when Muslims were best at every good thing under the sun. Over the past few centuries it is unfortunately not the case for many Muslims. However, it is encouraging that there is now a positive realisation in many quarters that good parenting is an obligation they can ill afford to ignore.

There is no doubt that the modern West, after sailing through the turbulent periods of the Renaissance and Reformation, has become an amoral and permissive society. The pull of Jahiliyyah is immense and the younger Muslim generation are caught between two opposing cultures: one at home and the other in the wider society. What have made things difficult for Muslims are their internal weaknesses, 'poor parenting' being a major one. The general ignorance, complacency and indifference of many Muslim parents are disturbing and could be a recipe for the psychological alienation of their children leading to social disaffection and spiritual emptiness. This may already be happening. A significant section of young Muslims seem to be experiencing an erosion of Islamic values and Muslim cultural moorings. As a result, an increasing number of parents are becoming worried, as they think they are 'losing' their children in the sea of modern Jahiliyyah. This, according to some, may lead to an impending crisis for the Muslim community in the West. It depends on how Muslim parents can best stand up to the challenges and address the issue of raising children within the positive ethos of Islam.

Children have their basic rights to receive physical, intellectual and spiritual nourishment from their parents. Parenting is not merely parenthood. It is a dynamic and challenging enterprise. Positive parenting is fundamental to raising children in any community. It is pro-active and responsive, rather than reactive. Islam's approach to life is holistic. That includes the parental responsibility entrusted by Allah. With its transcendental value-system and its crystal-clear focus on life, Islam has its unique way of preparing the younger generation of human beings for their future roles. The hadith that 'no parent can give the child a better gift than good manners, good characters and a good education' puts a heavy burden on parents to invest in their children. Parents are in charge of their children. They are fathers or mothers, educators, mentors, guides and role models to their sons or daughters. In order to perform all these jobs at the same time they have to build relationships with their children on the basis of love, respect and loyalty. After the years of parenting, they have to leave behind that role and become their children's trusted 'friends' in the difficult years of entering adulthood. It is a weighty responsibility, emotionally involved with their future hopes and aspirations. If they mess about with their futures the cost is too high and can rarely be made up, although the gates of Allah's mercy are never closed. Good parenting pays off, in this world and in the Hereafter.

Parenting in the West is complex and thus needs serious attention. It is joyful, enterprising and adventurous as well. Numerous books are available on this subject, but books written from an Islamic perspective are very few indeed. If Muslims want to a) safeguard their Islam, b) build their families and communities and c) work for the common good of humanity in the West, parenting should be brought to the forefront of their agendas. Conscientious members of the Muslim community should start a broader movement of 'positive parenting' without delay. *The Greatest Gift* is my humble contribution in this endeavour to Muslim parents or aspiring parents who would take parenting as a challenge and a mission to help a new generation of human beings grow up according to the model of the right-acting predecessors of Islam.

I have endeavoured to make the book reader-friendly, and not an academic or scholarly one. Neither is it a manual or a handbook. The principle followed is holistic and preventative, rather than piecemeal and curative. Human life is complex and as such there could be many approaches to addressing an issue, depending on cultural or other variations. Unless specified in the Shari'ah, any opinion in the book should be taken in that light and should not be taken as judgmental.

My passion to write this book is to create more awareness in as many Muslim parents as possible. It is an attempt to regenerate the Muslim communities of the West through 'common sense' parenting. This is a 'parent to parent' book, not an 'expert to layperson' one. My credential is my fervent desire to be a better parent. I rely on the forgiveness of Allah for my shortcomings and pray that He accept this humble work.

Organisation of the Book

This book is structured in five Parts, consisting of eighteen Chapters. These Parts are arranged in such a way that the reader can feel at ease by reading them independently or interdependently.

Part One (Chapters one to six) sets the scene of parenting as an obligatory task by clarifying the purpose and mission of life, emphasising the importance of parenthood and parenting, elucidating the danger of 'poor parenting' and spelling out the role of education and training in fostering Muslim personalities among children. This Part could be taken as the theoretical basis of parenting and read independently.

Part Two (Chapters seven to nine) stresses the importance of marriage, family building, forward-planning for parenthood, the shared responsibilities of husband and wife, the need for the Islamic rites and acts of worship and the obligation of nurturing of a young child physically and emotionally in a pleasant home environment.

Part Three (Chapters ten to twelve) explains the challenges of school years, the importance of good schooling, a basic understanding of the school system in the UK and the necessity of sound development through balanced education at school and home.

Part Four (Chapters thirteen to sixteen) deals with the challenges of adolescence in the context of the modern amoral and consumer culture with its numerous social ills, the importance and methods of motivation, the need for parental role-modelling with a view to enthusing children to enter fully prepared into the world of responsibility.

Part Five (Chapters seventeen and eighteen) summarises some of the important aspects of the book and tells that the price of poor parenting and the prize of positive parenting are too obvious in this world. The ultimate success or failure is in the Hereafter. Muslim parents cannot afford to take chances, as a second chance rarely comes.

ACKNOWLEDGEMENTS

This book is the outcome of a long-term involvement in youth and community work in Britain. Many people, including the very young and old, have contributed to the ideas contained in it.

They all deserve my sincere thanks. The decision to write a book on parenting was further enhanced when I came across a respected elder who 'lost' his daughter (mentioned anonymously in Chapter One). I was not sure how to console him at that time. I pray to Allah that no one falls in that situation with their children. The pressure within me to start writing became stronger when I was approached by the Witness Pioneer network, an Internet based virtual organisation, to run a course on some social issues for their virtual school. I made up my mind to run the 'Islamic Perspective of Parenting' course. I am indebted to them for giving me that opportunity through which I learnt a lot while running it. I am also grateful to Dr. Jamil Sharif of Webstar Plc, London, who decided to run the same course on their Salaam web page with additional on-line question and answer facilities. In the same way, my participation in a week-long Facilitator Course on 'Strengthening Families and Strengthening Communities: An Inclusive Parent Programme' by the Race Equality Unit (REU) in London was useful.

I express my deep appreciation for the contribution of my wife, Sayeda, for her understanding, support and her contributions to the writing of the book. In spite of the pressure of life, her excellent family management and sense of humour continuously encouraged me to sit with the computer. I am grateful to our four children, Rima, Raiyan, Labib and Adib for their enthusiasm during the process of writing. Rima and her friend Zakiya, both in their teens, spent time in going through the first draft and making valuable comments from their perspectives as young Muslims.

I am grateful to Dr. Hasan Shaheed and Rumman Ahmed for their valuable comments on the first draft. I am indebted to Ruqayyah Waris Maqsood and Dr. Jameel Qureshi for their invaluable comments and suggestions on the final manuscript. I am also indebted to a number of Ulama of the Islamic Forum Europe for helping me to find references from the Qur'an and books of hadith. May Allah shower His blessings on all of them.

Author's Notes

1. The book is an educational and social one. Although broad Islamic principles are highlighted, it is not meant to be a book of Fiqh. I have followed a broad Islamic principle, i.e., anything not forbidden in Islam is acceptable. The book is about facing the challenges of parenting 'from an Islamic perspective'. It is not meant to be a book of 'Parenting in Islam'.

2. The translations of the Qur'anic verses are based upon *The Meaning of the Glorious Koran* by Mohammed Marmaduke Pickthall and *The Noble Qur'an* by Abdalhaqq and Aisha Bewley.

3. It is established practice among Muslims to mention the supplication ﷺ – peace and blessing be upon him – after the Prophet Muhammad's name and this will be the practice here. Similarly, in the same manner, other prophets' names are followed by ﷽ - peace be upon him – and names of the companions of the Prophet Muhammad ﷺ are followed by ﷺ *radiy'Allahu 'anhu/'anha* – may Allah be pleased be with him/her.

4. This book is written primarily for Muslims in the West.[1] However, most examples are taken from Britain and, specifically, from the South Asian Muslim community. I think this should not jeopardise the common appeal of the book and I hope any reader can benefit from it. I am aware that the nature of this book may lead non-Muslim readers to erroneous view as to how Muslims perceive the West. The attempt to criticise the modern West has been done within a context and as objectively as possible. In the same manner, the East or the Muslim world has been criticised. The purpose is to put forward the best of the two. I apologise if I have failed in that objectivity.

Notes

[1] It is accepted that the word 'West' is not limited within a geographical boundary. "Geographically, the West includes Europe, North America, plus other European settler countries such as Australia and New Zealand. The term is now universally used to refer to what used to be called Western Christendom. Historically, Western civilisation is European

civilisation. In the modern era, North Atlantic civilisation or European-American civilisation is universally referred to as Western civilisation". (*The Clash of Civilisations and the Remaking of World Order, by Samuel P Huntington, pp46-47, US, 1997*).

"The 'West' is a political configuration, a cartel of advanced industrial and post-industrial states that are both capitalistic and secular and, above all, bound together by a strategic alliance with the United States". (Elizabeth Liagin, *Waning of the West: Birth Deficit and Economic Decline, Impact International*, Vol. 31, No. 3, March 2001, London.

An Obligatory Task

Executive Summary

- Modern human beings are lost in a wilderness. From being the 'emissaries' of their Creator on earth we have chosen to be the 'slaves' of the creation. Without prophetic guidance, in belief and action, we are on the path of self-destruction.
- Many of us Muslims, the 'best community' (Qur'an 3:110), have let humanity down in recent centuries by our degeneration on all fronts. Our predicament today has unfortunately made us underdogs in many places.
- The Islamic worldview is based on the concepts of 1) *Tawhid* (unity of Allah), 2) *Risalah* (the message through the prophets) and 3) *Akhirah* (human beings' accountability to Allah and eternal life in the Hereafter).
- Children are a 'trust' or 'test' for human beings from Allah, for the continuation of the human race. They should never be 'unwanted' or a 'burden', even in the most difficult situation.
- The hadith, 'every new born is born in *fitrah* (the natural state or Islam)', tells us of human beings' innocent journey on earth. The concept of children of Adam being burdened with 'original sin' does not have any place in Islam. The proper nurturing of children is important for their success or failure.
- Effective Islamic education that promotes the intellectual and creative exercise of knowledge is vital for the creation of good human beings. Value-free education targeted to

produce good citizens, may be successful in terms of material progress, but enslaves people to their whims and desire.

- As amoral consumerism and sexual permissiveness are embedded in the Western educational system, Muslim children are caught between two opposing cultures and are in danger of losing their identity. Muslims must work hard and forge links to promote a value-rich educational system in the midst of the dominant and uncreative Western educational system.

- The companions of the Prophet Muhammad 鐺 were the best generation in humanity because of their actions. The first three generations of Muslims led a civilisation that liberated human beings from slavery to mini-gods and brought them into slavery to the One: Allah. They were 'monks by night and knights by day'. They created an enviable world on the bases of worship, freedom, justice, accountability and responsibility.

- Muslims today have a civilisational duty to recreate the world mirroring the Prophetic model and in that endeavour we Muslim parents must train our children vigorously to build Muslim character among them.

1. Human Beings are in Loss!

By the declining day, truly the human being is in loss - save those who believe and do good works and exhort one another to truth and exhort one another to endurance. (Qur'an 103: 1-4)

THE PREDICAMENT OF MUSLIM PARENTS

An American Muslim writer, Jeffrey Lang, mentions the agony of a middle-aged Muslim father, Muhammad, in one of his books, *Even Angels Ask*. Muhammad 'lost' his son by the time the young man turned sixteen. "Muhammad was a truly devout Algerian Muslim who had done everything to raise a good Algerian Muslim son. But his son was not an Algerian; he was as American as apple pie, and whatever used to work back in Algeria had failed in America, as it did for so many others". When the writer heard the terrible news from the father, he was shocked like many others and contemplates why it happened. Then this thought gradually settles in his mind and he says to himself, "I was not convinced that he had lost his son, because I was not sure that he had really found him".[1]

Like Muhammad in America, we come across Muslims in the West who are joining the ever-increasing list of parents of 'lost' children. The number seems to be on the increase recently, not because the parental care of children has diminished but because of the perilous metamorphosis the emerging Muslim community is undergoing. Often, parents, especially from immigrant communities, open their hearts in their old age to someone they trust and express their pain and frustration at the 'betrayal' of their grownup sons and daughters. Incidents of bringing 'families into disrepute' by teenage boys and girls spread rapidly in the community only to frighten younger parents, some of whom, afraid of losing their own 'sweeties' in future, begin to 'tighten the grip' on the little ones. Does this work? Where does this lead?

IF I HAD ONLY BEEN A BIT FARSIGHTED

Some time ago, a respected personality in the Asian community invited me to his house. The tone of his voice was new, something I had not heard before. When I knocked at his door, he opened the door with a smile I still remember. I realised he was forcing himself to smile and that brought his inner psychological pains and trauma to the surface. He was not the same jovial person I used to come across every now and then after he 'returned' to Islam from his 'days of ignorance'. I was bewildered for a while. We sat down looking blank, none of us uttering a single word. Suddenly, tiny teardrops appeared in his swollen eyes. He was vividly trying to control his emotion. His cracked voice muttered as if it was coming from a faraway land, "brother can you advise me what to do?"

By that time I had managed to gain some energy and requested him to tell me exactly what had happened. It was similar to stories I have heard a number of times from others. As I was listening to how his daughter had 'finally' parted with him and started living with a non-Muslim man without marrying, the cold sense of unease was running up and down my spine. I am a father too. My children are growing as well. I still remember his monologue, "I don't blame anyone except myself. I was her biological father, but what did I give her except physical nourishment? I myself was ignorant; if only I had been a bit farsighted then!" I was lost for words. There was little I could say to console him - what could I say in that atmosphere! Neither did he expect much from me.

Why should Muslim parents in the West worry so much about their children? Why does the Muslim community feel so vulnerable about their future generation, especially at a time when they are the largest religious minority in some countries and Islam is portrayed as the 'fastest growing' religion on earth? Is it because Islam and the West are incompatible, or is something going wrong with present day Muslims?

The question is: as a universal religion is Islam going to fail its adherents in coping with life in a minority situation, such as in the West? Or, does it mean that Muslims have no other choice but to 'readjust' their religion and assimilate to mainstream Western culture? It would be very naive to think along these lines. Past experience shows that as adherents of a universal *deen* Muslims had no problems living as a minority in any land. Why is it becoming so difficult now? The answer is both historical and religious - while Islam remains a universal *deen* with the power to liberate and uplift a nation, the Muslim ummah has unfortunately degenerated to a condition when we probably cannot now claim to be rightful inheritors of our glorious past. The overall situation of Muslim communities across the world leads some thinkers to question whether Muslims themselves have become like the *Ahl al-Kitab* of the past. On reflection in the mirror of Islam, conscientious Muslims would come to the same conclusion, i.e.,

Muslims are failing, not Islam.

Obviously, for Muslims, the table has turned. While other nations have progressed and some established their material superiority by hard work over the last few centuries, albeit with the help of knowledge and intellectual freedom practised by Muslims in the middle ages, the Muslim world has slid into chaos and disintegration in the last few hundred years.

WESTERN SOCIETY: ITS NATURE AND IMPACT

Western society, especially after the Second World War, has undergone a rapid social transformation that has given rise to material prosperity on the one hand and amoral values and a consumer culture on the other. This has given rise to uncontrolled freedom in sexual behaviour in the society. For a long time women in the West were at the receiving end of society, suffering from inequality and injustice. Some slight redress was only brought about through the brave and courageous struggle of many campaigners. Social and political rights for women were only established in the first half of the 20th century, largely due to commercial pressures demanding that women come into the market as consumers on the one hand and labour on the other. However, in the second half, the campaign to 'liberate' women from male domination and empower them with basic rights was taken over by the proponents of radical feminism who, in their zeal, are, in fact, doing a disservice to women. While western women feel they have made quite a lot of progress in many areas of life, the social pressure on them to conform to modernity has made them vulnerable to exploitation.

Society consists of men and women. The progress of any society depends on the progress of both sexes. Have women got their equitable share in the West? The answer is - better than before, but not exactly. Even after half a century of campaigning for women's rights they are still discriminated against in many places. Most importantly, they have become losers in their womanhood. The pressure on them to accept social demands, mostly set by men, and in particular men in the marketing and advertising industries, is tremendous. They are encouraged to dress, work and adopt lifestyles promoted by these men. They have to look attractive, work harder than men and, in many instances, live as single mothers, because men often tend to abdicate their responsibility.

Marriage, as an institution, is fast losing its significance. 'Living in sin' is no longer treated as a sin. The overt caricatures of and animosity towards divinely ordained values and the promotion of moral relativism and permissiveness are taking their toll. The proliferation of the consumer culture and the entertainment industry is eating away at the spirit of innocence among the youth. Some are involved in addiction to drugs, alcohol and in petty crime. Many children are losing their childhood in broken families. The display of erotic advertisements in public places, the mass circulation of pornographic tabloids and what previously would have been 'censored' films on television and cinema screens are inviting people towards a more self-indulgent way of life. The glorification of extramarital sex and the practice of homosexuality are taken without ambivalence. They have become the essential ingredients of modernity and progress. In the wake of this proselytising force most in the society have, regrettably, taken a defensive strategy.

The seeds of this wrongdoing were strategically sown by a few, professionally nurtured and scientifically presented as the panacea for material progress. Many of those seeds have now grown into trees and are bearing the fruit of moral erosion, disintegration of family-structure, paedophilia and even worse They are now multiplying and becoming widespread, thanks to the proselytising power of globalisation. Promotion of vulgarity is now very skilfully done, directly or indirectly, through innovative creativity. The allurements of free sex, the strenuous effort by a hardcore minority to present homosexuality as a natural 'sexual orientation', and present female models as nothing more than 'sex objects' causes a further proliferation of the evil, destroys 'family bonding' and contributes to eventual social disintegration. Society is changing to such an extent that the sort of behaviour that would have dumbfounded people a few decades ago is now being taken as the norm.

THE MUSLIM PREDICAMENT

In this climate, the first generation of Muslim immigrants have undergone immense psychological upset in adjusting to the 'alien' environment of the West. On the other hand, later generations of Muslims are struggling hard to cope with the two 'opposing' worlds - the traditional inward-looking 'cultural Islam' on one hand and the highly materialistic, developed and complex Western lifestyle on the other. The small indigenous Muslim community in each Western country is struggling to contribute toward a positive image of Islam. The prevailing educational system of the West, based on a secular view of the world, and the social pressure to engage in self-indulgence are having an impact on Muslim youth.

It is now acknowledged that a section of children born to Muslim parents in the West may be falling into a pit of social, moral and spiritual disorientation. It is not surprising if some of them turn away from the great teachings of Islam in their behaviour and practice. A couple of decades ago it would have been difficult to believe this, but the reality is now haunting Muslim parents and social thinkers. The social and religious anchors that kept the Muslim community at an enviable advantage can only slacken if Muslim parents do not take a pro-active stance in guiding their children. Already there are reports of underachievement among Muslim youth in education. Bangladeshi and Pakistani children, most of whom are Muslims, achieve low grades in the GCSE[2] Fewer of them study degrees in the universities[3]. As a result of underachievement in education and other factors, unemployment rates among them, on the basis of ILO definition, are high[4]. This has left them with their average household savings very low[5]. The latest major research carried out by the Policy

Studies Institute (PSI) in London paints a depressing picture of Bangladeshi and Pakistani communities in Britain[6].

The increased use of drugs and involvement in gangsterism and crime among a section of Muslim youth are also causing concern in many Western cities. The summer 2001 riots in some cities of northern England have also further exposed the problems faced by Muslim youth, although there are complex religious and socioeconomic factors, including racist provocation from far-right groups, behind these callous events, Muslims need to ask themselves whether their youth are able to maintain proper Islamic *adab* while expressing their frustration and anger. Some soul searching among the parents and community leaders is needed.

The rise in the number of Muslims in Britain's prisons is another area that is creating anxiety within the Muslim community and the Prison service. Every community has its share of criminality, but it needs serious thinking and hard work when a community has a disproportionate share in it. The *Times* in London wrote on September 13, 1999 that,

> For the ones left behind, however, the prospects are dire. Their parents, often deeply conventional, are ill equipped to differentiate between a child yielding to the natural temptations of teenage western culture and a juvenile delinquent in the making. Rebellion against the security, which their families, cultures and traditions offered, may help to foster a gang mentality, above all in those without the skills needed to get more than a menial job. Falling between the stools of immigrant communities and British society, many land up in prison.

The *Independent* in London commented on January 10, 2000,

> Amid one of the country's most conservative Muslim areas, arrests for dealing in and using hard and soft drugs have tripled in four years.

Although Muslims constitute less than 3% of the British population, they now make up about 7% of Britain's more than 65,000 prison inmates[7]. The appointment of a Muslim prison adviser is evidence of this problem. In recent years Muslims have come across the presence of 'gay Muslims' in Britain, some of whom are even reported to be promoting homosexuality within the Muslim community. It is difficult to know whether this irreligious trend among Muslims is a matter of fashion or conviction. Whatever the number, it is better to be aware of the menace so that necessary precautions can be taken. Parents and community leaders should be well aware that powerful secular-liberal 'evangelists' are looking for more converts from among Muslims to weaken the very foundations of Islam.

THE THREAT

With unfortunate ignorance and passivity shown by many Muslims and complacency and indifference by the intelligentsia, the sense of frustration may spread within the Muslim community and the younger generation may have to pay a high price. In a social climate of sexual indulgence and moral permissiveness, young Muslims find it difficult to cope with the prevalent youth culture and grow up as sound Muslims. Due to environmental factors and possibly the lack of proper teaching of Islam there is a trend towards a weakening in practice of Islam among young people[8]. Western society is equipped to deal with its own social ills, albeit with the secular model, and has created some safety-nets for its own 'problem kids'. It is true that Muslim youth have the same right to use these facilities as everyone else, but, are Muslims equipped to create their own culturally-sensitive safety-nets for those youth who need material support and Islamic nourishment? Not yet. For this they need forward-planning, organised effort and dedicated people, which are all generally lacking at the moment.

It is time the Muslim community accepts that there are potential dangers ahead. Muslims cannot afford to behave like ostriches with their heads in the sand pretending nothing is happening. The real battleground for Muslim communities in Western countries and elsewhere is now the eradication or reduction of poverty, poor housing, educational underachievement, racialism, Islamophobia and discrimination. Muslims have become used to getting a bad press in the West. What we specifically need today is to build dynamic communities, mosques being centre-stage in our lives. Community mosques led by tolerant, educated imams and management committees should be able to engage the young and the old in order to address the specific needs of the community. Certainly this requires good leadership with honesty and Islamic virtues, far from corruption and complacency.

Muslims, like many other minority communities in the West, face a challenging future. With racism and Islamophobia alive in most Western countries, many young Muslims lack confidence and self-esteem. They are growing up confused and torn by conflicting emotions, some deeply sure of their identity. We may come across students of Muslim origin in school and university campuses, who feel embarrassed when they are greeted with the basic Islamic greeting, 'As-salamu 'alaikum' (peace be on you). Some even feel unease in identifying themselves as Muslims. Others are even perplexed with their Islamic names. Their numbers may be insignificant, but they represent a section that is growing who have doubt and uncertainty in their lives.

Muslims in the West are a significant minority. In some countries they are officially acknowledged as such. In most countries remarkable work is going on to promote faith and community harmony. Many Muslim bodies are trying hard to portray a sound picture of Islam to non-adherent Muslims and non-Muslims. In spite of all the difficulties, Islam still dominates Muslim cultural life and is the centre of life for the majority of Muslims. It is also heartening that many in the younger generation are rediscovering their roots in Islam and trying to assert their identity as Muslims, although they may be lacking in proper knowledge and understanding of Islam. While these are commendable, there is no room for complacency. With downward social and religious trends in the wider society, a big worry haunts them - how many generations will it take for them, like others, to be assimilated into the melting pot of secular culture? The question is a major one.

2. Children: A Divine Gift or an Unwanted Burden?

Our Lord, give us comfort in our spouse and children and make us a good example for those who ward off (evil). (Qur'an 25:74)

Too Many People on Earth!

When the high profile birth of the world's 'six billionth' child in Bosnia reached the media on 12th October 1999, there was a mixture of fun and apprehension in various camps. It was a media event designed to publicise the campaign against population growth in the world. Those who are engaged in the movement for worldwide population control took the opportunity of painting a disturbing picture of an imminent disaster on the globe. In their myopic worldview these 'hordes of humans multiply at astronomical speed in geographical dustbins', whereas, 'historically important nations' are struggling to survive in terms of human reproduction. Unfortunately, they are the people who possess disproportionate wealth and wield unparalleled power in the world. It is now widely known that, in their camp, a few hundred billionaires, mostly from the US, exercise colossal financial and political muscle in the modern world. Likewise, some five hundred corporations in the US, Europe and Japan control more than three quarters of the world's volume of Foreign Direct Investment and half of world trade.

The *Independent* of London once came up with data that suggested, "across the world, real incomes have risen sixfold in the last one hundred years, but they are distributed more unfairly than ever". The brutal reality is that the North Atlantic countries have most of the world's wealth, while people in the poorer nations live under the poverty level. This unfortunate north-south divide of the planet is undermining the fabric of human society. It is not surprising that these developed countries, most of which were colonial powers in the past, have the lowest rates of population growth ever. It looks certain that population growth is inversely proportional to the economic growth of a country in modern time. In some western countries, e.g., the UK, deaths will exceed births by 2027[9], because the birth rate per 1000 has decreased[10], and abortion for all ages has risen over the decades[11]. The question raised by some champions of the West looks simplistic - as two hundred and fifty babies are known to be born every minute, can the world cope with so many people? They are unfortunately like intolerant passengers on a train who always try to block new people entering their compartment for fear of lack of space or loss of comfort.

As the population growth of the developed countries is either stagnant or in decrease, they see, in the population rise of 'other nations', their own eventual decline and loss of power. It is now an open secret that their massive campaign for worldwide population control is more to do with the politics of containing numbers than feeding people from their mountainous food reserves. This stems from a very materialistic and narrow view of life in which greed and selfishness override principles of human equity.

THE STORY OF POPULATION CONTROL

When the Reverend Thomas Malthus wrote an essay on the *Principle of Population* in 1798 saying that world population would always grow more quickly than the food supply and thus lead to increased poverty and vice, the main impulse for worldwide population control was given. Charles Darwin took this up a century later in his The Descent of Man, in 1891 and he even wrote:

> Thus the weak members of civilised societies propagate their kind. No one who has ever attended to the breeding of domestic animals will doubt that this must be highly injurious to the race of man.

The twentieth century global campaign of population control was given momentum by two women across the Atlantic, Marie

Stopes in England and Margaret Sanger in America. With the advent of the 'Sexual Revolution' after the Second World War, the campaign for 'population control' has entered a new phase. There is now disparity in population growth between the developed countries of the West and the underdeveloped countries in the rest of the world. The latter have much higher annual rates of population increase than the former[12].

'Population control' has now a 'humane' face in the name of 'family planning' and is pushed by the UN onto its member countries. It is not difficult to imagine who set the UN agenda on this. There are donors and there are receivers. All are equal, 'but some are more equal than others'. Those who are at the receiving end of economic misery are obliged to follow the 'international norms' in everything, including family life. The UN conferences on this issue in Cairo, Beijing and New York, are now milestones in the UN's effort to disseminate the idea of 'women empowerment', which they think would lower population growth. The psychological pressure is so great that even a massive developing country, and ironically a veto power, like China has adopted a 'one child per family' policy, which has, in effect, given rise to widespread infanticide. This is reminiscent of the inhuman practices of pre-Islamic Arabia in which baby girls were buried alive or mercilessly killed, albeit for different reasons.

ISLAM'S VIEW ON POPULATION ISSUE

This is not to argue that there should not be any planning of family for otherwise parents would keep on producing child after child, irrespective of the mother's health or whether they could rear and educate the youngsters properly. This is an issue that every sensible parent feels important. But what people in the developing world object to is the coercive nature and politicisation of the subject. In this issue the questions that should come first are: how should human beings value the arrival of babies in this world and what place do they have in a planet belonging to all?

Life, in Islam, is a covenant from Allah, and a divine gift. Every human being is unique and thus valued. Life in itself is a miracle from Allah, a mixture of body and spirit. To parents who crave for a child and suffer from the tragedy of barrenness, this has a special meaning. Modern genetic engineering's continuing success in identifying the singular characteristics of individual human beings testifies to the complexity and marvellous nature of life. Life is an interwoven pattern of characteristic features. Life is beautiful, varied and wonderful. With extraordinary unity in its meaning and purpose, it is unmistakably well-defined. No two human beings are the same; even identical twins have singular features of their own.

Life starts from Allah's love for creation. A tradition of the Prophet Muhammad ﷺ mentions that of Allah's mercy He retained for ninety nine parts for His believing slaves on the Last Day, and the remaining part He distributed among His creation in this life. Mercy is at the heart of biological continuity. Human beings cannot create life; it is only at Allah's discretion, but Allah has given them the ability to participate in His creative process through sexual intercourse. One of the fascinating things about human beings and other animals is their love for their offspring. Allah, in His infinite wisdom, created man and woman as a pair and blessed them with love between them. Children are the products of a physical union in which love should be at the heart in the man-woman relationship. Those who are ignorant about Allah's design on earth have stooped to lowness in their thinking that human reproduction is purely biological and thus merely fun.

It is this love from the divine fountain that has created passionate feelings and emotions between human beings. The love that exists among other creatures is also drawn from this unimaginably huge, and in fact infinite, reservoir. Who need to be reminded about their mother's love for them? A Russian proverb tells that a 'mother's love will draw up from the depths of the sea'. The following incidents which occurred during the time of the Prophet Muhammad ﷺ are both inspiring and illuminating.

The Prophet's wife A'ishah, may Allah be pleased with her, narrated that a poor woman came to her with two little girls. 'I gave them three dates to eat. She gave one date to each of her daughters and raised the third toward her mouth to eat. The daughters finished their share and were looking at her. She divided her date and gave them a piece each.' (A'ishah) said, 'I was quite surprised at the incident. I told the story to the Prophet ﷺ. The Prophet ﷺ said, 'Allah has decided the Garden (saved her from the Fire) for this'. (Al-Bukhari and Muslim)

Abu Hurayrah ؓ narrated: 'I heard the Messenger of Allah ﷺ saying, "Allah divided mercy into one-hundred parts and He kept ninety-nine parts with Him and sent down one part on the earth, and because of that single part His creation are merciful to each other, so that even the mare lifts its hoofs away from its baby animal, lest it should trample on it."' (Sahih al-Bukhari)

Usamah ibn Zayd ؓ said: 'The Messenger of Allah ﷺ used to put me on (one of) his thighs and put al-Hasan ibn 'Ali on his other thigh and then embrace us and say, "O Allah, please be merciful to them as I am merciful to them."' (Sahih al-Bukhari)

THE GIFT OF CHILDREN

Children are gifts from Allah and the parental craving for children is universal. Couples having difficulty in conceiving, because of infertility or some other reasons, often fail to come to terms with reality and some become psychologically distraught and even schizophrenic. They are the people who can comprehend the meaning of parenthood. People often overlook the emotional and impulsive reasons behind a woman's decision to go for a test-tube baby. Although many 'modern' men and women tend to ignore the divine will behind the mystery of creation, they are puzzled by the complexity, yet harmony and balance, in nature.

> **The kingdom of the heavens and earth belongs to Allah. He creates whatever He wills. He gives daughters to whoever He wishes; and He gives sons to whoever He wishes or He gives them both sons and daughters; and He makes whoever He wishes barren. Truly He is All-Knowing, All-Powerful. (Qur'an 42:49-50)**

Every soul on earth has to perish. This is the only truth that everybody is forced to admit. But human beings are born with the inner desire to live longer and live on, if possible, in their progeny. This desire is alive in the hearts of all, from kings or dictators to ordinary people in the street. The history of warfare and the rise and fall of empires - all point to the fact that human beings try to live longer through their progeny. As such, children are a test for their parents.

> **Beautiful for humankind is love of the joys (that come) from women and offspring, and stored-up heaps of gold and silver, and horses branded (with their mark), and cattle and land. That is the comfort of the life of the world. Allah, with Him is a more excellent abode. (Qur'an 3:14)**

> **Know that your wealth and children are a trial and that there is an immense reward with Allah. (Qur'an 8:28).**

> **You, who believe! Do not let your wealth or children divert from the remembrance of Allah. Whoever does that is lost. (Qur'an 63:9)**

CHILDREN AS A 'TRUST' AND A 'TEST'

A child is a Trust from Allah. With the joy of parenthood come trial, temptation and test. Excessive and blind love for children leads to unfairness, injustice and tyranny. It also brings ruination to the children themselves. Failure in parental responsibility is one of the worst betrayals in the eyes of Allah.

> **You, who believe! Do not betray Allah and His Messenger, and do not knowingly betray your trusts. (Qur'an 8:27)**

Children can raise the status of parents in the Hereafter when their rearing and care are entered into for the sake of Allah alone. Mothers bear them in their wombs, sacrificing their comfort and undergoing physical and psychological discomfort for over nine months. Then, after their birth, parents bear the burden of rearing them, vulnerable and completely dependent beings, for so many years. They love, sacrifice, compromise and rearrange their lives according to the needs of these tiny creatures. They do these willingly with contentment and bright smiles on their faces. All the pains of their hard work and stress evaporate with one innocent smile from the baby.

Muslim men and women know the meaning of life. Their love for children is not blind. They put food into their children's mouth and, in the same way, feed them with spiritual nourishment. They teach them to grow up as 'Muslims', obedient and willing slaves of Allah. Their 'parenting' encompasses all that is good for their children in the world and in the Hereafter. This raises their status in the eyes of Allah. In this mundane world they are blessed with tranquillity and pleasure in life; in the eternal world they will see the fruits of good parenting.

> A slave will have his rank raised and will say: 'O my Lord how has this come about for me?' He will say: 'Through your sons after you, seeking forgiveness for you.' (*Ahmad* and *Ibn Majah*)

> When the son of Adam dies his actions are cut off except for three: A continuing sadaqah or some knowledge from which benefit is derived or a right-acting son who makes supplication for him.' (*Muslim, Ahmad*)

In order to pass the test in their parenthood Muslim fathers and mothers must plan for their families. The Islamic view on 'planning for the family' is guided by:

- the general encouragement to have children and
- the necessity to safeguard mothers' health and raise the children properly

This needs planning, preparation and a determined effort to establish a right-acting family from the moment a man and woman decide to marry. Educated parents with sound knowledge of Islam understand the necessity of gaps between pregnancies. They are also frightened to limit the number of children just for fear of poverty or for any other selfish reason.

3. Nature or Nurture?

That man can have nothing but what he strives for; that (the fruit of) his striving will soon come in sight; then will he be rewarded with a reward complete. (Qur'an 53:39-41)

FISH OUT OF WATER!

Many millions of Muslims now live in the West in the midst of a culture that is often not compatible with Islamic values. The West itself has transformed by leaps and bounds, especially after the Second World War. For centuries the worldview of the Islamic civilisations and the West had difficulties in adjusting with each other. With the decline of religious influence in the West and intellectual stagnation in the Muslim world, the gap has widened. Many Muslims, disadvantaged in their homelands and affected by post-colonial uncertainties, have settled in relatively affluent Western cities and are finding themselves caught up in the complexities of modern Western life. To many it is an abode of uncertainty, the life of a 'fish out of water'. The situation of the native East European and Balkan Muslims is rather painful in the wake of the colossal tragedy that befell them in the last decade. Converted Muslims constitute a significant proportion in some countries, but they have their specific disadvantages and are yet to form an influential entity. They are finding their life not less difficult than others in their own homeland.

PLANTS IN A POT

A highly educated immigrant Muslim professional couple once told me about their two university-going children in voices filled with resentment and resignation. Their resentment emanated from a longtime observation of the 'unsocial behaviour' of their own children and the children of their friends. What is wrong with these young people? They mentioned that the children would never on their own come down from their rooms and talk to their family friends, who were mostly from their country of origin. Whenever there was any family guest they would withdraw into their small rooms. They said that they had now resigned themselves to the fact and adjusted themselves to the apathy and indifference of their children toward their own 'roots'. At the end of the discussion, they sounded a bit philosophical, "we are a displaced people with our roots neither here nor there. Our children are like uprooted plants struggling to survive in a new pot".

I am not sure whether their observation is accurate. Even if it is, do plants not survive in hostile environments, if proper care is taken? As far as human beings are concerned, we are not only capable of adaptation but are also able to influence events in extreme difficulties, if we really want. What really matters is our iman in Allah and high expectation of Him, and our physical and intellectual fitness and stamina. Of course, not everybody or every nation can manage to survive and sustain themselves in hostile environments. Muslims, in the various high points of history, not only survived and sustained themselves in new lands, but also displayed exemplary human and Islamic qualities, so much so that they were able to change hearts and influence history. They either lived in harmony without any fear for their future or welcomed the indigenous people into the common brotherhood of Islam within a few generations. What led to their successes in those periods of history and why do present-day Muslims think that they are failing now?

Here arises the issue of the enormous responsibility of Muslim parents in Western society. This is a divine task, a strategic and visionary one for all Muslim parents. I would rather call it a civilisational duty. We have twin tasks or missions in our lives, which we need to take passionately on board or else, we will face severe consequences in future. On the one hand, we have to quickly improve our adaptability, adjust to the minority status we enjoy in the environment of the West and work for the common good of the society without compromising basic Islamic principles, and on the other, we have to undertake the great burdens of raising our children on the prophetic model so that they can become witnesses for the Truth in the society.

EARLY SHOCK OF SCHOOLING

I personally know of some South Asian parents who, at some stage in their lives, took the painful decision to pack up and leave Britain. They planned to live in their countries of origin, especially in the ages when their children started going to the Junior Schools (8-11 years) in the UK. Why? Most of them mentioned that they had been "shocked" with the dismal, "so what", "I don't care", behaviour and attitude of their young ones. They realised that suddenly these young people had turned into 'monsters'. That, they complained, was due to the twin effects of schooling and watching TV. One of them grudgingly mentioned that TV, to him, was a 'Terrible Virus' that enters into the minds of the youth and destroys their innocence.

Could these parents settle in their countries of origin with their children? Unfortunately, not. The worst that happened to those who took the daring decision to go back was the damage done to their children's careers, and their whole futures. After spending some years in their own countries they came back to Britain, each with different sad stories. In the meantime, the children had lost the most vital periods of their education. The problem is that if parents fail to take care of their beloved ones in their formative periods and blame the system, the outcome is obviously a failure.

PARENTING: A MONUMENTAL TASK

Parenting is an enormous job. It demands emotional, psychological and spiritual maturity. It combines the jobs of parent, teacher, mentor and spiritual guide. Providing the child with decent food, clothing and shelter is the minimum. Parenting is much more than that. It is a life process and, as such, a learning one for parents as well. Here an adult human being becomes directly responsible for another individual, however small, and helps develop a new life, full of challenge. No educational institution can ever provide the direct training for parenthood in the way that the practical life experience of being a parent demands. Letting children grow into men or women is the essence of parenting.

Of course, parents have limitations and as such cannot be 'perfect' in their rearing children. No parent will be caught ought on the Day of Judgement for unintentional weakness in rearing and educating their children, as human beings are born with natural frailties.

Allah desires to make things lighter for you. Human being was created weak. (Qur'an 4:28).

But, parents need to be better aware that on their weak shoulders rest the burdens of raising 'human beings', Allah's emissaries on earth. As they start the journey to parenthood, a new family emerges and gradually pushes aside the existing family. The family becomes the microcosm of the community, a wider world, where duties and responsibilities need to be exercised in accordance with the commands of Allah. Love, passion, compromise, sacrifice and other human features tie the members of the family together with a sense of purpose. The family is a small unit of a society or a nation in any civilisation. In Islam, the duties and responsibilities are overriding and well-defined. The Prophet Muhammad ﷺ has mentioned

Everyone of you is a shepherd and every one is responsible for what he is shepherd of. (Sahih al-Bukhari and Muslim)

Parenthood is a creative struggle to accommodate a newcomer in a world where everything needs to be shared in the family. It is a journey through new experiences that leads to the increased maturity and the accountability of the parents. The journey is one-way, full of bends, curves, and ups and downs. But it is the sense of consciousness that makes parenting a lively, challenging and enjoyable enterprise. Positive parenting requires a determined and planned effort. Serious and honest parents acknowledge their shortcomings, learn through the process and endeavour to disseminate the same to their children. As time passes, life rolls on and one set of parents are replaced by another, who were themselves once children. This cycle of parenthood continues till the end of the world.

Parenthood is a historic journey that brings challenges and rewards in one's life. At the start of a journey all parents are expected to know their destination and how they are going to reach there. The destiny of Muslim parents is exalted, i.e., preparing their children for a great role as emissaries of Allah on earth, the way is in the prophetic models. Life is vast and as such fathers and mothers must complement and share their responsibilities so that children get the best of their nurturing. Confusion or lack of planned efforts in this process will end up in tears and failure, for both parents and children.

Parenting could be the most pleasurable and worthwhile engagement in life. But planning and preparation are fundamental for that pleasure. 'If you fail to prepare; prepare to fail'. Teachers who want to succeed in providing the curriculum in a disciplined and safe environment, have to spend a considerable amount of time in preparing and planning their lessons. Likewise, a parent's long-term plan is absolutely vital for the development of children's physical, intellectual, moral and spiritual life. We all subconsciously do some planning in our life, but most often ignore that in bringing up our children. Those who plan, are rewarded in the end.

'The hand that rocks the cradle rules the world'. Nations that cater for the proper nourishment and development of their children outperform others. The existing generation passes on its historical and civilisational heritage to the new generation which, in turn, does the same for future generations. This is the desired continuity and those who can maintain this with enthusiasm and efficiency, keep their elevated position on earth. Those who fail lose out.

Positive Parenting: A Creative Endeavour

The importance of positive parenting, cannot be overemphasised. Plants in the nursery and children in the home and school 'nursery' have striking similarities. The culmination of a plant is a healthy tree with flowers and fruit. Similarly, the culmination of a child is a successful human being, a fully balanced person. Islam is an opportunity for all human beings to grow up as responsible emissaries of Allah on earth. In that respect, parenting is a divine responsibility. As uncared for or less-cared for plants normally grow with deformity, children with little or no parental care can grow up with psychological deformities and distorted lifestyles. Parental care does not simply mean providing children with good food, dress, shelter and emotional support. It includes proper education and the inculcation of good behaviour towards other human beings and the entire creation. Those who create havoc in society and become menaces to humanity are generally known to have had unfavourable upbringings.

Here the question of 'nature' and 'nurture' arises. What about genetically determined characteristics in children that are thought to influence or limit their abilities to learn? Is a human being's fate genetically destined? This is a wider religious and philosophical question. Islam has a clear teaching on it, but this is not relevant in this discussion. Whatever the argument, these questions should not mar the issue of rearing the children through positive parenting, or else, the whole purpose of education will be meaningless. While genetic influence has an important place in children's lives, acquired features dominate their external and functional behaviour. In a causal world human beings need to concentrate on what they can achieve through their efforts and build where they are. We are not responsible for failure when we have tried our best. According to Islam, Allah will reward us for our effort.

ACQUIRED OR NATURAL?

A teacher was teaching Genetics in a Science lesson. Before starting the lesson, she hurriedly wrote on the board, 'make a list of the acquired and natural characteristics found in human beings'. The handwriting was not that clear. So, pupils ignored it. After the rollcall when the teacher read what she wrote on the board and asked them whether they have finished the list, everyone was quiet. It was a bit unusual. She then asked the question again.

Suddenly one of the pupils, known in the class to be very blunt, spoke up from the corner. He said, 'Miss, I understand now. The natural features are – colour of hair, tongue rolling, ...err... and the acquired qualities are ...O, yes, good handwriting'. The whole class burst out in laughter.

One can raise the issue of societal influence, especially when prevailing social norms have overwhelming influence on its members. This definitely has its effect in raising children. In an environment where moral permissiveness and sexual promiscuity are encouraged, the effect of good individual parenting may be small. In such situations, the West African proverb, 'evil enters like a needle and spreads like an oak tree', probably holds true. As human beings are social, the tide of amoral social norms may temporarily wash away many values.

But giving up is an affront to human potential and dignity. It is true that people are susceptible to natural weaknesses. It is also true that general pessimism can creep in a negative social environment, but human beings have the ability to overcome mountainous obstacles provided they have iman in Allah, commitment and physical stamina. History has shown that those who were determined to face the challenges, succeeded even in extreme hardship. However, those who easily give up are sidelined by the wave of adversity. As human beings, passive reaction to any historic obligation and resorting to fatalism are reprehensible. It is obvious that infectious diseases transmit faster, but health does not. Likewise, social ills have the capacity to spread quickly among people, but, at the same time, goodness has its universal appeal. Thus, as a new emerging community, Muslims need to learn how best they can cope in those situation and effectively deal with those ills. They have the opportunity to interact with others and collectively fight the common evils in the society. Human beings need reminder and encouragement for common good.

Positive parenting is essentially a way of engaging the younger generation to create a better future for all. Like any constructive endeavour it is an uphill task for which parents have to plan. Children, with their dynamic and creative features, are their partners. Virtue is the collective property of human beings and it needs nourishment for its survival and growth. Positive parenting can effectively sow the seed of virtue in a society. The rest is with Allah.

4. Watch over the Fire!

O you who believe! Safeguard yourselves and your families from a Fire whose fuel is people and stones. (Qur'an 66:6)

FIGHTING THE FIRE IS A HUGE JOB

This verse above has the essence and meaning of the divine responsibility laid upon Muslims, i.e., enjoining good and forbidding evil in the society in which they live. It is their social obligation to those with whom they have close links. As children are the closest in one's life, this has direct implications and special significance for them. Parental duty is at the heart of Muslim life. For a sound and healthy continuity of the civilisational legacy every parent has to transfer the spirit and broad message of Islam to their offspring. If an individual parent cannot cope with this great and demanding task for some reason, the community has to create such a network such that nobody in the ummah falls through the net. Like any other community, there will definitely be some weakened and even lapsed 'Muslims'. But the rest should not leave them alone, and the wider community should endeavour to establish the necessary infrastructure to lend them support. For an individual Muslim parent home is an immense obligation. However, it is a collective and mutual accountability from which nobody can pull out. Although, according to Qur'an, nobody bears the burden of others nor are they burdened with unbearable burdens, individual human beings have a wider responsibility involving their families and communities, their nations and humanity in general.

...What each soul earns is for itself alone. No burden-bearer can bear another's burden. (Qur'an 6:165)

25

Allah does not impose on any self any more than it can stand. (Qur'an 2:286)

This is a divine mercy for human beings.

Family, in the Islamic context, is far wider than the so-called modern 'nuclear family' or even the extended family. The Qur'anic term *ahl* or 'family' can mean 'people of the same faith' or 'comrades'. In practical day-to-day life it means people close to oneself - relatives through blood or marriage, neighbours, dependants, friends, colleagues, etc. It includes people who share one's race, tribe, culture and faith. As a result, the Muslim responsibility for their 'family' is immense, one that encompasses their life-mission.

HUMAN BEINGS AS SOCIAL BEINGS

The human being's solitary arrival on and departure from earth is from a divine decree, but children's arrival is linked with the two caring and loving people who passionately expected the new arrivals and provided them with support and nourishment from impulsive emotion and unfathomable love. The relationship between parents and children is at the heart of a family. This then broadens and encompasses brothers, sisters, uncles, aunts and others. That is why, in any society, the closest in blood have more right over the others. The old saying, 'human beings are social beings', represents a fundamental precept of human obligation toward each other, as well as human longing to live a communal life. Psychologically, people could be loners or bent on individualism, but that does not take the social responsibility off their shoulders. Consequently, helping people or serving the community is the doorway to securing the pleasure of Allah and bringing happiness in the society. Those who can serve others with no desire of return are the best people on earth. According to the Prophet 鸞, they are the leaders of the community.

And they give food, despite their love for it, to the poor and orphans and captives; (saying) We feed you for the sake of Allah only. We wish for no reward nor thanks from you. (Qur'an 76:8,9)

The leader of a people is their servant. (*Sunan at-Tabarani* and *ad-Daylami*)

The spirit of Islam is encouraging to Muslims in such a way that they are even prepared to die for Allah, rather than to live selfishly for themselves. Here lies the hidden reason of Islam's lightning success of winning people's hearts in its early period. Self-centredness and 'individualism' have very little to do in a caring society. These are departures from basic humanity and make a society avaricious and dangerously competitive. They are features of materialistic societies in which human beings vie with each other to succeed and triumph. This gives rise to the 'survival of the fittest' that makes some super rich and powerful at the expense of the majority. In contrast, Islam advocates social responsibility without, of course, endangering individual creativity and innovation. In Islam it is abundantly clear that a selfish and miserly person has little chance of entering the Garden.

In the end, a society comprising such people cannot sustain its prosperity and growth, because of the hatred and anger engendered against the privileged. Countless social problems creep in and cripple this society.

THE FIRE AWAITS!

In a world of cause and effect there are rewards and sanctions. The sanctions and rewards in this world are minuscule, but they are mere tests or warnings. The earth is not meant to be the human being's permanent abode. Allah has created our ultimate residence either in the Garden or the Fire. The Fire that Allah mentions is a fearful one. It has been elaborated in many places of the Qur'an. Allah, in His wisdom, has made the matters that lead to the Fire tempting and those leading to the Garden onerous. According to a Hadith Qudsi, the Prophet Muhammad ﷺ said:

> When Allah created the Garden and the Fire, He sent Jibril to the Garden saying: 'Look at it and at what I have prepared therein for its inhabitants.' So he went and looked at it. Then he returned to

27

Allah and said: 'By Your glory, no one who hears of it would stay away from it.' Then Allah surrounded the Garden by hardship and asked Jibril to go again and have another look. So he went and looked at it again. Then he returned to Him and said: 'By Your glory, I fear that no one will enter it.' Allah then asked Jibril to go and take a look at the Fire saying: 'Look at it and at what I have prepared therein for its inhabitants', and he found it was in layers, one above the other. Then he returned to Him and said: 'By Your glory, no one who hears of it will enter it.' Then Allah surrounded it by all kinds of lusts and asked Jibril to take another look. This time the angel Jibril said: 'By Your glory, I am frightened that no one will escape from entering it.' (*At-Tirmidhi, Abu Dawud, an-Nasa'i*)

This illuminating account tells the whole story of human beings' perilous journey on earth. The road to the Garden is an uphill one and the road to the Fire is slippery and downhill. Human beings' tendency to libertinism and promiscuous behaviour because of material prosperity leads them toward perpetual doom and downfall. This is the Fire promised for the ungrateful slaves of Allah in the Hereafter - since ingratitude is the same as *kufr*. Allah, in His divine mercy, has granted His slaves conscience and God-consciousness so that they can counterbalance this.

It is difficult to comprehend the Garden or the Fire in the human intellect, but we can experience them analogously in this world. In the present day, many who have surpassed the levels of prosperity of previous ages and attained the height of celebrity, have realised how 'Hellish' one's life can become. The highest rate of suicides being in the developed countries are just tips of the icebergs of human beings' tormented lives. When we ignore the signposts and warnings in our lives, what better can we expect? On the contrary, many ordinary people living in huts and in poverty symbolise an enviable happiness in life.

Happiness is from within

On August 31, 1997, when Princes Diana of Britain died in a car crash in Paris there was worldwide anguish which was reflected in the media. The people of Britain were shocked by her death. Diana was a celebrity. Her royal position, charismatic personality and accessibility to the common people contributed to her high renown in the world. Only a few years prior to that, she was envied as the happiest woman on earth - two handsome young sons, a king-in-waiting as husband, and great wealth and beauty. She represented, as many people thought, an earthly 'Diana', the Greek goddess. But nobody knew what was going in her heart. She was being eaten away from within and when her tormented life was flushed into the public domain, people realised how disgruntled she was with her world. Her desperate attempt to run away from her 'Hellish' life ended in the tragic accident.

THE BALANCING ACT

The world and its belongings are made attractive in order that people do not run away from it and forget their responsibility as the best of the creation. If they did so, the purpose of being human would be missed. The temptation of attractive things - women, wealth and the other things mentioned in the Qur'an, has been embedded in human nature. However, Allah has prescribed how to live with these tempting things and how best to use them.

> To humankind the love of worldly appetites is painted in glowing colours: women and children, and heaped up mounds of gold and silver, and horses with fine markings, and livestock and fertile farmland. All that is merely the enjoyment of the life of the world. Allah! with Him is an excellent abode. (Qur'an 3:14)

It is a balancing act, like walking the tightrope. Losing balance due to indifference and apathy or selfishness and greed brings disaster. Only a clear iman in the unity and omnipotence of Allah, and a full consciousness of Allah's commands and adherence to them can save human beings from doom, i.e., torment in this world and eternal Fire in the Hereafter.

PREPARING FOR A HOLISTIC LIFE

Muslim parents raising children as a minority in a hostile environment have a formidable task before them. Their job is to imbue a holistic view of life in the innocent minds, so that they know how to translate it into practice. The goal of Islam is to create a world where human beings are liberated from the clutches of ignorance, Jahiliyyah. That includes the liberation of the mind before anything else. Being a Muslim challenges the human mind and intellect to come clean with an objective outlook so we can think clearly. Contrary to the common perception today, being a Muslim demands intellectual exercise in every area of knowledge, including even aesthetics and zoology. Islam's assertive approach to life encourages Muslims to take an active role in intellectual and social enterprises. It urges Muslims to participate in, interact with, engage in and influence society's common good. It has a positive vision to encourage human beings toward a full submission to Allah, our Creator.

The parental role is to prepare children with this broadest aim in mind. Muslims in the past played a pivotal role in the world, even where they were insignificant in number, a tiny minority. They were pioneers in passing on the message of submission to Allah, to their own children on one hand, and to the rest of humanity on the other. As a result, they were rewarded with unparalleled success. Millions of hearts were bonded in a common purpose of servitude to Allah. Together they expanded the frontiers of a civilisation dedicated to the divine, without coercion. As rivers and tributaries join a sea, human beings in multitude converted to Islam. Islam quenched the thirst of desolate hearts. Once human hearts were conquered, societies braced themselves for natural change in all areas of life.

Positive parenting in a stable family environment can do miracles. There is no room for compromise with the basic tenets of Islam. Of course, most parents do need flexibility and adjustments in real life. But they must be forthcoming, honest and sincere with their children. Integrity is never to be negotiated. If parents do fail in adhering to the right Islamic disciplines for some reason, they must openly admit it and clarify to the children so that they understand the context. In any case, parents must keep on trying to stay within the limits of Islam and draw closer to Allah.

All these are tests in real life. Excessive love for children should not deceive Muslim parents and drive them away from the divinely ordained responsibilities. Extremity of love for or apathy towards children are recipes for misfortune. Those who are blessed with children or adopt some should always remind themselves that these youngsters can emancipate them from the Fire or throw them into it. The Fire is lying in wait for those who are careless.

5. Education and Building Character

"My son, do not associate any partner with Allah. Associating others with Him is a terrible wrong"... My son, establish prayer and enjoin right and forbid wrong and be steadfast in the face of what befalls you. That is certainly the most resolute course to follow. Do not turn your cheek from people out of haughtiness and do not walk with arrogance in the land. Allah does not love any one who is boastful. Be moderate in your tread and lower your voice. The most hateful of voices is the donkey's bray." (Qur'an 31:13-19).

SOCIAL NORMS AND MUSLIM PERSONALITY

What sort of person does Allah want a Muslim to be? To what extent can a Muslim parent contribute toward creating that person in his or her child?

A child's person is decreed by Allah, and to some extent its development is then dictated by family norms and the dynamics of society. How much it is influenced by parental genes is not relevant to this discussion. Societal norms and ideology have an influence on any human being. Every people wants to mould its future generation in its own image. As such, minority communities, whether faith or race based, face apparently insurmountable barriers, especially in countries where the majority culture is proselytising and in some cases coercive. In the melting-pot culture, minority communities are meant to be assimilated into the dominant life pattern of the majority over a few generations. Fortunately, most Western countries have been accommodative towards the emerging minority communities. The issue of multiculturalism and pluralism is creating interesting debates in many of them. Although there are elements who will only be pleased with their monocultural version by getting rid of 'others' or by their total assimilation into the majority community, this is rejected by most. Only time can tell where this debate will lead us.

Modern Western society has developed by leaps and bounds in technological advancement and institutions. Life has become fast, competitive and complex. With the rapid rise of materialism, the concept of divine purpose and accountability for life are all but lost. As a result, modern Western societies are losing many values and norms human beings hold dear in other parts of the world. There do not seem to be any absolute value and norms of life. Everything changes according to the needs and demands of people. While societies are creating needs, the needs in turn are influencing societies. In this respect, the West is rooted in its Graeco-Roman past, which had little to do with revealed knowledge since whatever there might have been were already of considerably antiquity in ancient times. Although Judaeo-Christian values made inroads into that Greco-Roman culture and our society displays some discernible Judaeo-Christian features, it is visibly marginalised in the wake of the overwhelming materialism of post-Renaissance Europe. This has given rise to consumerism and libertinism in the minds and behaviours of people.

In the moral maze, spiritual bankruptcy is the outcome. A vacuum has been created by the weakening of religious and spiritual influences and is now filling up with values and norms that would have created uproar in the past. The alternative powerful 'religions', such as Secular Liberalism and Market Capitalism are as proselytising and intolerant as some religions used to be in their dark ages.

Social consequences aside, the West has devised effective methods of passing on values, or their lack, to future generations. Its educational system is the springboard for the continuation of its position as a 'developed' society. It has so far succeeded in this goal. Being in the forefront of intellectual and technological achievement, they also wield tremendous influence over poorer nations in all areas of life.

EDUCATION: THE WESTERN PERSPECTIVE

Education transmits a philosophy of life to new generations and prepares them to serve, whether they serve Allah, themselves, their families or the nation. It links generations together. An educational system reflects the prevailing attitudes, the cultural and historical legacy of a country. It always takes into account the norms and values of mainstream society. Concepts comprised under citizenship, such as loyalty, liberty, justice and fairness, are, of course, important in disseminating education among the younger generation, but, they can never be balanced and wholesome if knowledge of human purpose on earth is ignored and excluded from education. Without balanced and comprehensive knowledge, prevailing materialist values and philosophy dominate the educational system and affect the younger generation directly.

The basic precept to which Western education has been reduced is to produce 'good citizens', primarily to increase or sustain economic productivity and play their citizenship roles. All of statecraft and social might are geared to this end. It is important to the powers-that-be that education be always at the centre of public debate in the West, and that buzz words like 'standards', 'excellence' and 'performance' be used extensively by experts and educationalists. As a result, teachers experience immense pressure to produce better educational standards in schools, colleges and universities. As teachers are always under pressure due to structural changes, paperwork and criticism from the top, this also has its adverse effects.

The fear that, in recent times, many Western countries are falling behind a number of developing countries elsewhere, has created a sense of urgency among policy-makers. The concern has also risen because of increasingly antisocial behaviour among the younger generation, such as bullying, juvenile delinquency, racism, drug abuse, alcoholism, and teenage pregnancies, etc. In some Western countries, they are now growing at alarming rates and creating big holes in confidence of the capacity to move forward. These are also proving economically costly.

Needless to say, these problems in the educational world are not isolated from what is happening in the wider society. They are the products, as well as causes, of many social diseases. For a sound civil society they are challenges from within. But, instead of adopting a holistic approach, Peacemakers in the West are resorting to piecemeal solutions by attempting to address the issues in a manner which is only skin-deep. Merely improving educational standards for young people cannot allay the fear or solve the problems.

The Christian denominational schools and private schools constitute a powerful block in their own right in many Western countries. Compared to state schools, they have generally better performance and discipline. It is true that they have a relatively more prominent moral and religious ethos, especially in the Catholic schools. But, in the context of wider social diseases their impact is limited. They are only a few cogs in the same wheel.

The idea of good citizenship in Western education produces limited notions of history, geography, language and ethnicity. Although it is expected that by being a good citizen one learns the civic responsibility of one's own country, the impetus in the end is toward becoming more nationalistic. A good citizen of, say Britain, may not turn out to be a good citizen in Germany. On the other hand, it is often forgotten that, in modern pluralist societies, people may prefer to identify themselves in different manners, e.g., by their faith or culture. Finding little room in the not-so-wide concept of citizenship, these groups can feel disaffected, disadvantaged and excluded. At the same time, even minorities within one group can feel themselves marginalised. History has also shown that citizenship can have different meanings and different dimensions in different periods.

Education in the West is predominantly task-centred where tasks, not the learner, are given prime importance. Only recently, is the pupil-centred approach being given importance in some areas of education, e.g., Special Educational Needs (SEN). With a bit of religious education students could probably be aware of various faiths and cultures, but become susceptible to more confusion about life. With rising social pressure and peer influence, the moral, ethical and spiritual dimensions have been sidelined. They have been compromised by the needs of society. In the absence of exemplary role-models around them, young people are tempted to imitate those who have name and fame but little balance in their lives.

In the postwar West, the situation has worsened since the powerful liberal secular camp has succeeded in creating an environment in which the concepts of individual freedom and self-fulfilment are given paramount importance. They often clash with the interests and wellbeing of the wider society. Religion and culture are not rejected outright, but have only a subordinate role in determining social policy. Empirical knowledge, based on 'facts', dictates the value-system of life. To diehard secularists, religion is outdated and illogical, and promotes an irrational attitude to life. Religion is no longer the 'opium' of the people, because humankind has invented far more powerful 'opiates' in which to indulge. So, it is demanded, young people in educational institutions should not be overburdened with the age-old 'dogmas' of religious teaching!

As an outcome of society's post-modern disengagement from religion, the educational system is promoting a self-indulgent and value-free philosophy of life. Young people have little opportunity or access to knowledge leading to the knowledge of their accountability and responsibility to their Creator. Life is governed and conditioned by the desire to survive and succeed. At best, human beings are rational animals in this philosophy, albeit intelligent ones.

The long-term effect of sidelining universal and transcendental values in education has always proved disastrous. History has witnessed the appalling atrocities carried out by 'good citizens' of some countries on others, e.g., the Holocaust in Nazi Germany and the genocides in Cambodia, Rwanda, Bosnia and Chechnya. The list is long. Hitler, Mussolini, Stalin and leaders like them were probably considered the best citizens of their countries in their lifetimes. That is why, Iqbal, the philosopher poet of the East, cried out and reminded the world that 'withdrawal of religion from public life gives rise to the atrocities of Ghenghis Khan'[13]. What he meant by religion was a universal faith with transcendental values, not the one full of bigotry and fanaticism. Ignorance and excessive enthusiasm in any religion can also bring disaster for human beings.

An educational policy based on the philosophy of market-driven expediency may succeed in producing more and more capitalist entrepreneurs, but has an inherent weakness in overcoming any social disharmony and injustice that would ensue. The focus in this policy is on the commercialisation of life. 'The effect of government reforms in education is to put schools squarely into the market place, where heads and governors find themselves managing not only the resources and curriculum but increasingly also the disparate values of a customer-driven culture[14].

In this educational model, Muslims and other faith communities are worse off. For Muslims, our undiluted faith in revealed knowledge is indeed demanding and uncompromising. How we should adjust and compromise without betraying our principles is a dilemma. Muslim educationalists should come up with some agreeable solutions. It seems that Muslims in the West have genuine reasons to worry about the education of our future generations. We have an uphill task in raising our children in multicultural and pluralist societies without compromising the principles of Islam.

POSITIVE ASPECTS OF WESTERN EDUCATION

On the other hand, modern Western education has proved effective in providing the younger generation with key skills for the competitive life, such as, communication and information-processing skills, reasoning and problem-solving skills, social and life skills, and the creative thinking and evaluation skills, but all of the above geared to survival and success in a purely secular society.

Although lacking in the spiritual dimension, the West's material success lies in this educational system that gives young people confidence and self-esteem as worthy citizens of their country. It is important to note that pre-university education has been given prime importance in the West, as it provides the foundation of a nation. Their balanced curriculum includes wider subjects, such as arts, science, humanities and social sciences as well as varieties of social and life skills. With 'Citizenship' being included in British secondary education in 2002, young people will be taught civic responsibility in a modern social context. Western education also continuously addresses the problems of under-performance through improving literacy and numeracy, reduction of class size, ensuring equal opportunities for all, improving school leadership, teacher training, inspection of schools and education providers and use of ICT in an effective and efficient manner. There is an urge to maintain set standards and accountability, as they are considered an essential for success.

There is also an effective partnership between teachers, parents, businesses, the voluntary and statutory sectors as well as its implementation with proper planning and funding. These are the positive aspects of education provision any minority community should appreciate and whose benefits they should try to maximise. But these measures are not themselves alternatives to or cures for the social and moral ills that prevail in society.

'ISLAMIC' EDUCATION: BUILDING GOOD HUMAN BEINGS

In addition to engaging in the fight for standards in education the most important thing for young people is the inculcation of a strong foundation, moral and spiritual roots, to which they are anchored from the very beginnings of their lives. There have been some attempts in certain countries to include these in the curriculum, but they are generally weak and, once again, the main objective is to produce 'good citizens' for a liberal secular society. The concept of producing good human beings is missing altogether.

How can young people become both good citizens and good human beings without having in them the conviction and stability based on firm belief in the all-powerful and ever-vigilant Creator, to Whom all people will return on the Day of Judgement? How would they know that responsibility and sense of accountability in this life are at the core of their liberation from their own whims and desires? Without incorporating these in the educational system and a determined effort to disseminate them, this expectation will remain pure idealism.

The main focus of education in Islam is 'child-centred' and bent on preparing young people for roles compatible with the purpose of their creation on earth. As human beings are put in charge of the affairs of this world, it is an immense responsibility. As such, education should focus on the continuous maintenance and development of harmony and justice in society as well as in the environment in order to bring us toward self-surrender to Allah. Imbalance in nature and deviation from justice bring calamity. Effectiveness, standards and structure in this model are also of prime importance for without them the above objectives will remain daydreams.

Education, in the Islamic framework[15] is intrinsically linked to the revealed justice of Islam. As a result, there is clear unanimity among Muslim scholars that education should aim at familiarising the individuals with their:

- individual responsibilities in life,
- relationships to other creatures,
- responsibilities towards the human community,
- social relations,
- relationship to the universe and phenomena and possibly their exploration of natural laws in order to utilise them,
- to deepen their appreciation of the Maker's creative wisdom which is apparent in the creation.

Therefore, education should be a continuous process of transmitting knowledge and values in order to promote the intellectual, moral, spiritual and physical development of young people enabling them to cope with the challenges of contemporary modern society and grow up as balanced and motivated individuals. There should be harmonious development of mind, body and spirit. On the one hand, education should help equip children with the required skills and experiences needed to meet the challenges of modern competitive life and on the other it should prepare them to live as good human beings serving others in diverse societies. With effective dissemination of these tasks, young people can attain genuine success in this life and salvation in the Hereafter.

STRUGGLE TO MAKE EDUCATION ISLAM-FRIENDLY

It is clear that the religious or theological education prevailing in the West is out of touch and is inadequate to face the challenges of the modern Jahiliyyah that is created from within the society. In fact, it has little positive influence in shaping the lives of young people and may well drive them further away. Society remains geared to secular materialism. Offering a bigger chunk of time for 'Religious Education' in the curriculum is not going to produce any miracles. What is essential is to address the issue from a wider perspective - material, moral and spiritual. Without a deliberate insertion of higher values, derived from revealed knowledge, into the educational ethos little is going to change.

For example, take 'sex education'. Primarily it is dealt with in the light of information about reproduction and in terms of the promotion of 'safer sex' among people who supposedly consent to take part in the sexual act. The focus is primarily to reduce 'Sexually Transmitted Diseases' (STD) and unwanted pregnancies. The institution of marriage, which forms the basis of the man-woman relationship according to the practices of all civilised societies throughout history, hardly comes into discussion at any stage. In most cases, this is not only ignored but looked down upon. As a result, sex education classes are either embarrassing or provocative to young children, especially in the mixed classroom environment. A confused ethos and uncomfortable environment becomes a recipe for an irresponsible sensual life pattern. This 'laissez faire' sex education, which starts from Junior school age, instead of achieving its stated objectives, is giving rise to sex-related crimes and burgeoning teenage pregnancies in the Western countries.

Nobody ever denies the importance of proper knowledge of this primary topic, as the sexual drive is so strong in youth, but what needs to be emphasised is a deeper understanding of and responsibility in sexual behaviour. This could be taught under the broad heading of 'Parenthood', 'Parenting' or 'Family' by those who are knowledgeable, responsible and intellectually mature. Once this could be done, a fresh air of sanity would blow on this issue. Likewise, all other areas of knowledge could be refocused in the light of the human being's responsibility, accountability and sense of and justice on earth.

THE COMMON GOOD OF HUMANITY AND THE MUSLIM ROLE

Muslims cannot expect this happening in the foreseeable future in the West, but this is an area we cannot ignore. Muslim parents and educationists have a duty to take the initiative in forging links with other like-minded people from all spectrums of society. People having common grounds concerning human values need to join hands together to work in harmony with others. The Qur'an is explicit about the necessity of this joint challenge and harmonious coexistence between people so that we explore commonality in order to build a peaceful world.

> 'Say: O People of the Scripture! come to an agreement between us and you; that we worship none but Allah; that we associate no partners with Him; that we erect not, from among ourselves, lords and patrons other than Allah. If they turn back, then say: Bear witness that we have surrendered to Him'. (Qur'an, 3:64).

Human beings now face common problems globally. The world has been witnessing for so long the catastrophic effects of virulent nationalism and ethnic strife, the spread of weapons of mass destruction, massive migration, the refugee crisis, the ecological and environmental disasters, and the spread of deadly diseases such as AIDS. All these make it imperative for sensible people on earth, Muslim and non-Muslim alike, to work together for a better place in which to live. As we now live in an interdependent world, evils of common concern should be fought together.

The physical world has now become quite small. The human being's natural diversity of race, colour, religion and geographical location is now considered an essential human heritage, but, unfortunately, the gulf between people of differing backgrounds is widening. The post-cold war era is experiencing unparalleled human suffering due to injustice and double standards on the one hand and tyranny, arrogance, incompetence and corruption on the other. If they are not challenged effectively, the coming age will bring further agony and injustice to humankind. A new dark age may envelop us all.

People of conscience are genuinely worried about the future of the planet, which needs better management with wisdom and sensitivity. Our survival and prosperity on earth are now a collective endeavour that needs good human beings. Who is going to take the lead in nurturing and fostering these good people? As the 'best community' (Qur'an 3:110), Muslims naturally have a monumental responsibility. A model of education from an Islamic perspective, if properly framed, has the potential of tackling these issues. It is encouraging that in a recent survey education topped the priority list of concerns among Muslims in Britain. It is time their concern lead to pragmatic action and Muslim academics act seriously to devise achievable plans. Muslims, on the one hand, should take full responsibility for educating their children with a broader Islamic ethos and, on the other, must also keep the dialogue open to influence the educational system of the societies in which we live.

It is difficult and challenging, but not impossible. Most Western countries are now pluralist and multicultural. Diverse and rich religious and cultural values are increasingly taking root in these lands. As a result, people with moral and spiritual values have the opportunity to assert them in the educational system. However, we must remember that the mere incorporation of some religious aspects within the system is not going to work, although it might create a positive environment in the beginning. A gradual but consistent penetration of values into the system is important. It needs strategy, consistency and hard work and, above all, patience and perseverance. Once a concerted effort is made on all fronts, the fruits can be reaped later. Generations would then grow up with a sense of responsibility rather than recklessness, conviction rather than doubt and humility rather than arrogance.

A Big Stake

Young people need stability in their lives. Those born and brought up with physical and emotional care as well as love and warmth in stable families have the unique potential to deliver the same to the wider community. On the other hand, those born to irresponsible parents or raised in unstable environments suffer most and can contribute very little to society. Even more, they become a burden on society. Deprivation is not only economic and social, it can be moral and spiritual as well. The former creates chaos in the society, whereas the latter brings confusion and eventual destruction. No nation can prosper with social strife and internal instability.

What is needed is the determination and courage of strong-willed people in the educational as well as voluntary and public sectors. In this, Muslim parents have a challenging role to play.

6. Creating Muslim Personality

Muhammad is the messenger of Allah and those who are with him are firm and unyielding towards all deniers of the truth, (yet) full of mercy towards one another. You see them bowing and prostrating seeking Allah's bounty and His pleasure. Their mark is on their foreheads from the traces of prostration. (Qur'an 48:29)

The (faithful) slaves of the Beneficent are they who walk upon the earth modestly, and, when the foolish ones address them, answer: 'Peace'. And who spend the night before their Lord, prostrating and standing. And who say: Our Lord, avert from us the doom of Hell. It is wretched as abode and station. And those who, when they spend, are neither extravagant nor mean, but take a stance midway between the two. And those who do not call any other god together with Allah, nor take the life, which Allah has forbidden, save in justice, nor commit adultery... (Qur'an 25: 63-68)

MONKS BY NIGHT, KNIGHTS BY DAY

The above features of the companions of the Prophet Muhammad ﷺ tell of those unique Muslims who will ever remain as role models for humanity till the end of the world. Qur'an mentions many more qualities of these people in eloquent language.

In the decisive battles against the Romans during the time of the Caliph Umar ؓ, the Muslim soldiers, although always outnumbered by the enemy, proved mysteriously indomitable and strong-willed opponents. The Roman commanders were baffled as to how the once barbaric and irregular desert army could display such vigour and chivalry against a battle-hardened regular Roman army. They sent some informers to see how the Muslim soldiers spent their time in the leisure periods, especially at night. As drinking and womanising were the common practices of the conquering Roman army, the generals were perplexed and frightened to hear the stories of those Muslims. This is what they were informed:

> One informer said, 'They are knights by day and monks by night. They pay for what they eat in territories under their occupation. They are the first to salute when they arrive at a place and are valiant fighters who just wipe out the enemy.'

> Another testified, 'During the night it seems that they do not belong to this world and have no other business than to pray, and during the day, when one sees them mounted on their horses, one feels that they have been doing nothing else all their lives. They are great archers and great lancers, yet they are so devoutly religious and they remember Allah so much and so often that one can hardly hear them talking about anything else in their company.'

> The third said, 'You will find them prayerful; during the day you will find them fasting. They keep their promises, order good deeds, suppress evil and maintain complete equality among themselves".[16]

Such were the characteristics of the first generation of Muslims who, within a few decades, conquered lands beyond Arabia and brought an extraordinary social revolution in the history of humankind. They made the mountains move and rivers give way in their search for human liberation from the imprisonment of the desires and whims of the self, and there desire for, above all, the human heart's surrender to Allah. They were the first "Qur'anic generation", as Syed Qutb of Egypt put it. They were the people who were once stooped in Jahiliyyah and barbarity, but whom Islam revolutionised and elevated to the peaks of human perfection. The Prophet ﷺ, the Qur'an and Islam changed their hearts, moulded their character, eradicated their ignorance and reconstructed their society in the noblest fashion.

They were the Arabs who were on the verge of self-destruction owing to their lawlessness, vulgarity, stupidity and, to use the

Qur'anic terminology, Jahiliyyah. Allah says, 'You were upon the brink of an abyss of fire, and He did you save from it' (Qur'an 3:103). They were people despised by the then superpowers, the Persians in the East and the Byzantine Romans in the West, to such an extent that neither of them even felt like taking them over. Within decades of their transformation from Jahiliyyah to Islam they smashed the superpower arrogance of the Byzantine Romans and the Persians, liberated their lands from their oppressive kings and won the minds and hearts of millions for Islam.

How did they do it? What was it that created miracles in their lives? To understand it one has to understand the message of Islam and the person of the Messenger of Allah ﷺ. From the moment Allah Almighty placed Islam in their hearts they became a totally different people, equipped with:

- a deep understanding of Islam, the meaning of life and contemporary challenges,
- the deepest relationship with Allah and love for the Prophet ﷺ,
- liberated minds, which they filled with visionary ideas for the good of humankind,
- the characteristic features of Muslims,
- unwavering commitment for Islam and balance in life.

An Enviable World

They created a world in which a young woman could travel alone between two distant places within Arabia without any fear for her life or chastity. They created men and women who could challenge their Caliph, the conqueror of empires, in the public gatherings of the Friday prayers. That was the most open, transparent and inclusive society humankind has ever created. They were people who on the battlefield offered their last sip of water to fellow Muslim brothers whom they thought more needy. They created a society where wrongdoers, who were the smallest in number a society can think of, rushed to the Prophet ﷺ to be punished in the world rather than suffer the Fire in the Hereafter.

They were those who possessed compassionate hearts that cared not only for human beings but other living things and the environment. They were people whose leader (Caliph) shared the ride on one camel with his slave on a journey to Jerusalem. When the Caliph was entering the city it was the servant's turn to ride. When the servant offered his turn to the Caliph, the latter refused saying, 'the honour of Islam (i.e., being a Muslim) is enough for us.' They established a world order that was not only just but based on compassion and spiritual elevation. Allah promised victory for those who would live by Islam, and the generations that grew up with the Qur'an fulfilled that promise.

They created individuals and a society of which mankind can feel proud. They are the role models for human beings till the Day of Judgement. Allah, the Exalted, lovingly mentions about them:

> **'The forerunners - the first of the Muhajirun and the Ansar - and those who have followed them in doing good: Allah is pleased with them and they are pleased with Him...' (Qur'an 9:100)**

They were people who deserved this glad tiding from Allah, not that they were the 'chosen' people by birth, but they earned it through their sweat and blood, firm belief and action, and loyalty to Allah and His Messenger ﷺ. Their passion for the Akhirah (Hereafter) and maximisation of the worldly tools to reach their goals had perfect balance. They made a conscious decision to serve humanity in their physical and spiritual need. They preferred to die for Allah, rather than to live for their own selves. They were people who challenged the existing order of the Quraysh aristocracy, Arab arrogance and the superpower haughtiness of the Persians and the Byzantines. When success kissed their feet in their mission they used to prostrate before their Lord. Their success was not for narrow self-interest but for humanity, and above all for the pleasure of Allah.

How could they revolutionise their characters and became so creative, wide-hearted and open-minded within months and years of their acceptance of Islam? How could they become so entrepreneurial and dynamic from their historic and deep-rooted tribalism and barbarism? This will remain history's biggest paradox. What was the role of Muslim women in this miraculous transformation? Contrary to the present worldwide confusion regarding the role of the sexes, Islam's assertive and holistic view on life gave women the confidence to share responsibilities in a stable and tranquil environment.

THE ESSENCE OF MUSLIM CHARACTER

In psychology, 'Personality' is the integrated and dynamic organisation of the physical, mental, moral and social qualities of an individual that manifests to other people in social interactions. It comprises their impulses and habits, interests and complexes, the sentiments and ideals, opinions and beliefs. According to some, 'Personality' is the supreme realisation of the innate idiosyncrasies and self-affirmation of a human being.

The Muslim character during the time of the Prophet ﷺ emanated from their firm conviction of *Tawhid* (Oneness of Allah), *Risalah* (Prophethood and all of the revealed shari'ah and Sunnah) and *Akhirah* (Hereafter). This conviction continuously polished and refined their characters through the close association and supervision of the Messenger of Allah ﷺ, the 'touchstone' of human character.

The characteristic features of those early Muslim men and women are mentioned in the Qur'an and ahadith. Like compassionate physicians they carried out sharp operations on the diseases of human souls, showing full care and sympathy with the 'patients' but not with the diseases. The contrasting aspects of their characters created of them consummate beings who pulled everyone towards them with a magnetic attraction, except those who were bent on evil. Their glowing faces and appearance displayed their peaceful heart and spiritual fulfilment.

The concept of Muslim character is thus intrinsically rooted to the deep understanding of human duties and responsibilities on earth, irrespective of gender differences. The well-balanced and complementary gender roles made all of them a powerhouse of Islam's inner strength. Muslim women, from the advent of the Prophet's mission, participated fully in the creation of the ummah. Muslim mothers, sisters and wives were fully in tune with the Prophetic vision and, with full responsibility, kept Muslim families in full order and provided the sustenance for future conquerors and scholars of Islam.

The Muslim character is rooted deep in knowledge and conviction - the knowledge that elevated human beings to a status higher than other creatures, including angels, knowledge about Allah, the angels, the prophets, the revealed books, the Last Day, the Decree of good and evil being from Allah alone, the world, the creation, and about themselves and their surroundings. The Messenger of Allah ﷺ has emphasised knowledge so much that one wonders how Muslims could have stooped so low in ignorance as we have today. 'Wisdom is the lost riding beast of the believer' and Muslims are asked to grab hold of it wherever they find it. Acquiring basic and essential knowledge of Islam is obligatory for every Muslim, man and woman. Knowledge widens horizons, gives conviction and creates tranquillity in the mind. Conviction drives a human being to action, gives steadfastness, patience, perseverance, dedication and consistent commitment in life.

The Muslim character thus has an inner reservoir of strength that emanates from Allah's limitless treasure and it has its external manifestations. It is like an oak tree that has a strong root in the soil and branches widespread in the sky. Muslims are people who watch each moment of their life and ask themselves whether they are using their time meaningfully. They utilise their time in a self-assured and confident manner to enjoin good and forbid evil. They use their eyes, ears and other senses to observe, learn and educate themselves every moment of the day. They use their knowledge and develop their skills to make sound judgements, honour truth and do justice to all, including themselves. They harness the material and spiritual benefits from each moment's existence through consciousness and a feeling of gratitude to the Kind and Merciful Creator.

Muslims are ever vigilant of what is happening around them and in the wider world. They read the signs of Allah in nature and learn by looking closely at the technological development of the world and its impact on human life. Muslims are not only fully aware of modern people's latest gadgets, such as the Internet, mobile telephones and other high-tech tools, but can utilise them effectively for the benefit of mankind. The hallmark of Muslim character today is shaping our lives in the image of the companions of the Prophet ﷺ, rather than to pander to the whims and fancies of people engrossed in Jahiliyyah.

Muslim character does not fit with the bigotry, fanaticism, extremism, terrorism, passivity, lethargy, miserliness and narrowmindedness that we often see among us present-day Muslims. A Muslim can never be inward-looking, self-seeking and ill-mannered. The Qur'an and Sunnah strongly mentions the necessity of balance in Muslim character.

> **In this way We have made you a middlemost community. (Qur'an 2:142)**
>
> Beware of excessiveness (*ghulu*) in deen. (People) before you have perished as a result of (such) excessiveness. (*Sahih Muslim*)
>
> He who is deprived of leniency is deprived of goodness. (*Sahih Muslim*)

How can a Muslim possess such negative features, which are the recipe for disaster for any community, let alone the 'best community' (Qur'an 3:110). Aren't Muslims raised for the good of humankind, to save human beings from the pitfalls of Jahiliyyah?

FEATURES OF A MUSLIM

The building blocks and features of Muslim character are modelled on the character of the Messenger of Allah ﷺ, which was the Qur'an as his beloved wife A'ishah, may Allah be pleased with her, observed, as well as on the behaviour of his companions ﷺ. Ac-

49

cordingly, Muslims have distinct attitudes toward life. This dictates their character and external manners. Their character shines through their appearance and behaviour, and right action becomes embedded in their nature. As they are conscious of their responsibility in the world they illuminate themselves and others with the light of knowledge of Allah, the Sunnah of the Messenger of Allah ☀, virtue and good manners. The emphatic call of the Prophet ☀ to Muslims to attain and exercise good manners is a weighty one.

> Usamah ibn Sharik ☀ narrated: 'We were sitting in the presence of Allah's Messenger ☀ so quietly as if birds were perched on our heads. Nobody had the courage to open his mouth. In the meanwhile a person came and asked the Prophet ☀, "Among Allah's slaves who is the dearest to Him?" The Prophet ☀ replied; "One who has the best character".' (*Ibn Hibban*)

> The Prophet ☀ was asked, 'Which Muslim has perfect faith"? He answered, "he who has the best character'. (*At-Tirmidhi*)

> 'Abdullah ibn 'Amr narrated: 'I heard the Prophet ☀ saying, "Should I not tell you who among you is the most likeable person to me and who will be the nearest to me on the Day of the Judgement?" He repeated this question two or three times. The people asked him to tell them about that person. He said, "He among you who has the best character".' (*Ahmad*)

> The Prophet ☀ said, "I have only been sent for the purpose of perfecting good character". (*Al-Muwatta*)

> The Prophet ☀ has also mentioned, "My Lord has taught me good manners and He has mannered me well". (*As-Sam'ani*)

Muslims are testimony to a permanent involvement with, and infinite self-sacrifice for Allah, and striving to establish Islam which in its essence is social justice and the welfare of human beings and even matters such as a clean environment. We are witnesses to and against mankind, as the Prophet ☀ was witness to and against us. Our Jihad (utmost struggle) is to promote good and equity and the brotherhood and sisterhood of Islam. Muslims are the symbols of hope for mankind.

MUSLIM

A Muslim guest speaker was once giving an introduction on Islam to some non-Muslims. Knowing the background of the audience, he devised a simple acronym that clarifies some of the features of a Muslim. As he wrote the following in the flipchart

M for Moulding life in the way Allah wishes
U for Understanding the world and Islam
S for Surrendering to Allah
L for Linking with Allah
I for Integrity of character
M for Motivation to work for Allah and serve His creation

one woman hesitantly asked him, 'but, are they found in the present-day Muslim?' The speaker was taken aback and, after a pause, answered, 'That is why we are in this mess today.'

PARENTAL ROLE IN BUILDING MUSLIM CHARACTER

"Our personality comprises not only the physical body but also the mind and the heart, feelings and attitudes, character and be-haviour."[17] "What Allah requires of you, in Qur'anic vocabulary, is for you to be Mu'min and Mujahid. A Mu'min is one who is true and firm in his faith in Allah. A Mujahid is one who strives his utmost, with all the means at their disposal, to gain Allah's pleas-ure."[18]

The (true) believers are only those who believe in Allah and His Messenger and have left all doubt behind, and who strive with their wealth possessions and their lives. It is they, who are true to their word. (Qur'an 49:15)

Building Muslim character needs constant and conscious train-ing and practice. Effective training requires competent trainers with excellent qualities in whom people can put their trust and confidence. A trainer possessing exemplary character can infuse attachment to the learning process. The Prophet Muhammad ﷺ was the best trainer in humanity. His was the perfect example, the role model, of good character to be emulated till the Last Day. Allah, the All-Merciful, has Himself testified to his perfect character in the Qur'an:

You have an excellent model in the Messenger of Allah, for all who put their hope in Allah and the Last day and remember Allah much. (Qur'an 33:21)

A Messenger has come to you from among yourselves. Your suffering is distressing to him; he is deeply concerned for you; he is gentle and merciful to the believers. ... (Qur'an 9:129)

'Abdullah ibn 'Amr said: 'The Messenger of Allah ﷺ was neither ill-mannered nor rude. He used to say that the best among you are those who are best in their character.' (*Al-Bukhari*)

Can Muslim parents train their children effectively? The answer must be 'yes'. If parents do not feel comfortable in all aspects of training their children, they should seek help from others in the community. Muslims never claim perfection, as human beings are created with a lot of frailties. We have strengths and weaknesses. What Allah wants is the hard work and continuous effort to improve. The Prophet ﷺ has said:

Allah has prescribed excellence in all things. (*Sahih Muslim*)

It pleases Allah that when any of you does anything, (he) should perfect it. (*Al-Bayhaqi*)

Allah admonishes us to improve, enhance, reinforce and consolidate good qualities and as such Muslim parents should consistently try to instil these features in their children day in day out. Thus, *Tazkiyah* (the purification of the self) or *Tasawwuf* (Sufism), both of which mean the effort to purify the self from bad qualities and to develop the noble qualities, is essential in building Muslim character. Muslims, through the conscious attempt to help the needy, feed the hungry, shun evil and enjoin good, doing all of them for the sake of Allah alone, are rewarded by Allah to the extent that their souls become compliant to Allah's mercy (Qur'an 87:14-15, 89:27, 91:9, 92:18-20)

TRAINING METHODS TO BUILD MUSLIM CHARACTER

Religion is a contract between the slaves and their Creator. In Islam this contract entails two types of relationship - one between the human being and Allah, and the other, between the human being and creation. This relationship comprises essential rights and responsibilities. A Muslim life is essentially a life of continuous effort and struggle to implement Allah's commands on earth. The human being's success or failure depends on effective dissemination of those commands. However, we can only make efforts to the best of our ability. What we achieve in this world, although that affects our lives, is immaterial to us, because our ultimate gain lies in the Hereafter. This does not mean that we carry out our work with lethargy and inefficiency in this world.

Parents are not only providers and protectors - remembering that Allah alone is The Provider and The Protector - but teachers, educators and role models for their sons and daughters at the same time. Parents, especially mothers, have a closer association with their children than anyone else. Raising a successful generation of Muslims depends on hard work, and the training they provide their babies from the time their lives start in the womb. In this process they themselves are highly benefited and rewarded by Allah. For effective teaching, teachers must know the subject, grasp it, digest it and try to teach in the most effective way. In the same way parents must make use of all the techniques that are found in the Qur'an and the Prophet's Sunnah to produce dynamic Muslims in the modern world. In their attempts to rear the children they should try to emulate the Prophet ﷺ as mentioned in the Qur'an, which is 'to recite to them His revelations and purify them, and to teach them the Scripture and Wisdom' (Qur'an 62:2).

Most parents love their children. Some children may be more beloved to parents than others, as was in the case of Ya'qub i and Yusuf i. However, parents must be balanced and fair in dealings with and upbringing of their children. As conscious slaves of Allah they must play the role of *Murabbi* (trainer, wise counsel) in emulation of the Prophet Muhammad ﷺ. The following methods[19] are known to be most effective in training children.

i. Advice, Persuasion and Reminder - All the prophets and wise people on earth adopted this basic technique to train their people. The Qur'an mentions Luqman's excellent advice to his son. However, for maximum benefit, advice should be timely, relevant and, ideally, frequent. The Prophet Muhammad ﷺ advised people, individually and collectively, in a way that had lasting impact on them. Parents are in an excellent position to do this day in and day out or at suitable intervals.

ii. Parables and Storytelling - The Qur'an tells the stories of past nations in an eloquent manner with a view to teaching people so that we reflect and learn. The parables, such as a 'good word' for a pure tree and an 'evil word' for a bad tree mentioned in the Qur'an, penetrate people's hearts (Qur'an 14:24-26). 'Isa (Jesus) ї and the Messenger of Allah ﷺ also used similar parables to clarify things to their companions. On one occasion the Prophet Muhammad ﷺ used a comparison between a human being's capacity to use knowledge and the soil's response to rain. Parable, metaphor and story reverberate in human memory for a longer period and help them understand the meaning of life. Muslim parents should be the source of good parables and stories. Bedtime stories for younger children have proved effective in all cultures.

iii. Role Modelling– the Prophet Muhammad ﷺ has been sent as the model for humanity (Qur'an 33:21). He took part in mundane work with his companions, e.g., in building the mosque at Madinah, in digging the ditch for the siege and on many other occasions where he was no different from his companions. He was the perfect father, husband and companion. Role models have tremendous influence on the attitudes and actions of a child. Parents can be the nearest role models for their children.

iv. Rewards and Sanctions – Allah has created the Garden to reward people who have true iman in Him and do right actions, and the Fire to punish people who reject iman and do wrong actions. The Prophet Muhammad ﷺ used to give recognition to the good works of his companions and sometimes chastised or disciplined them for wrong or unacceptable behaviour and action. The story of the three companions who were penalised for showing indifference to participation in the expedition to Tabuk is an example. Rewards and sanctions are effective tools to teach young children about the reality of life.

Muslim parents should be in a position to train their young ones with enthusiasm and liveliness. They must appreciate the techniques mentioned above and adopt practical ways to train them for the future. Of course, the training has to be age-appropriate and compatible with the children's emotional and intellectual needs. One does not have to be an expert in all areas of knowledge. Sincere parents, even if they are unlettered, can become effective trainers of their children.

Muslims in the West probably have little chance in the near future to see Islam shaping the societies in which we live. Given the extent of materialism in the developed countries, it looks a mountainous, a near-impossible, job at present. However, if Muslim parents can motivate themselves to become catalysts of change by adopting Prophetic methods of training their children, there is definitely a hope in the regeneration of Muslim youth, who later on, can play a strong role in shaping their future. Allah helps those who help themselves.

NOTES

[1] *Even Angels Ask - A Journey to Islam in America*, P7, Amana Publications, USA, 1997.
[2] Social Focus on Ethnic Minorities - A Publication of the Government Statistical Service, HMSO, August 1996, p34.
[3] Ibid, p37.
[4] Ibid p46 (27% in 1995, i.e., 3-4 times higher than that of the indigenous population).
[5] Ibid p49.
[6] *Ethnic Minorities in Britain: Diversity and Disadvantage*, The Fourth Na-

tional survey of Ethnic Minorities by Policy Studies Institute, London 1997.

[7] www.homeoffice.gov.uk/rds/pdfs/chapter6.xls

[8] *Young Muslims in Britain: Attitudes, Educational Needs and Policy Implications*, Muhammad Anwar, The Islamic Foundation, UK 1994, pp33-34.

[9] *Social Trends* 25, HMSO, 1995, p21.

[10] Ibid, p46.

[11] Ibid, p51

[12] *1998 Demographic Yearbook*, United Nations, New York, 2000

[13] 13th century Mongol conqueror known as the 'scourge' of the world

[14] *Educational Values for School Leadership*, Sylvia West, p13, Kogan Page, 1993.

[15] *Curriculum and Teaching Education*, Ed. M.H. Al-Affendi and N.A. Baloch, Hodder and Stoughton, p16 1980

[16] Excerpts from *Islam and the World*, Abul Hasan Ali Nadwi, IIFSO, 1983

[17] *In the Early Hours: Reflections on Spiritual and Self Development*, Khurram Murad, p2, Revival Publications, the UK, 2000.

[18] Ibid, p5.

[19] *Meeting the Challenge of Parenting in the West: An Islamic Perspective*, Dr. Ekram and Mohamed Rida Beshir, pp61-91, Amanah Publicatiions, US & *Raising Children in Islam*, Suhaib Hasan, pp51-55, Qur'an Society, London.

Parenthood and the Age of Nurturing

Executive Summary

- Human beings want children for spiritual, emotional and biological fulfilment, social status, for solace and for many other reasons. Whatever the reasons, Allah intends human continuity till the end of the world.
- Conception is perceived by human beings mistakenly as an accident but it is a miracle from Allah. The burden of pregnancy is heavy for women. Although traumatic, it can be a pleasurable experience. The hadith, 'The Garden lies at the feet of the mother', has underlined the elevated position of the mother an in Islam.
- Muslims plan for family. So-called family planning for enjoyment of life's passing pleasures or for fear of economic hardship is against the dignity of the human being. Contraception occurs in the circumstances agreed by husband and wife, if Allah wills.
- The birth of a child, boy or girl, is a blessing in Islam. There is no priority of boy over girl or vice versa. Parents should follow the excellent Islamic customs at the birth of a child, and during the first week of the birth.
- The period of pregnancy and the early years of children are important for the sound health and formation of their character. Nutritious food, sound health and the moral and spiritual lifestyle of the mother are essential for their later Islamic character.
- Husbands should try to be near to hand during pregnancy, and during the birth and rearing of the child. This strengthens the bond between the couple.

- As children grow, parents also become more attached to them. Parents must keep in mind that their children not entice them towards the world. It is important to maintain a balance between love and responsibility.
- The early years of children are daunting for and demanding upon parents. The home should be a positive environment where their character is moulded. TV or computer games should not replace the parental presence. Parents should teach their children from an early age and supplicate Allah for their Islamic upbringing.
- Children should be exposed to good habits, in manners and behaviour. They should be protected from anything negative, especially in their early life. Parents need to sacrifice their own bad habits for their child.

7. Journey to Parenthood

O Lord, grant me by Your favour an upright child ... (Qur'an 3:38)

My Lord, bestow on me a right-acting child!... (Qur'an 37:100)

MARRIAGE, FAMILY AND PARENTHOOD

The inspiration to become parents starts from the moment one decides to marry. Marriage provides solace, comfort and pleasure to two human beings. On the other hand, it also teaches compromise and sacrifice in order to live together under one roof. The sort of spouses people wish to marry tells what sort of children they want to have. Truthful, honest and believing men and women will look for those very same qualities in their partners. On the other hand, indecent partners will naturally cling to one another (Qur'an 24:26). As the urge for parenthood is embedded in human nature, most human beings long for children. Marriage is the best divinely ordained method of fulfilling this urge.[1] Children are the products of physical love between a man and a woman.

Marriage is for a divine purpose. It is the best legal outlet for sexual fulfilment.[2] Allah has created everything in pairs and blessed them with physical and emotional attraction between the opposite sexes. The Islamic way of life leads young people toward lawful marriage, which satisfies spiritual, sexual, emotional and social needs. Celibacy, unless for some unavoidable reasons, is not allowed in Islam. In permissive societies, teenage romances, encouraged by social and peer pressure, often end up in illicit physical relationships between socially and psychologically immature boys and girls.

Marriage is a social contract between two human beings of opposite sex and an institution that encompasses the joy of the relationship between a man and a woman in a family. A stable family with a lifelong commitment between the spouses produces romance that can be long-lasting, enduring even after death. Blessed children add joy to this relationship. The Prophet Muhammad ﷺ has asked Muslims to marry early and start families in order to lead balanced lives on earth. He also advised Muslims to have children so that families multiply and his ummah becomes large on the Day of Judgement.

The arrival of a child raises the issue of parenthood and parenting in a family. While the former is primarily a biological process, the latter is a conscious act of raising children in the mould of the deen. In a family, there are rights and responsibilities between family members - between the parents, between the parents and children and between the children. In an extended family, this is further widened. A blessed family is built on love and mercy, respect and honour, steadfastness and forgiveness, justice and fairness, honesty and integrity, openness and clarity, mutual consultation, loyalty, sacrifice, liveliness and many other features.

PREPARE BEFORE YOU EMBARK

Why do people want children? As modern human beings have changed so much from the traditional outlook of life and become more complex, the answer to this question has become multidimensional, such as:

- to look for solace in loneliness
- to take pride in numerical strength and in social status
- to immortalise themselves and live longer through the children
- to make sure they are looked after in old age
- to create something which remains in their ownership
- not to miss out on the experience
- to use the opportunity before the biological clock runs out
- for biological and emotional fulfilment
- to surrender to fate or 'accident'

The journey to parenthood has thus divergent objectives for different people, depending on their outlook on life. A Muslim's desire for children is dictated by the teachings of Islam. It is to take part in the creative process of Allah so that humankind can play the role of vicegerency on earth. Good deeds and right-acting children are essential investments for parents after their deaths.

The decision to become a parent is thus a challenging, but necessary, one. It is a pleasant adventure on the one hand and it carries physical, psychological and financial demands on the other. Raising children has become an expensive enterprise, educationally and socially. Raising a child is an achievement and no achievement can be gained without some pain. With money, sweat and toil human beings prepare to bring new people into the world and raise them, only to see that they demand their places in the family and replace them in time. What is so pleasant about it? Self-seeking, individualistic people will find it hard to take this on board, to have children. Even if they decide, they cannot afford more than one or two, no matter how affluent they are. Glamorous, high-society women with a materialistic and carnal outlook of life will find pregnancy costly to their health and social demands.

Stepping onto the road to parenthood is a unique and adventurous journey, fascinating for the newly married couple with their first baby. One can gain knowledge from others or information from books, but it is a real life experience. However, natural instincts in the man and woman teach them how to cope and succeed. What is important for successful parenting is insight as well as an open and exploratory mind. Conscientious couples learn from seeing others and from that they produce good planning.

In Islam, physical, emotional and psychological preparedness and willingness to become parents is important for embarking on the journey. A journey full of ups and downs needs mature understanding and a deep sense of responsibility. As mentioned earlier, Muslims prefer early marriage, especially in permissive societies, for many reasons. Marriage between two responsible adolescents, with full support from their families and the people around them, gives them confidence to embark on a shared life. A unique transformation occurs in their life and they start thinking, not merely as separate people but also as a couple. In time, they acquire more wisdom.

The psychological demand to become parents arises instinctively in a married couple. Inhibition of this demand for selfish reasons does not produce good results in the long run. The arrival of a child is almost always a joy for the couple and it works as a further bonding between them. Many marriages have withstood strife and breakdown just because of the arrival of tiny babies who, with their innocent looks, want their parents not to let them down by their individual self-interests. They become bridges and symbols of the link between the parents. On the other hand, marriage in materialist societies easily collapses because many couples fail to prepare themselves to accommodate to the 'burden' in their lives or are too busy with their careers. There are also self-seeking women who are too conscious about their physical 'beauty' and do not want to lose it or their 'fun time' because of someone else.

Arrival of a new member in the family does need extra preparation and amenities. But human necessity depends on individual's attitude to life and, to some extent, on the sociocultural surrounding. The wisest suggestion is that one should not wait for 'perfect' financial or social conditions, as the perfect time very rarely appears in one's life. *Tawakkul* (reliance on Allah) solves many problems. Of course, a husband and wife need to work hard in order to minimise financial and other difficulties as much as possible. Both before and after their utmost endeavours, the result is with Allah. Tawakkul should be accompanied by the utmost effort and constant supplication to Him (Qur'an 3:159).

BEYOND BIOLOGICAL FULFILMENT

Allah has permitted Muslims to enjoy the world. Lawful enjoyment of wealth and the fruits of marriage are gifts from Him. Allah's design for human continuity is through the natural process of procreation. Men and women fit in this design and fulfil this process through their physical relationships. Allah has mercifully attached joy and fulfilment to physical love so that His design never falters. What is the Muslim approach to this biological phenomenon? As Muslims' lives are dictated by continuous conscious remembrance of Allah, in joy and in sorrow, we are asked to offer supplication even when we approach our spouses for physical union. While sexual passion drives human beings mad, Muslims do not need to suppress it. They simply need to regulate the passion and use it in the way Allah has prescribed. Many cultures consider 'sex' taboo, and some religions still consider it as something that hinders 'godliness' and advocate celibacy, which they think can only be attained through self-torture. While some strong-willed people may succeed in suppressing this natural urge, others fail and live deceitfully. Islam, the *Deen al-fitrah*, (religion of the natural condition) encourages human beings to enjoy their lives, albeit, with simple conditions - by working within Islamic guidelines and by showing gratitude to the One Allah, Who has allowed us the enjoyment.

As a reward for their gratitude to Allah, Muslims receive all the benefits, i.e., on the one hand, love, romance, tranquillity and biological fulfilment and on the other hand, those pleasant fruits from Him, children. The following supplication tells of the purity of Islamic way of life

O Allah, Keep us away from the shaytan and keep the shaytan away from whatever You bestow upon us. (*Sahih al-Bukhari, Muslim, Abu Dawud* and *at-Tirmidhi*)

Muslim parents ought to be forward looking. They not only ask for immediate gains in life, but look beyond this mundane world. Success in the eternal life in the Hereafter is their ultimate goal. They know that, on the Day of Judgement, they have to stand in front of Allah with their progeny at which time they are either going to be leaders of the right-acting or of the wrong-doing people. Their supplications thus reflect those of the virtuous people in the past. Sincere supplications always find a response from Allah, as in the case of the prophet Zakariyya i.

Then Zakariyya prayed to His Lord and said: 'O Lord, grant me by Your favour an upright child. You are the Hearer of prayer.' And the angels called out to him as he stood praying in the sanctuary: 'Allah gives you the good news of Yahya, who will come to confirm a Word from Allah - a leader, chaste, a Prophet and one of the righteous.' (Qur'an 3:38-39)

CONCEPTION AND THE BURDEN OF PREGNANCY

Creation is in Allah's hand, but men and women are partners with each other in the process. According to modern science, only one in millions of sperm from the male body joins with one single female egg and fertilises it to cause conception. This minuscule and fragile creation, the embryo, then takes shelter in the protected place in the woman's body called the uterus. During the next nine months the warm and well-protected embryo grows in its watery liquid in the womb, which acts like a cushion. The embryo receives nourishment and oxygen from the mother's blood through a flexible tube, the umbilical cord. As the cells multiply, the embryo begins to take on the shape of a human being. After about eight weeks, it has legs, arms, eyes, ears and a mouth. Within three months, all the different types of cells form a complete human being, which at this stage is known as a foetus.

According to science, from conception to the birth of the human being is pure accident, but, in reality, it is the scheme of Allah. The baby's stages of development in a tiny crammed space in the mother's dark womb, from conception to birth, point to the fact that Allah's plan is supreme. The selection of a baby's gender and the parity between men and women, from the beginning of human creation, are the manifestations of Allah's wisdom and justice on earth. Human beings have no control over it. They take everything for granted and probably have some ability to study with a feeling of awe the complexity of creation. Allah, the Lord of the universe, has His own plan as to how to run the world. There are some who do not plan for children, but apparently inadvertently keep on getting them. There are others who are serious about having children, but have none. There are people who want boys - or girls - but Allah decides otherwise. On the other hand, there are 'lucky' ones who get whatever they want. On the face of it, this may confuse us. Whatever we get or fail to get is a test in this life. Mere success or failure in this life does not guarantee ultimate success or failure in the Hereafter. Success there depends on right action and, above all, on the mercy of Allah.

The life in the womb is a link between the world of the spirit and the earthly life. Before coming to this world, in the world of the spirit, all human beings made a covenant with their Lord.

When your Lord took out all their descendants from the loins of the children of Adam and made them testify against themselves, 'Am I not your Lord?' they said 'We testify that indeed You are!' Lest you say on the Day of Rising, 'We knew nothing of this.' (Qur'an 7:172).

According to a tradition, after four months of conception Allah bestows spirit on the tiny being and predetermines its life. This means nevertheless that, as we do not know what is lying ahead of us, we must work to the best of our ability to achieve our destiny. Muslims are thus continuously active in the world. Fatalism is against the deen of Islam.

> The creation of each of you is gathered in the belly of his mother for forty days as a drop, then later he is a blood clot for the like of that, then later he is a morsel of flesh for the like of that. Then the angel is sent to him and breathes the spirit into him, and he is commanded with four words: with writing his provision, his lifespan, his action, and whether he is happy or grievous. (*Sahih al-Bukhari* and *Muslim*)

Pregnancy is a heavy burden for a woman. Carrying a live creature as an extended part of her body is an arduous job. It is physically stressful and emotionally demanding. The whole pattern and style of her life needs readjustment and adaptation. The mother's body readjusts along with the growth of the baby. She loses the tenderness of her skin. The demand for more and more space within her body makes her tired and weary. Sometimes she cannot sleep, as the growing baby wants to move inside her. She needs lot of extra nutrition for her tiny guest. The last two months of pregnancy prove even harder for the mother to physically cope, as the baby becomes heavier to carry around. Then there is the fear of the pain of delivery. All these led to some Christian and Jewish beliefs that women are punished for the sin of Eve at the beginning of human creation. Nothing is further from the truth.

Sharing household and other jobs with the husband is crucial, especially in the last few months of pregnancy. It would be cruel if the mother did not get extra support at home. Unusual anxiety or physical exhaustion can have adverse effects on both mother and baby and can even lead to miscarriage. Children are trusts from Allah and to both father and mother, so both need to work in harmony, especially in the last days before delivery when uncertainty and anxiety tend to creep in. Labour pain is traumatic and needs Allah's mercy to overcome. Once again reliance upon Allah is the key and supplication is the medicine. Human aptitude for taking risks in order to get rewards works in favour of the mother, who fortunately receives psychological backing and courage as the date of delivery nears. An increased sense of awareness prepares her body to be in tune with the demand. Reasonable exercise, meditation and breathing practices are essential.

Food, habits and the emotional feelings of the mother all affect babies, not only their childhood, but throughout their lives as well. Only a happy and healthy mother can produce a healthy baby. For an unhappy and weak mother childbirth is a risky enterprise. Research has shown beyond doubt that consumption of drugs and alcohol and smoking cigarettes are hazardous for babies in the womb. In Islam this is not only wrongdoing, but criminal as well, as it hampers the foetus's life. A child has a right to be born healthy. The future of Islam lies with the conscientious Muslim mothers who shun these practices even under extreme social pressure. The devastating result of these on babies has further been established from the results of research by a team from Edinburgh University, Scotland. They have found that 'babies of mothers who smoke are more vulnerable to the lethal disease, Meningitis.'[3]

A JOYFUL PREGNANCY

Anxiety for the balanced growth of a baby in the womb is natural for both mother and father, but, the only thing they can do is take more care and supplicate Allah, Who lets babies grow in a good fashion and nurtures them in the womb.

> **It is He Who fashions you in the womb as He wills. There is no god but Him, the Almighty, the All-Wise (Qur'an 3:6)**
>
> **Surely, We created man in the finest mould. (Qur'an 95:4)**

While mothers worry for their babies in the womb, the babies seem to have no worries about their mothers. It is exciting how modern science has shed some light on what babies do in their small world. The fact that after four months of conception the baby is no more a lump of flesh, but a human being, is important. Babies hear their mothers' heartbeats and voices, they kick and stretch and they relax. As they need food to survive and grow, they are also in tremendous need of spiritual food. Their mothers' virtuous and positive thinking, recitation of the Qur'an, offering of prayer and sadaqah, conscious supplication to Allah - all these provide spiritual food to the baby. Whatever a mother says, does or thinks has bearing on the awake creature. It is illuminating that human beings of spiritual elevation and worldly might in Islam were born to mothers who cared for them while they were in the womb. Modern research also agrees on this. The following research finding is intriguing.

> 'An observational study programme of mother-child relationships at Edinburgh University in Scotland has been operating for the past twenty years and found that babies whose mothers do not sing to them are at risk of growing up unable to communicate and express emotion'.[4]

Whether the quoted research is reliable or not, the importance of communication with the baby in the womb is undeniable.

Mothers' sacrifices and their pivotal role in the life of a human being have put them in a high position of respect. The hadith, 'The Garden lies at the feet of your mother', tells a great deal about how Muslims should value their mothers. That does not leave fathers on the sidelines. Parents mean mother and father. It is true that mothers take most of the day-to-day burden of childcare and they generally have more skills in this, but it is also true that fathers have a significant role to play in raising the child. Parenting is a cooperative business and partnership is essential. While the maternal instinct dictates mother-child interaction, the connection between fathers and babies can be very strong indeed. A father's being at hand but not actually present during the birth and his emotional feeling for the mother in her pain increase his bond with the baby. It has been clearly shown that it is unadvisable for men to be present during childbirth for many reasons, not the least of which is the effects that witnessing the tremendous indignity his wife suffers can have on their marital relationship. While the father and the mother complement each other in terms of their needs and talents, the baby in its utter dependence on the mercy and provision of Allah, experiences most of its needs being met by the agency of the parents.

Given the context of living with Iman and the fulfilment of the requirements of the deen, which in our situation means to exert oneself with everything at one's disposal to establish Islam in our lives and communities, Muslim parents can work significantly towards the Garden by caring for the foetuses in the womb, rearing the babies after their birth, nurturing their courtesy and practice of Islam, providing them with a sound Islamic education as they grow older, and facilitating their entrance into the world in the best way. In the same way, Muslim children can please Allah to some extent along with fulfilling the same demands that are obligatory upon their parents, by being loyal to their parents, obeying them and helping them in their need. This is a part of the cycle of life.

FAMILY PLANNING OR PLANNING FOR THE FAMILY?

Children are gifts from Allah and they are taken as trusts. The idea of 'unwanted children' comes from a cruel materialistic philosophy of life. As the life of believers is determined by their seeking divine good pleasure, they are ever happy with their lot, including the gift of children. Believers always ask for goodness from Allah and surrender themselves, even though the result does not fit in with their plans. This voluntary submission to the will of Allah is the essence of Islam and this protects human beings from unnecessary agony and frustration.

Where does then the idea of 'family planning' come from? Without going into theological discussion, which is beyond the scope of this book, one can easily observe that the modern campaign of reducing the rate of childbirth is rooted in a political agenda of some people in the developed world. This has been discussed elsewhere in the book. The Islamic perspective of 'planning for the family' emphasises two essential points: a) a general encouragement to have more children as they are treated as gifts from Allah and b) the necessity to safeguard the mother's health and raise the children as Allah's emissaries. From the moment a man and woman decide to marry each other, this needs planning, preparation and determined action to establish a right-acting family. Not having a child may be essential for some couples, but it should not be generalised. Limiting the number of children just for fear of poverty or for any other selfish reason does not befit Muslims.

Allah's design on gender parity maintains human continuity. Parents may prefer a boy or a girl and ask Allah in supplication what they want. People have tried in the past and are trying today to influence the gender of the baby by resorting to 'expert advice'. But does it help? Muslims should never pin their hopes on the preferred gender of the baby, lest they become frustrated. No one, except Allah, has the power to decide what is in the womb. (Qur'an 3:6, 42:49,50, 75:37-39)

Both men and women are the emissaries of Allah on earth. Although they have distinctive roles in the successful management of the world, they will stand before Allah on the Day of Judgement with the same questions facing them. Allah has designed the world in such manner that it can only proceed if men and women are complementary to each other, neither competitive nor unequal. The issue of a so-called 'inferior or superior' gender does not arise in Islam. The story of Maryam and her mother is illuminating in this respect.

> **Remember when the wife of 'Imran said, 'My Lord! I have pledged to You what is in my womb to be devoted to Your service. Please accept it from me. You are the All-Hearing, the All-Knowing.' When she gave birth, she said, My Lord! I have given birth to a girl' - and Allah knew very well what she had given birth to, male and female are not the same - 'and I have named her Maryam and I seek protection for her and her offspring from the accursed Shaytan.' And her Lord accepted her with full acceptance and caused her to grow up in goodly growth... (Qur'an 3:35-37).**

Child rearing is a demanding job that starts with pregnancy. As the child grows in the womb the short-term goal is to care for the physical and psychological exhaustion of the mother. But, from the very beginning, the question both parents need to ask is: what kind of human being are they going to aim for and for what kind of world? This long-term objective will drive the parents to plan and prepare for the future. It might look far-fetched, but it is vital. If Muslims want to recreate a civilisation on the basis of revealed knowledge they must think further ahead than others.

In a world of Jahiliyyah, the new generation of Muslim youth needs to be thoughtful, creative, competent, courageous and confident. They need to be proud of being Muslims. They need to be forward looking and accommodative but strong-willed. They cannot afford to become impulsive, passive and defeatist in the face of challenge or failure. Parents who want to cultivate these aspects of their children's character need to start from the day they know about pregnancy and map out their future strategy. Once again, the basic ingredient in these short-term and long-term objectives is partnership and harmony between the mother and father.

In order to successfully carry out their parental jobs there needs to be a natural spacing between the children's ages. Allah does not overburden His slaves, so why should human beings do it to themselves? The health of the mother and effective raising of children in Islam are vital. If a husband and wife genuinely fear that they cannot cope with too frequent birth of children, Islam has the latitude for them to take a joint decision on that with Allah's fear in mind. Building Islamic character in children is a divine obligation. To ignore this would be wrongdoing on the part of the parents and fatal for the ummah.

8. A New Arrival in the Family

Every child is born in a state of *fitrah* (the natural condition)...
(*Sahih al-Bukhari, Muslim* and others)

A TRAUMATIC, BUT FULFILLING PROCESS

A Muslim's every act is an *'ibadah* (worship or servitude to Allah). What else could be more rewarding than being at the creation of a new slave of Allah on earth and welcoming him or her? Nine months may not be that long, but for babies in the womb it completes an extraordinary stage of their journey. It is a journey through which a 'spurting fluid' (Qur'an 86:6) is fashioned in the safe lodging of the mother's womb (Qur'an 23:12-14) and grows bigger and bigger to become a human being. As human beings are not meant to be confined in a tiny space, we need the wider physical world in order to go through the process of tests and tribulations for which we are destined.

The birth of a baby is attended by a mixture of anxiety, excitement and expectation. For mothers it can be a dreadful but fulfilling experience. Allah has given them unusual resilience, strength and courage to bear the burden, discomfort and pain. A new life in their lap is a dream come true for both parents. It can be the ultimate experience of 'togetherness' for a couple, both of them working in unison to bring a new creature, the fruit of their love, into the world.

Healthy pregnancy generally leads to a natural, drug-free labour, ending in natural birth, but it all depends on Allah's mercy. Although parenthood is a matter of preparedness from the time one plans to marry, birth initiates the real-world experience of parenting. Labour can be a traumatic and painful physical, as well as psychological, experience for a woman.[5]

Meeting the newborn babies as they make their first cry on earth for a mother is like witnessing the most wonderful and radiant sight in life. The first loving skin-to-skin contact with the baby can be ecstatic for her and is vital to the meaningfulness of parenting. The tender hug of the mother assures the baby that, 'you are the most loved one on earth. We are there to help you out.'

Looking at tiny newborn babies who start their struggle to survive in the new environment with feeble heartbeat and breathing, is an experience that reminds us of our vulnerability on earth. It refreshes our memory of how helpless we were in the beginning of our life-journey and how Allah showered His mercy on every stage of our existence. It also teaches us to value our own parents. That is why parents, who find their grown up children ungrateful to them, express their discontent by making comments, such as, 'you will only realise what we did to you when you get a child'.

ISLAMIC CUSTOMS AT THE BIRTH OF A CHILD

The arrival of a child in a family is a glad tidings that needs to be conveyed and shared (Qur'an 3:39, 37:101). A newborn baby is welcomed by the family and the community with open arms. As a cultural custom in South-Asian communities, sweets are often distributed among close family and friends at the earliest convenient time. Muslims parents and elders have instinctive *du'a* (supplications) for the new ones. The supplication of Maryam's mother in this regard is unique (Qur'an 3:36).

> When a child was born in a family, A'ishah, may Allah be pleased with her, would not ask whether it was a boy or girl, but rather she would ask 'Is it complete and sound?' So, if she was told that it was, she would say, 'All praise and thanks belong to Allah, Lord of the worlds'. (*Sahih al-Bukhari*)

Whatever the joy, Muslim parents and close family members never forget their tasks[6] immediately after the birth. As babies arrive in the new wider world, spiritually pure but bodily impure, they need to be cleansed and dressed. The tasks are as follows,

i) *Adhan* – some of the schools recommend that a male adult, father or someone close in the family, should recite the *adhan* (call for collective prayer), in the right ear. It is mentioned in a hadith that the shaytan runs away at the sound of the *adhan*. In the world of the spirit, human beings declared their instinctive readiness to accept Allah as their Lord (Qur'an 7:172). The first sound to reach the babies' ears should thus be the declaration of Allah's greatness, so that the sound always reverberates in their memories and settles in their beings. The mother of the faithful A'ishah, may Allah be pleased with her, mentioned, 'I saw the Prophet ﷺ call the *adhan* in the ear of al-Hussein ibn 'Ali when his mother, Fatimah, gave birth to him'. (*Ahmad, Abu Dawud* and *at-Tirmidhi*).

ii. *Tahneek* – It is considered by some an excellent practice to give a bit of small chewed date or a sweet substitute, e.g., honey, to newborn babies, so that they start their lives with the taste of sweetness. As life is a complex and difficult journey that has adversities and hardships, this sweet start may be useful for babies at the beginning of their journey.

A'ishah, may Allah be pleased with her, said 'Newborn children used to be brought to the Messenger of Allah ﷺ and he would supplicate for blessing for them and rub a chewed date upon their palates.' (*Sahih Muslim, Abu Dawud*).

iii. Removal of Hair – The way of the Prophet ﷺ is to shave the baby's head completely, preferably on the seventh day after birth. It is also advised that the weight of the hairs be balanced with silver and the weight of silver is given in sadaqah to the poor.

When al-Hasan ؓ was born, he (the Messenger ﷺ) said to her (Fatimah): 'Shave his head and give the weight of his hair in silver to the poor.' So, she shaved off his hair, weighed it and its weight was a Dirham or a part of Dirham. (*Ahmad* and *al-Bayhaqi*)

iv. *'Aqiqah* – It is a Prophetic tradition to perform the *'aqiqah* for a baby and some say that it is on the seventh day after its birth. Some regard the Islamic practice as sacrificing two sheep for a boy and one for a girl, but the school of Madinah as transmitted by Imam Malik holds that a single sheep suffices for both. As the birth of a child is a happy occasion, friends and families are invited to celebrate the occasion by sharing in the meat.

Every child is held in pledge for its *'aqiqah*, which is sacrificed for him on his seventh day and he is named on it and his head is shaved. (*Ahmad* and *Abu Dawud*).

Whoever has a child born to him and wishes to offer a sacrifice then let him sacrifice two sheep for a boy and a single sheep for a girl. (*Abu Dawud* and *an-Nasa'i*)

With the child there is *'aqiqah* [a word for the hair on the head of the newborn child and possibly also for the foreskin], so spill blood for him and remove the harm from him. (*Sahih al-Bukhari, Ahmad, Abu Dawud, at-Tirmidhi*)

Unfortunately, this Sunnah is not given enough importance in the Muslim communities of the West, probably because travelling to an abattoir is time-consuming for many people. Many Muslims find an easy solution by sending money to their relatives in Muslim countries who offer sacrifices on their behalf. As a result, a great occasion for communal happiness is missed.

v. Circumcision – Circumcision is an accepted practice deriving from Ibrahim ﷺ. Some people regard it as correct to circumcise the child on the seventh day, but there is considerable disagreement about this and the early practice of the people of Madinah, as recorded by Imam Malik, is totally against it, deferring it for some years and preferably until the child loses his first teeth. It is now accepted that circumcision is a better way to prevent some diseases among males. The following tradition tells about the Sunnah of Muslim life that gives an amazing emphasis on cleanliness of the human body since a baby starts the journey of life. Obviously, cleanliness of the soul is equally important.

The *fitrah* (the natural way) is five: circumcision, shaving the private parts, trimming the moustache, clipping the nails and plucking hair from the armpits. (*Sahih al-Bukhari, Muslim*)

vi. Naming – Children have the right to good names as they will carry them for the rest of their lives. Muslim parents always try to give their children good names. Names should be linked with the father's name and have to be meaningful. Praiseworthy names are those that mean slaves of Allah or of His attributes. They could also follow the names of the Prophets and the notable Muslims of the past. Names should not be such that have negative connotations or are marred with meaninglessness. The Prophet Muhammad ﷺ used to change any name that had unpleasant meanings. This is the reason why most new Muslims change their names after accepting Islam.

Call them after their fathers. That is closer to justice in the sight of Allah. And if you do not know who their fathers were then they are your brothers in religion and people under your patronage... (Qur'an 33:5)

The most beloved of your names in the eye of Allah, the Mighty and Magnificent, are 'Abdullah and 'Abd ar-Rahman. (*Sahih Muslim*).

THE DEMAND FROM A NEWBORN BABY

The demand from a newborn baby is enormous and unrelenting. Parents, especially mothers, can sometimes go crazy from lack of sleep and exhaustion. On occasions, they may become frustrated by the cry of the baby, especially when they do not know whether it is because of hunger, loneliness, the pain of wind or sickness. Whether first time or expert, most parents come across moderate to severe crises in rearing their infants. Learning to take physical care of babies, e.g., nappy-changing and bottle-feeding, comes through practice. But, what overwhelms parents are the relentless demands, constant pressure on time and worry about their health. As the routine of the parents is altered because of the extra demand, less sleep and shortage of rest can create fatigue and postnatal depression. Fathers need to watch out and share the burden with sensitivity.

On the other hand, these demands have their joys as well. Babies have a magnetic attraction because of their innocent looks, smiles and sounds. Their dependence on their parents give fathers and mothers worth and importance in human life. This can only be felt in the heart. Whatever the demand, parents, especially mothers, should provide physical closeness and skin contact in order to give them security and peace when they need it most, in their tender age and in a world which is totally new to them. A child, of course, should not be made unnaturally dependent on parents. A gradual and natural programme for independence needs to be adopted from the very beginning. This requires careful planning for positive parenting. The practical task of parenting requires professionalism and basic skills.

Babies learn how to communicate meaningfully with others. They recognise mother, father and other members of the family and gradually learn to behave accordingly. They see, observe, respond and learn. Their hands and feet also participate in their action. Countless pieces of information about the meaning of the world pile up in their small brains and tend to overwhelm them. All these are in the process of building their unique characters. Babies are dependent on others, but are not ignorant or totally helpless. They know when they are happy, hungry, tired or in pain and they signal these with their smiles, cries or body movements. The maxim, 'health is wealth' is terribly important for babies. Parents must take their young children's physical wellbeing and safety, etc., very seriously. Such should be their spiritual and intellectual upbringing. The formation period of a human being's earliest journey in the world should have a strong grounding on all these fronts.

Newborn babies are fully dependent on adults. The only way they can communicate is crying when they are angry or uncomfortable and smiling when happy. They like to be rocked and talked to. Mothers are in the forefront of this effort to make sure that the baby is clean, well fed, loved and protected. The first two years are crucial for rearing a child. Muslim mothers are asked to suckle their babies for this period (Qur'an 2:233). There are reasons for this. Breast milk is now scientifically proven to be the balanced and perfect food for babies. Moreover, the physical touch of the baby with the mother during breastfeeding creates a strong relationship between the two. This helps create a lifelong love between mother and child. However, it is completely acceptable for mothers to hire or utilise foster mothers to suckle the child.

Parents are human beings and not all cope well under stress, but they should not give up. They should always make an effort to become good parents and work to the best of their ability to rear their children. Children simply cannot survive without adults. As parents wield overwhelming influence over their young children, this can make them feel giddy with power and lure them to assert too much control over the young ones, which will prove dangerous in the end.

Effective rearing of newborn babies rests with the conscious responsiveness of the parents. They learn this by watching the babies, listening to them and waiting for their reactions. Babies' ranges of signals are limited and they can only communicate with parents if they recognise their signals. Thus, forming secure connections with babies is most important, especially for mothers. It would be unfortunate if Muslim women were tempted to shy away from their tasks as mothers before this connection is secure. This would result in their losing the joy of rearing children. Unless absolutely required, Muslim mothers should not let their children be raised by professional childminders, many of whom are non-Muslims, without taking exceptional care in the choice of the person, insisting on a Muslim, and exercising a great deal of supervision of the childcare process.

We cannot expect our children to grow as Muslims when our young ones spend most of their formative time with those who know very little about Islam, no matter how professional they may be. It would be extremely unwise in the long run. In some cases, it is even economically not prudent for mothers to work outside, as money paid for child-minding is very high and Islam has burdened men to earn for the family and they cannot avoid this responsibility.

The wrong action in not providing maintenance is enough to waste a person's deeds. (*Ahmad* and *Abu Dawud*).

If a father finds it really difficult economically to sustain the family during the early years of child-rearing, the mother can step in with part-time or temporary work to help out, if she wishes. However, this needs serious mutual consultation between husband and wife. In any case, the work and its environment should be decent. It must be kept in mind that rearing children is never inferior to working outside the home for an employer. Muslim parents who consider it thus should prepare for the eventual consequences, i.e., the future casualty of losing their children if they prefer to follow the materialist way of life. It would be unfortunate if they failed to raise their future generation in Islam.

The way parents look after their babies has profound consequences for the way they grow as human beings. As their survival depends on parental care, so their psychological wellbeing depends on how they are nurtured. Parenting thus requires accurate awareness of and interpreting and communicating with the baby and responding to its various needs - physical, emotional and spiritual. How can parents make sure that they are growing with full balance in these? An excellent practice for parents in this period is to recite the Qur'an for them, engage in meaningful talk and make du'a for their successful future. This not only helps the babies, but the parents themselves. The verbal communication in the Words of Allah influences them spiritually and reduces the parents' exhaustion.

As the babies grow, the demands on the parents change. No sooner do the parents learn the delicate art of responding to their demands, e.g., rocking them to sleep, than they suddenly realise that they have entirely new children in their hands - toddlers. It is in this period when safety issues become more prominent. Children are naturally curious. They put things in their mouths, noses and ears. As such, all dangerous items, small or large, should be out of their reach. They should not be left on their own or unsupervised at this time. All parents must learn a few basic rules of first aid and use common sense in times of emergency. It is better to be safe than to be sorry. The demand is ever changing and the pressure is varied. It requires extra patience to take care of an active toddler. Of course, the pressure and hard work have their adventures and benefits as well. The joy and pleasure, the innocence, the fountain of love, the chance to watch the unfolding mystery of life - all are rewarding, albeit for those who look for meaningful pursuits in life.

All children have the basic right to suckling, sustenance, affection and education from their parents. Islamic civilisation was built and maintained by generations of Muslims who were serious in giving these rights to their children. Deviation from this was not accepted. An incident during the caliphate of Umar points out the importance of these rights.

A CHILD'S RIGHTS OVER PARENTS

A man came to the second Caliph with his young son, complaining that his son was disobedient and insolent to his parents. Instead of admonishing the boy 'Umar ﷺ calmly asked him what the matter was. The boy replied by asking, 'Do I not have rights over my father? Are there not certain things which he should do for me?' 'Umar ﷺ replied that the child naturally has rights over his parents. When the boy asked to hear some of these, 'Umar ﷺ said, 'When a man wishes to marry, he should marry a virtuous woman to be the mother of his children. When Allah Almighty blesses him with a child he should give him a pleasant name. He should teach the child Qur'an and Sunnah. When the child reaches the age of maturity, he should arrange for his or her marriage.' The boy was listening quietly and then said, 'My father did none of these for me. As far as my mother is concerned, she belonged to a certain group of immoral people. I do not wish to name these people, but they are known for their illegal sexual relations. When I was born my father named me Khunfasa (black beetle). As a result, wherever I go I am taunted by other children as being a cockroach. My father did not arrange for my Islamic Education. I have never attended a mosque or a school, and I have no knowledge of Qur'an or Sunnah.' When the boy had finished his complaint 'Umar ﷺ turned to the father and said, 'You have severed relations with your son before he severed relations with you.'[7]

SIBLING EQUALITY

New arrivals in the house naturally get full attention from all the family. As a result, elder brothers and sisters can feel a little left out. The previously youngest ones, who had probably so far monopolised parental attention, can be confused or even jealous. Parents have to be sensitive about this and assure them, according to their age and intellect, that the share of their love has not been reduced. In the beginning, newborn babies should not be left alone with their immediate elder siblings and parents need to watch out that the older ones do not harm them in any way. The elder children should be given some sort of 'ownership' of the newborn babies. It is just a matter of time until things settle down and the brothers and sisters learn to accommodate themselves and begin to create a lifelong relationship.

In a sound family environment elder brothers and sisters can be of enormous help to the parents in rearing the new one. Children can speak in their special language and can sometimes communicate faster with their siblings. They can also relieve their parents of many day-to-day activities. However, parents must make sure that the elder children do not become solely childminders and that their education is not hampered.

It is un-Islamic to discriminate negatively between a boy and a girl. The gender of a child should not bother parents, as it is decided by Allah. Sons and daughters must be treated equally in terms of affection. In pre-Islamic Arabia and some other ignorant societies daughters were symbols of embarrassment and were treated in a shameful manner. In the days of Arab Jahiliyyah some fathers even buried their young daughters alive. It is an irony that many societies even today do not welcome the birth of daughters in the same way they do their sons. Islam has put an end to this shameful and discriminatory custom. Unfortunately, this pagan custom of killing daughters is now practised in a different manner - some modern parents do this through the abortion of female foetuses. Let human beings hear what the Qur'an says about this abhorrent practice.

And they assign daughters for Allah - Glory be to Him! And for themselves, whatever they desire; When one of them receives the good news of the birth of a girl, his face darkens and he is filled with inward grief. He hides himself from the people, because of the evil of the good news he received! Will he keep her with dishonour, or bury her in the earth? Verily, evil is their decision! (Qur'an 16:57-59)

When the baby girl buried alive shall be questioned, 'For what sin was she killed?' (Qur'an 81-8,9)

In the beginning of children's lives there is simply childhood and the issue of boyhood and girlhood becomes distinct later on. The features and thus demands diverge as the children gradually and naturally acquire and absorb their masculine and feminine qualities. Obviously, during their formative years as females and males, mothers and fathers should respectively address specific issues. Conscious parents carefully watch out for the developmental phases of their children and make sure that equity is maintained. Boys and girls are not the same, but no one is superior to other except in taqwa. On the Day of Judgement human beings are accountable to Allah on the basis of their actions, not gender. The teachings of the Prophet Muhammad ﷺ on this is manifest in many traditions. As he did not have any surviving son, his behaviour with his daughter Fatimah, and his other daughters, may Allah be pleased with them, was exemplary.

Treat your children equally. (*Ahmad, Abu Dawud* and *an-Nasa'i*)

Whoever takes care of two girls until they reach adulthood he and I will stay on the Day of Rising– and he interlaced his fingers (*Sahih Muslim*).

PASSING ON THE TRUST OF IMAN

Holding babies in the arms is exhilarating and one of the most emotionally fulfilling experiences in life. Getting to know newborn babies in the first few days and weeks is also thrilling but goes far beyond catering for their daily needs. Watching babies grow and thrive is most rewarding. Babies also learn about their parents, the family and their surroundings. As they gradually occupy their place in the family, it becomes an unforgettable experience for the elders to watch tiny human beings making sense of the world around them. In the process, parents become more mature and responsible in their lives. Child-rearing is an interactive and dynamic process of life. It is as joyful as it is challenging.

Children are a source of vigour to the heart, joy to the souls and pleasure to the eyes. However, wealth and children are adornments to human beings (Qur'an 3:14,18:47) that lure them towards the worldly life. Many forget their roles of bringing their children up properly owing to their intense love for them. This can bring unfortunate results in the end. Parents are for the protection and physical care for their children till the time they attain maturity. They are also for passing on their life experience to their young ones. Parents from successful nations carry on these jobs with the fullest responsibility and seriousness.

Muslim parents are obligated to pass on the *amanah* (Trust) of iman and vision to their children from the moment the young ones are conceived. They need to have well thought-out targets and action plans for children from their tender age, so that they can grow with balanced Muslim characters. Only then would the future generation of Muslims be able to bear witness to the Truth before humanity. It looks like a mountainous job, especially in the West, but there is no shortcut to this great task. For conscientious Muslims it is a challenge worth taking.

9. Infancy and Preschool Nursing

If you have a child then treat him like a child. Play with him like a child and do not impose yourself on him like an adult. (*Ibn 'Asakir*)

A CHALLENGING START

As babies grow in physique and intellect, their world starts widening beyond the world of parents and siblings at home to include more and more people around them in the society. The surrounding environment keeps on imprinting diverse pictures on their memory and helps building their characters. In the first few years babies grow steadily and change rapidly. The cooing and babbling sounds that come from their tiny mouths, the smiles that shine on their faces and the innocence that emanates from them exert a magical attraction on all around them. Every day they master new skills, speak new words and understand new concepts through interactions with others, games and other activities. By the time they are sitting and crawling they learn how to make mess of things. Within a year they are used to doing a lot of mischief and getting on other peoples' nerves. They become ever more active and, as such, need protection from a lot of household dangers when they walk, run, talk and poke into anything they find interesting. Some children become little terrors at home. Every member in the family should be aware of the safety rules and every home with an infant should be child-proof. This, naturally, makes high demands of the parents. However, in spite of all the tensions, all parents remember their children's early years with affection.

This is the time when parents have a tremendous role in their rapid physical growth, intellectual development and their spiritual quest. Children take life as an adventure and work on impulse as they are not yet ready to grapple with the thinking process. They play and through this they learn life skills. In order to teach them the reality of life and contain some of their natural impulsive behaviour a number of do's and don'ts may need to be used with them from childhood. This is important for their safety as well. But too many do's and don'ts can impede their intellectual development. As such, parents need to be sensitive and should only establish those rules that are essential. Even then they should make sure that children learn and the rules do not hamper their natural development, creativity and innovative power. Parents should refrain from shouting, frightening and physically punishing. Children should gradually be led to be able to understand that the basic rules are for their safety, sound development and social acceptability. A verbal comment or look of parents should be sufficient at this stage of life.

Children are unique. They gradually grow into their characteristic nature. Some are calm and some are restless. Getting to know young children, to 'read' them, is relatively easier than getting to know older people, as children are generally expressive and forthcoming in their natures. They cannot conceal their feelings and their innocent looks and impulsive actions generally tell everything about them. Many children cry a lot and want continuous company from someone. Some cannot sleep on their own, as they always need someone at their side. Many children force their way in to stay with their mothers at night. As every child is different, mothers have to adapt and sacrifice more for such ones.

Mothers in industrialised societies are advised to make sure that their children sleep in the cot and, if necessary, in another room. They are advised to ignore their crying so that children understand that they must sleep separately and learn to live alone. Mothers should not spoil their children by answering all their cries, but for the baby, who grew inside her body, physical closeness with the mother is essential. Mothers who always keep their babies separate at night cannot do justice to their loved ones. By being harsh to them in this most important phase of life some mothers loosen the bonds with them. Muslim parents, especially mothers, need to make sure that their children are emotionally satisfied. As for cry, they need to ascertain whether it is because of anger, hunger or pain. Sometimes they cry on purpose to attract the attention of the adults or to get something. Conscious parents nurture their little ones with utmost care and try to mould their characters with delicate precision. Good Muslim parents should treat parenting as a mission. They are aware of the fruits of parenting and price of negligence.

PARENTING STYLES

Conscientious Muslim parents have to deal, on the one hand, with their children's immediate demands and, on the other, their balanced growth as Muslims so that they can confidently play a positive role as Allah's emissaries on earth. By investing time, energy and attention in the early years of the children, parents can reap dividends later. What are the techniques of parenting? Research has shown that there are three broad styles of child-rearing, e.g., a) authoritarian, b) permissive and c) authoritative. They produce different types of child behaviour.[8]

• Authoritarian

In the authoritarian style, parents try to shape and control their children through orders, i.e., do's and don'ts, obedience to authority, work and tradition. Children are judged by how well they conform to the set standards. Creativity and personal accomplishments are probably not rejected outright, but have little recognition. This military style of discipline from the very earliest childhood has an impact on the personalities of the children and influences their future behaviour towards other human beings. As a result, children can lose the joy of childhood, become withdrawn and turn out to be timid. If they are shouted at or punished, it has an impact on their self-esteem and they will lack creativity and self-discipline. Research has found that this technique is worse for boys than girls. By fervently pursuing strong-arm techniques to raise their children in Islam some Muslim parents unwittingly follow this technique and unfortunately lose out in the end.

• Permissive

On the other hand, with the permissive style, parents give in to their children's impulses and actions. There is little demand on them and any idea of punishment or sanction is frowned upon. Parents do not try to discipline them, nor do they use overt power to achieve their objectives. As a result, children tend to be immature and low in self-reliance. They cannot cope with social responsibility and independence. In permissive societies, where most first generation immigrant parents have little clue about the dynamics and complexities of the societies in which they have settled, this technique has devastating effects on future generations. Some Muslim parents adopt this style because of their own lack of confidence. This is now creating serious concerns among the Muslim communities in the West.

• Authoritative

With the authoritative style, parents try to lead their children in a rational manner and give them lot of space, but at the same time explain things at important steps and keep the reigns in their hands. There is room for consultation, give-and-take and accommodation. It is an assertive and positive style of parenting where power is used when necessary, but is generally avoided. Parents expect their children to conform to the demands set, but they accept freedom and independence. Children brought up in this style are generally happy and self-reliant and grow up with the ability to meet the challenges of life. They become socially responsible, dynamic and friendly. They also become positive-minded and can take on the challenges of life. This is a middle-of-the-road parenting technique and Muslims are broadly expected to raise their children in this style.

'The mumin is the mirror of the mumin…' (*Abu Dawud*). Parents are genuinely their children's mirrors. By carefully observing the parents a child can realise whether they have affection and respect for and trust in him. If they feel contented and confident in their parents, they will grow confidently as good human beings, Muslims of the modern age.

THE FORMATIVE PERIOD

From the age of one, children's reasoning ability starts developing. The natural praise and recognition from their loving parents and elders make them feel good about themselves and reinforce their competence and enhance their abilities. Their self-confidence drives them toward acquiring practical skills, such as wearing shoes and blowing their noses. They also learn how to communicate orally. In a sound family environment they learn that they must be good to get recognition from their elders. However, the valid concept of good and bad needs to be inculcated in them with clarity.

• Avoid the Freudian Pitfalls

How should Muslim parents deal with the psychological development of their little ones? Unfortunately, under the influence of Freudian psychoanalysis on the behaviour of children, this has lost genuine focus. Freud's perverted analysis of child behaviour has led modern human beings to believe that, between the ages of three and six, every child wants to possess the parent of the opposite sex. This so-called 'sexual self-consciousness' of the child is thought to be important 'to form satisfying relationship with the opposite sex and, indeed, to establish and maintain a satisfying self-image and satisfying attitudes to the world and life in general'.[9]

Like the concept of human beings' original sin, this concept of the sexual attraction of young children towards their mother or father has sadly influenced modern minds over the past century and contributed to unrestricted sexual promiscuity in industrialised societies. Unfortunately, some apologetic secular Muslims have fallen into this pit. However, this dogma of modern Jahiliyyah has rightly come under vehement attack even from Western academics. An Islamic perspective has been given in 'The Dilemma of Muslim Psychologists'.[10]

At the same time, the influence of modern psychology, based on materialistic behaviourism, has led to the liberal approach of 'parents are always wrong' and 'children are always right'. This can only give rise to permissive attitudes in the parents and foster in the children a disrespect for them in the long run. Muslim parents must not fall into the pitfalls of this materialistic philosophy of life. Professor Badri refers to a very significant hadith on this, 'that even if they manage to get themselves into a lizard's hole, the Muslims will follow irrationally' (Sahih Muslim), that tells about the present Muslim predicament.

• Adopt Commonsense Training Methods

Parents do not have to be psychologists or expert educationalists to rear their children. What they need is commonsense and an elementary understanding of human behaviour to interact with them and contribute to their children's development. The parent-child relationship is a dynamic reciprocal one, but, in the beginning, building a reliable relationship is the parents' job. Understanding the stages of the children's physical, intellectual and emotional development helps in making appropriate demands on children. With the passage of time, children's innate skills and understanding of the world expand. They learn how to relate to other people, develop life habits and live as human beings. Parents need to spend time with them, study them and teach them the basics of life. The quality time they spend with their children helps them lead their children in their voyage into life. In this lively engagement, conscientious parents continuously enrich their own knowledge and experience. It is a two-way process. If parents respond positively to their children, with strong principles but flexible approaches, children will eventually develop into sociable and considerate people. All children are born with innate potential, parents need only to help them blossom, but parents should not hurry in such a process. Individual children take their own time.

Parents are the guides, and must function as *murabbis* - people who foster, bring up, train and give wise counsel - to children for their lives' journeys. They are the adults closest to the children who sincerely want to help them up above themselves. Their hard work, sacrifice, compromises, love and compassion for them are selfless - they want their young ones to fulfil their own ambitions.

Success of the children, both inwardly and outwardly, in the present life and in the next life, is the dream of all Muslim parents. They do not expect any reward from their children. Mothers in this respect are more selfless. As a result, some parents tend to push their children too much. Muslims always hope and pray that their children give them something that will ease their burden in the Day of Judgement. For this they need to train their children, from a young age, to become Muslims and good human beings. Parents receive reward because of the supplication of their adult children.

• Empathise with the Child

In order to train children effectively, Muslim parents must learn to empathise with them. The power of entering into another's personality and undergoing their experiences with creative imagination is the most important skill a trainer can acquire to utilise for the benefit of the trainees. The most effective trainers of human beings in history, the prophets, were successful in this endeavour. By trying to put themselves in their children's position, parents can understand the nature of their needs and learn to see their rapidly enlarging world. Empathy tells parents that children's day-to-day life, like everybody else's, is driven by love, fear, self-interest and other human characteristics. Through empathy and insight parents can build their children's sense of worth and encourage their involvement in decisions concerning their lives. This sets good examples for the child who thus learns how to empathise with others in life.

Children are different in temperaments. Variety is the gift of Allah. The world is beautiful, because it is inhabited by human beings with singular personalities. Children may grow up with personalities with which their parents probably do not feel comfortable, but that is the reality. It is essential that parents try hard to mould their children's character in the colour of Islam.

• Instil Islamic Spirit from the Start

Children generally utter their first meaningful words when they are about one year old. Between one to two years the average children learn about two hundred words. Development is faster after two years when they can connect words and develop thinking skills. What are the first few words Muslim parents should teach their babies? Should not the small slaves of Allah learn the word 'Allah' before anything else? If the words 'Allah', 'Qur'an', 'Alhamdulillah', 'Insha'Allah', 'As-salamu 'alaikum' and other phrases are a part of the parents' realities they will naturally repeat them before the children who will then learn them first of all. Language development is enhanced when the parents keep on talking to their infants in baby-talk, not normal speech. Parents should talk to them in meaningful and short sentences with good rhythm, such as, 'Bismillah' etc.. Reading good nursery rhymes and telling short stories and family incidents with verbal and body expression delight them and make them interested in learning. But beware of telling infants Islamic stories too soon because this will mean that they will remember them all their lives as 'fairy tales'. The best age for learning the stories of the prophets and the Messenger of Allah ﷺ and his Companions is after seven, when the child is old enough to understand something of the meanings of the real stories of real people. Conversation with young children may look strange, but it is an effective way to increase their language skill. However, one must keep in mind the subtlety of their abilities and should not overburden them with something they cannot bear.

MIND YOUR CHILD'S MATURITY LEVEL

A couple was rearing their very young child with all sincerity and seriousness. Both of them were educated and, as such, they were also learning from experience. On an academic level, they were quite familiar with child psychology and were carefully applying their knowledge to the young one. As both of them were practising Muslims, the first word they cherished to hear from their child was 'Allah'. As the child was growing and learning to speak it was a joy for them to hear nice words, though with amusing sounds, from his tiny lips. Even, hearing Allah as 'Aiyah' and Qur'an as 'Kunan' was a thrilling experience. In their zeal to teach him Islam from that early age they were talking about Allah, His mercy and His punishment. In that they unfortunately behaved like typical parents who normally frighten their children with some object or person in order to feed them or make them sleep. Did they depict a fearsome mental picture of Allah in the little one's mind? By the time the child became three he probably formed an image of Allah in his mental eye as someone to be feared. The parents did not realise that in the beginning.

The embarrassment came when the child joined his preschool nursery. The child's teacher was a lively lady and within days she easily made a good relationship with the little one. By observing the child over a few weeks she managed to discover that he was scared of something. By that time he had learnt how to express himself a bit and read some basic words. In a one-to-one discussion she asked the child why he was so scared. The answer was, 'because Aiyah is hiding and seeing me'. 'What does it mean? Why should he be worried if someone sees him from behind?' thought the teacher. She could not figure out what it was all about. She was waiting for an opportunity to talk to his mother. The occasion came and the teacher asked her whether she knew of any reason why her child was scared by something called 'Aiyah'. The mother realised that the young one had taken the brunt of their over-enthusiastic teaching about Allah. She avoided the answer and said that she would try to deal with it. The parents discussed the issue at home and devised positive strategies to take the excessive fear of Allah away from the little mind and put a loving and positive picture there.

NEED FOR A BALANCED DEVELOPMENT

Growing up is adventurous. Children love games and playing. Running, chasing, climbing, jumping, throwing and other physical activities develop their bodies and help their motor coordination. While doing all these they talk and talk. All children are different, they play differently and it is interesting that boys and girls play differently from an early age. Generally, boys play more outside games in larger groups and physically tough games in order to dominate others. On the other hand, girls generally play gentler indoor games. This natural inclination is amazing.

Games and other activities give them opportunities to learn about the world. Parents should obviously give importance to the physical aspects of their child, such as sound health because that enhances confidence and self-esteem. They should occasionally take their young ones out for fresh air and let them play freely. The Prophet Muhammad ﷺ was exemplary in giving importance to physical activities and fun. Even when older, he himself used to engage in innocent play with his young wife, A'ishah, may Allah be pleased with her, and showed interest in children's play. It is universally acknowledged that physical activities, play and intellectually stimulating games enhance children's creativity and confidence.

Children grow in size and shape rapidly. They grow in intellect, their brain develops faster than any other organs of the body. Scientists have found that, by age five, children's brain reaches nine tenth of an adult brain, although their body is still one third of adult weight. This is the best age for memorising Qur'an by heart. Many pioneering Muslim scholars, natural and social scientists, became *huffadh* in their early years. As they grow, the children pass through different stages of thinking. They can think in words and symbols and relate them in day-to-day life. This age is momentous for their intellectual development and language acquisition as they learn words faster. Meaningful Islamic stories are very useful at this stage. Gradually they learn how to think logically.

As children become more socially skilled, they develop self-awareness at this stage. Success and failure affect them to the extent that they sometimes become overconfident and at times confused. Parents need to protect them from experiencing un-necessary failure. Children take praise and blame seriously at this stage. Parents must devise strategies that help their young ones to remain assured and contented.

Physical, intellectual and emotional and social development should go hand in hand with children's spiritual development. Muslim parents, as Murabbi, should try to inculcate the growth of a holistic personality in them. A balanced approach between this world and the Hereafter gives them confidence and focus of life. This gives them determination and positive outlook to be dynamic and assertive Muslims. They then acquire tranquillity of mind and heart, which is essential for human beings' journey toward Allah.

• Reward, Discipline and Self-esteem

Children are like human 'raw materials'. Parents and elders make the 'product' i.e. 'human beings'. As they learn from the sur-roundings they need discipline. Discipline means teaching chil-dren how to behave sensibly and responsibly. Parental responsi-bility is to teach them in a way that they feel good when they behave well and feel bad when they do not. If this can be incul-cated in them from within, that will remain embedded in them for the rest of their life. There is a mistaken belief that the only way to discipline children is by punishing them. Sanctions should, of course, be used for disciplining a child but need to be used with proper judgement, consistency and fairness. Most impor-tantly, the same message should go from both parents. Different treatment from fathers and mothers can prove disastrous.

The most severe punishment for children is the disapproval of parents. Children need to have why they are being punished ex-plained so that they feel that their parents do not hate them, but simply want to correct them. Once punished for some reason, the child should not be burdened with an unnecessary sense of guilt. Moreover, punishment should only be used for serious misbehaviour. Otherwise, it may miss its objective. Nobody wants children to be defiant in the end. Crude punishment may stop children temporarily from doing wrong, but it does not teach them how to overcome the discipline problem. Muslims do not disapprove of physical punishment, such as spanking, but it has to be used in the proper context and only with the purpose of educating the child. Indiscriminate or inconsistent punishment drives away children's fear and can make them rebellious at a later stage. Shaming or belittling them, especially in public, does not help their self-esteem. The maxim, 'love in public, correct in private', is very important. Children must feel that their parents still love them even after the punishment.

Parents feel proud when their children achieve something, however small it might be. It is essential parents express their feelings directly and openly about their children's accomplishments. Genuine recognition heightens their self-esteem. On the other hand, any shortcomings of the child should not be seen as the end of the world. 'Never mind. If you work harder next time, you will do better', this type of sincere comment and encouragement from parents will help maintain their self-esteem. Wrecking someone else's self-confidence is easy: a simple negative look or comment is enough to lower it. Parents must be conscious of this. If children do something very silly, the best way to deal with it is not the punishment or threat of it, but to make them realise that doing wrong is in itself upsetting. As parents need to empathise with their children, they should be taught to empathise with others as well. Only then will they realise the value of others and understand others' feelings.

The magical way to reduce the discipline problem is to recognise, praise and encourage children's good behaviour. Once again, consistency and diligence are important. Muslim parents should make sure that they encourage those that are good in Islam, e.g., honesty, sacrifice, Islamic manners and courtesy. Recognition and praise should come from the heart and parents should learn the techniques of praising and rewarding. Indiscriminate, lavish and inconsistent praise do more harm than good. The golden rules are:

- use judgement as to whether praise or punishment is essential.
- praise or punish at the correct times.
- be diligent and consistent in praising or punishing.
- make sure your praise or punishment is genuine, not whimsical.
- maintain the level of praise or punishment according to the weight of the action.
- make sure children know why they are praised or punished.
- observe whether praise or punishment is working.
- there should not be any dearth of love, even after punishment.

• Manners and Habits

No father can give his child a better gift than good manners, good character and good education. (*At-Tirmidhi*)

As children grow under the eyes of parents and other adults, they develop their unique personalities. Some traits are inherited. Their physical features, such as height and colour of the skin, and mental characteristics, such as aesthetic talents are passed from the parents' genes. However, children's environment is as important as their genes. Their upbringing, health care, education, abundance or deficiency of love, family manners - all influence their growth and development and mould their personalities.

Parents have lots of expectations from their children and some try hard to make sure they are achieved. But no one knows whether they will be realised or not. As human destiny is determined by Allah, Muslim parents should endeavour their best to raise their children to make them better Muslims with a view to pleasing Allah alone. They must have open minds and a clear understanding of *tawakkul* and action.

In the post-modern industrialised world, where Muslim children are growing in relative material abundance, the predominant culture is, sadly, one of individualism, suspicion of authority and rebellion. Indulgence and immorality are not only accommodated but, in many places, encouraged and promoted. The lack of family discipline and absence of strong moral codes have led to sexual experimentation, the drug culture, violence and confusion in gender roles. The electronic media have made things worse and are globalising these vices. We parents cannot behave like ostriches hiding our heads in the sand and ignoring the realities of life. We also cannot keep our young ones insulated from what happens in society. By their very natures children want to know things, good or bad, around them. Muslim parents have to understand that social ills spread like viruses and have the power to engulf their children, unless immunised with Islam.

How can we respond to this challenge? The only way to survive the modern destructive trends is to instil in the children a deep sense of Islamic values and morals so that, as proud young Muslims, they can differentiate between good and evil. We must try to infuse in them a sound knowledge of Islam and contemporary society from the very beginning so that in future, as adolescents and adults, they do not run away from the society but interact, engage and influence it without giving in to the social vices. This is essential for the future of Muslims, not only in the West but everywhere in the world.

As mentioned earlier, the process of training should start from the days of the babies' conception in the mothers' wombs. However, from birth up to five years old has a special significance for children. At this stage, they absorb whatever messages are around them. These messages have a long-lasting impact on their brain. If they are Islamic in the broader sense, children's mental film absorbs them and helps create sound Islamic character later. If they are mixed or un-Islamic, children grow with confusion and distortion in their character. Let us start with nutrition for our children. Islam has made it clear that children have the right to be suckled for a maximum of two years of their life. This is not only the best food for their physical growth, but this also helps transmit some qualities to them. A contented Muslim mother thus builds up her child in the mould of Islam.

Imparting education is a gradual and natural process, not a coercive one. Constant use of Islamic vocabulary in the family environment encourages children to repeat these as well, i.e. in the case where the parents naturally talk about Allah and His Messenger of Allah ﷺ. However, there could probably be little more destructive than for the parents to artificially start attempting to speak in an Islamic vocabulary that is not naturally theirs. We all have reflexes, such as, sneezing and yawning. If parents clearly utter the word 'Alhamdulillah' when they sneeze and also remind children to say the same when they do it, it gradually becomes embedded in their natures. Most importantly, parents need to practise Islam and good manners themselves, as examples are better than precepts. Children in a house where parents are practising Muslims copy many of the practices of Islam and they have lasting influence on their characters. However, parents should also make sure that children are not overburdened with ideological fervour.

Education and training are pro-active processes. Parents cannot leave their children to learn on their own. Parasites or viruses grow quickly if they are left alone, but plants need care and nourishment to grow. Both under- and over-nourishment kill them. Human beings need trainers to help them develop human qualities. We need even basic training in how to eat, urinate, talk with elders and value other creatures in their own cultural context. Islam, as a comprehensive deen, has guidelines on all aspects of life. How would children know them without being told or trained? Allah u has forbidden some evils for human beings. How would we stay away from them if they are not explained to us properly?

As such, children need to be educated, reminded and guided in the early stages of their lives. Continuous training by effective trainers - fathers and mothers - is always the best way to produce results. Even some animals, such as dogs and dolphins, learn how to do certain things if trained properly. Parents must not forget that they are commanded to educate and train their loved ones so that they are imbued with exemplary Muslim character.

Innocent children need to be protected from evils because they move very quickly. Bad habits, such as swearing and using slang languages, can easily be picked up by them, no matter how careful parents are. Parents must be extra careful so that their children do not use foul words at home and they need to educate them about Allah's displeasure at this. Muslims are decent human beings who do not use 'vain or vulgar talk' (Qur'an 23:3).

• Home as the Nursery

Children are intelligent in identifying love, affection, anger, sadness and other human expressions. Even when they are little they can read the faces of their parents. Parental dealings have to be meaningful, especially when children are at a tender age. Parents need to openly display their positive feelings. They should maintain consistency in their behaviour. Mothers and fathers must be careful to deliver the same message to their children. Any gap or misunderstanding between them can give wrong signals to the children. Discipline is vital for their proper upbringing and teaching. Parents should not spoil their young ones by a desire to please them. Children have to gradually learn their limits. They should learn that they cannot get everything they want in this world. That does not mean that parents should only resort to do's and don'ts to educate them.

Children like copying adults. They wear their clothes and shoes and copy what they do at home. In a family where Islam is practised on a daily basis with the prayer, Qur'an recitation and du'a, children observe them meticulously and try to imitate them in earnest. Repetition of these practices has a lasting impact in their memory. Children are such keen observers that many of them methodically learn how to do the *ruku'* and *sajdah* of the prayer. Children's brains are like dry new sponges. Whatever is absorbed in their early years is imprinted for a long time to come. Parents must display exemplary behaviour and extra tolerance in order to give them a good education and the joy of childhood. They should try to create a learning and joyful environment at home so that whatever they see or hear is positive and infused with the Islamic ethos. The dealings of the Prophet Muhammad ﷺ with his dearest grandchildren, Hasan and Hussein, were full of love and mercy. On one occasion he was leading a congregation prayer and he lengthened his *sajdah*. When he finished the prayer the companions asked him about this. The Prophet ﷺ answered, 'My grandson rode on my back and I gave him time to play'.

Parents must remember that children are not adults and should not expect too much from them. Forcing children to do something or conform to parental wishes is counterproductive. This can end up in a strained relationship between them later. Instead, they should wait a little to allow children to mature and use persuasion so that they do things on their own volition. This tolerance of parents infuses similar qualities in their children.

Children need guidance and should not be left on their own to find their own way. It is true that natural instincts lead human beings to find their ways to survive. But children need nurturing. If Muslim parents fail to shape their character in their way, others will fill the vacuum and the environmental effect will turn them away from Islam. Responsible parents are like cautious potters who meticulously and sensitively engage in shaping their delicate raw materials for a wholesome outcome. All successful nations invest in moulding their future generation in their own way. When they were the teachers of humanity Muslims in the past succeeded in creating generations who were genuinely the 'best community' in the world. Unfortunately, this forward-looking vision has been absent from many Muslims for many centuries.

Positive parenting involves pro-active teaching with love and care, but with admonition, if and when necessary. All these should be in context. Parents should plan for disseminating knowledge and understanding commensurate with their children's ages and abilities. One cannot expect parents to have formal syllabuses as schools have, but conscientious parents have targets and focus in educating their children from the very beginning. They set their goals regarding children and make their home a nursery for them. Across civilisations homes were the best schools for humankind.

As discussed in the previous chapter, mothers working full-time outside the home and leaving their young vulnerable children in kindergartens commit an injustice to them. Before deciding to dump their children with strangers, Muslim mothers need to ask themselves what is more important in life. Those who out of necessity are compelled to work have their point and they must find ways to counteract this during their time at home. But those who prefer not to stay at home for fear of social stigma or those who underestimate child rearing need soul-searching before they loosen their bonds with their children. It generally results in the loss of authority over the young ones when they grow up. What can these parents expect from their children when they become old? We need a proper balance in our lives.

Young children reared and educated in non-Muslim kindergartens are exposed in their formative period to many practices which are alien to Islam and Muslim culture. They grow up with roots which are not well established. Instead of continually hearing words and seeing things related to Islam they grow up with the nursery rhymes and vocabulary of the prevalent amoral nursery education. While this may not be a point of concern to those who subscribe to the secular way of life, it has a lasting influence on the mental make-up of children. What they learn in the kindergarten influences their future development and fills their hearts with confusion about life. The worst that parents can do to their children is give them a confused start in life.

It is not expected that all Muslim mothers will employ the techniques of educational psychology per se in rearing their children, but it is essential that they become pro-active with them, engaging them with the ever-increasing challenges of life. Raising pre-school children is fun as well, if mothers take it that way. They should sing songs, recite age-appropriate poems and tell them stories about life. Stories from the Qur'an and from the golden period of Islam should not be repeated until the child passes the wakening of the intellect around the age of seven lest the child take the very real stories of Islam for fairy stories. Muslims in the West are now fortunate to have organisations and publishers that produce good quality children's books, cassettes, albums and animated cartoons. There are good storybooks around. Parents should use them as resources in their home nursery.

THE ISSUES AT THIS AGE

• Toilet-training and General Cleanliness

> Allah is Good and likes what is fragrant, He is Clean and likes cleanliness, He is Generous and likes generosity, He is Munificent and likes munificence. (*At-Tirmidhi*)

The concept of *taharah* (cleanliness) is important in Islam. It is a prerequisite for performing the prayers that lead to spiritual cleanliness. It is important that parents understand the essence of it before they teach their children. All parents are impatient to teach their children about physical cleanliness from a very early age. However, problems arises during the transition period when children leave their disposable nappies and learn to use the toilet. Parents should be prepared for accidents, however unpleasant they may be. Through fervent desire to keep the home pure, parents should not use coercive methods in this regard.

Toilet training is one of the most difficult things with children. Some learn it quickly, but others take time. Forcing toilet training is a big mistake, as this ends up in tears for children and frustration for parents. It can result in persistent bed-wetting and soiling in older children. What is the best age for it? Generally, children over two years, i.e., after the suckling period, learn this easily. Children have to attain a certain physical level of maturity and body coordination.

• Halal and Haram

The necessity of halal income is basic in Islam. In the same manner, spending in a halal way and consumption of halal food are absolutely important for Muslims. This is more so in the West where the notion of halal and haram can be different from the Islamic one. Halal and haram have wider meanings in a Muslim life, which is anchored in obedience to Allah. The believers are asked to eat of the good things (Qur'an 2:172, 20:81). It is mentioned in a hadith that which means, 'the flesh nourished from haram food will not have its place in the Garden, and the Fire is its abode' (*Ahmad, ad-Darimi, al-Bayhaqi*). Islam is a natural religion and most things on earth are halal, except for a few things mentioned in the Qur'an and Sunnah. As such, the list of haram things is limited. Over the centuries it has been shown that what Allah has categorised as haram are really detrimental to human body and soul.

Whatever the situation, Muslim parents are required to educate their children about the importance of halal and haram from their childhood. The concept should be embedded in their thinking process. Whatever the parents buy for their little ones, food or any other item, need to be checked according to the criteria of halal and haram. In consumer societies, Muslims should be extra careful of what is bought and consumed. Fortunately, producers in the developed countries are required by law to publish the names of the ingredients in their products so that consumers know what they are buying. On the other hand, as a result of positive Muslim campaigning in the social arena, the idea of halal and haram is rapidly spreading in Western countries and Muslim requirements are now being acknowledged in most places. But, this was not true a quarter century ago.

• Coping with Frustration and Tantrums

Life has both smooth and rough. Disappointment, frustration and anger are unavoidable factors in life. Not everybody can cope with them. Children consistently loved, cared and trained by parents are emotionally contented. But can they cope with the hard facts of life and frustrations that ensue from various sources? It all depends on the quality of parental upbringing and training. If children are not cared or loved sufficiently or they experience too many broken promises, they gradually give in to frustration. They lose control of themselves and become angry.

Moreover, if parents set bad examples to their children, shout and exhibit emotional outbursts in front of them, they learn this. Lack of patience, tolerance and steadfastness in the parents affects the child very negatively. In the Qur'an Allah has asked Muslims to seek help from Allah through *sabr* (steadfastness) and prayer (Qur'an 2:153). Wise age-old reflections, such as, 'patience is bitter but its fruit is sweet', 'patience is a plaster for all pain', 'patience is often better than medicine' and 'patience is the door of joy' are important in real life.

Parents need to watch when tension is built up inside their children and intervene positively before an outburst. They should teach them the necessary skills to release bottled-up feelings and techniques to contain their anger. They should be imbued with the love and fear of Allah. Allah dislikes anger and frustration. However, if in spite of all teaching, children do have a tantrum, parents should concentrate on containing it, rather than becoming angry themselves. Anger feeds anger and is like a fire that burns.

• Use of the TV and Computer

The struggle for survival in the real world keeps parents very busy. Many Muslims are occupied with the world of work amid prejudice and discrimination. The pressure of day-to-day jobs or businesses and the need for extra money to top up family income and meet other social demands strains them. Time becomes a rare commodity. As a result, many of them fail to invest the required amount of time with their children. In situations like these, TV can unwittingly take on the role of a baby-sitter in some families. Some parents, because of simple-mindedness, consider all children's programmes, such as cartoons, innocent. But, are they? Unrestricted and un-screened exposure to apparently harmless programmes can easily dilute the children's values and the ethos so carefully fostered by parents at home.

TV is regarded by some as an almost essential tool of modern life, and it is very influential in dictating our lifestyles, forming our opinions and moulding our personalities. The academic debate as to whether TV is helpful or harmful to children is widespread in the industrialised countries and it will not easily die out, but the fact of the matter is worrying. A Westerner spends, on average, three to four hours a day watching TV, i.e., more than ten years of his life watching TV! Young children having busy parents watch more.

TV may serve some useful purposes for children as entertainment and learning, but it eats up their time significantly, the time when they are not sleeping or playing. Is TV stimulating or educational? There is doubt about it, as it keeps children away from engagement with life. It is a one-way enjoyment. Instead of helping children to relax, TV leaves them more tense. It is believed to cause delayed acquisition of speech and poor health in very young children. It might have links with attention deficit disorder. TV is also seen by many as a tool that kills creativity. It makes people lethargic and unable to concentrate for some time after watching it.

Do children like TV? Research has found that children watch TV most often because they have nothing else to do. They also watch it when they are bored. Children generally prefer to stay in the company of others and if they are denied this, what can they do? For their young minds, finding no other creative outlets, TV can become addictive in the end. To some, TV can prove to be a 'Terrible Virus', much as in the way viral infection harms the human body. Once addicted, TV can prove destructive to the growth of children. Children who have less opportunity to spend time with their parents and/or other adults are at risk of spending their formative years looking at this 'idiot box', and as such can grow in a warped way. The advice to Muslim parents is unequivocal - unless it is absolutely essential for both parents to engage in full-time earning or study, parents should plan between themselves to make time for their loved ones, stay at home and engage with their children in creative activities. Children should not be left to the mercy of TV programmers.

TV is not the only 'enemy within' against the balanced growth of a child. Similar concern is now being shown towards computer related 'fun time' for children at home. The computer, with countless games and Internet facilities, is already having a disproportionate influence on the children of the developed world. Most children have got access to computer at homes before five. As sex and violence have now become tools of commercialisation, young children are exposed to numerous provocative materials on computer screens from mindless money-makers who do not care about the impact of their 'innovative' software. Young children at the preschool age are easily hooked on computers for hours every day and can lose their innocence at an early age.

Not everyone would proclaim these tools of modernism evil in themselves. If used in meaningful learning pursuits they could be most effective tools in the education and wholesome growth of children. Societies run on decent values are, in fact, utilising them for this purpose. Unfortunately, as modern societies are sliding lower in moral degeneration, these tools are being used by a powerful minority to propagate vice. As a result, Muslim parents need to be extra cautious in using TV and the computer at home so that they do not invite disaster in the young minds. Safety barriers need to be erected against the vices spread by this evil minority.

• Birthday Parties and Celebrations

'Happy birthday to you' is the song chanted in chorus amid cakes and candles in all birthday parties in the West. Birthday celebrations are one of the most important cultural aspects of the Western family and social life. From the first birthday onwards families, nurseries and primary schools arrange some sort of party where children look for fun while starting a new year in their life. As the years roll on they begin to understand that the day is losing significance.

It might be considered insensitive in society if anyone showed scepticism about the purpose of celebrating birthdays, but what exactly is the birthday and what does the birthday mean to a Muslim? And is it just a matter of celebration? These are the questions raised by Muslim scholars. In Islam's long history the birthday was not a matter that needed discussion. Where remembered by some parents, it was a matter of reflection and occasion to seek forgiveness from Allah for themselves and their children and to form resolve for resolute action in future. As Islam follows a lunar calendar, which is different from the solar one, birthdays fall in different seasons. Birthday celebrations only gained some importance among the secular Muslim elite in the later period of colonialism when they started parroting everything they saw in the West.

Birth in Islam is a serious matter. To Muslims this has three stages. One, when all human beings' spirits were first created by Allah in the world of spirit. Nobody, except Allah, knows when it was. Two, when individual human beings are conceived through the physical union of their parents. Three, when they are delivered from their mother's womb on earth, about thirty-nine weeks after conception. Which one is the human being's real birthday? As people generally fear to face the reality of existence, the delivery date is normally taken as the birthday. Here, the big question arises. What is there to celebrate for a day when human beings, as lumps of flesh and blood, were thrown into the world, totally dependent on others? Shouldn't we rather make this an occasion to reflect and show our gratitude to the Lord Who created is from nothing and kept us alive?

Islam has two unique celebrations in a year, Eid al-Fitr to celebrate the end of the month-long fasting and Eid al-Adha to commemorate the sacrifice of the prophet Ibrahim ﷺ and his son Isma'il ﷺ. Muslims are asked to make these occasions lively, enjoyable and meaningful. These two occasions have wholesome religious, social and economic implications. For children and women these have special meanings as the Prophet Muhammad ﷺ encouraged them to engage in them wholeheartedly in communal prayer. Apart from these well-defined celebrations, we Muslims are free to enjoy our lives with thankfulness to Allah and in good measure at any time. Taking these into consideration, if Muslims want to remember birthdays at all we should make them occasions to remind ourselves of our tasks on earth. Children need to be educated in this wholesome perception.

NOTES

1   It is permissible for a man to have children with his slave woman, but that immediately elevates her status and that of her children so that they may not be sold and are free upon his death, if he has not freed them before. Clearly this option is hardly open to many in this time. Ed.

2   See note above.

3   *The Daily Telegraph* (London), 12 June 2000.

4   *The Times* (London) 7 August 2000.

5   There is a fashion of men attending the actual birth, but that was never done traditionally either by Muslims or non-Muslims, and can have proven deleterious effects on the relationship of the couple. Many couples who have followed this route have never recovered their intimacy after the birth. Ed.

6   *Raising Children in Islam*, Suhaib Hasan, pp18-22, Qur'an Society, London, 1998, and *Manners of Welcoming the New Born Child in Islam* – Yoosuf ibn Abdullah Al-Areefee, Maktaba Darus Salaam (UK) 1996.)

7   *Raising Children in Islam*, Suhaib Hasan, Qur'an Society, pp31-32, London, 1998.

8   *Parenting: A Handbook for Parents*, Maureen Gaffney, et. al., Town House, UK, pp69-71, 1991

9   *Understanding Your Child: An A-Z for Parents* - Mavis Klein, Judy Piatkus

Ltd, p9, 1991

[10] *The Dilemma of Muslim Psychologists* - Malik B. Badri, MWH London Publishers, 1979.

The World of Schooling

Executive Summary

- Primary education is the bedrock of formal learning. So, choosing a good school is vital for children. Parents should help, guide and build confidence in them at the start of their school life.

- Muslim parents should become aware of what is being taught in the school and to what their children are exposed. They should watch whether their children like or dislike the school and why.

- Muslim parents should keep an eye on the numerous celebrations in school, many of which have little or no meaning from an Islamic point of view. They should make extra efforts to make Eid celebrations enjoyable, occasions of learning and public.

- Muslim parents should watch whether their children pick up offensive language and rude behaviour from outside. Manners and etiquette reflect character and a Muslim should try to be best in them.

- A proper policy of discipline should exist at home. Both too much control or laxity can spoil children. Young ones should be taught the basic teachings of Islam with warmth, love, understanding and justice from an early age.

- Muslim parents should leave no stone unturned in choosing a quality single-sex secondary school for their children for healthy growth of their character and better academic achievement.

- Compulsory school years are vital for the growth of children as balanced human beings. Muslim parents should consistently help them to acquire personal management and life skills as well as love for and commitment to Islam.

- A Muslim home should create a positive environment where children feel anchored, shun the temptations and pull of the permissive and value-less culture of the wider society. Parents should spend quality time with their children at home.

- Muslim parents should encourage their children to learn about Islam and socialise with good friends through supplementary Islamic schooling and involvement with Islamic and community activities.

10. The World of Schooling (Primary)

No father can give his child a better gift than good manners, good character and a good education. (*At-Tirmidhi*)

THE BEDROCK OF FORMAL EDUCATION

The statutory age to start school in the Western countries is, generally, five. In Britain, children start their formal education in the primary schools at this age and they go to secondary schools at eleven years of age. As primary schools provide the foundation of education, Western countries give them importance. Primary schools impart basic literacy, oracy and numeracy as well as social skills that give children the confidence necessary to start secondary education. There is competition to excel in world-class education that sometimes puts young children under tremendous pressure. However, we must acknowledge that some people believe that the supremacy of the West over many centuries is because of their creative and innovative educational system that begins with their primary schools.

As schools have to produce tangible results, especially in the curricular areas, teachers are obliged to work hard. Unless they are professionally sound, motivated and committed to educate the young ones they cannot withstand the pressures from the educational chiefs from above as well as demands in the classrooms. As such, both the style and content of teaching are important.

Education reflects the values as well as the influences of the society in which we live. A broad set of common values and purposes underpin the school curriculum. Teachers are the vanguard in disseminating, creating and maintaining these values across generations. They are catalysts of change in society, as they mould the personalities of the children in the shape of these values and norms. Primary teachers' delicate job of shaping the character of future citizens of a country in theory make them valued and respected in the society.

The future of the Muslim ummah depends, among other things, on the education of our children. But, can our young ones grow up and develop in the spirit of Islam within the Western educational system, which subscribes to overwhelmingly amoral values and norms? On the other hand, can the Islamic schools, which only serve a tiny minority of Muslims, educate young Muslims in a way that answers the historical needs of the ummah? It is difficult to say at this moment. First of all, in the powerful sociocultural context of Western countries the survival and growth of an alternative value system is a daunting prospect. Second, the lack of confidence among the Muslim population, because of various factors, makes things difficult for us. Being unaware of the system many Muslims expect miracles from Muslim schools. Competence and the broader Islamic perspectives of the teachers of these schools are of paramount importance and for practical reasons many schools are unable to provide these. Those who send their children to a traditional madrasah to produce an imam or hafidh of Qur'an have specific goals in their lives and are generally content with their children working in many mosques in the West. In any case, to whichever school children are sent, whether state-run, private Muslim or a traditional madrasah, parents need to be pro-active in moulding their characters.

In Britain, English, Maths and Science are the core subjects in both primary and secondary schools. A balanced curriculum with other foundation subjects - such as, ICT (Information and Communication Technology), D & T (Design and Technology), History, Geography, Art, Music and Physical Education - is followed in primary schools on the basis of two Key Stages, Key Stage 1 (age group 5-7) and Key Stage 2 (age group 7-11). For each subject and Key Stage, teachers follow programmes of study that outline the syllabus for the pupils. To ascertain the knowledge, skills and understanding of pupils of different abilities and maturity by the end of each Key Stage an 'Attainment Target' is set. Under the Education Act 1996, all schools should also teach their children RE (Religious Education) and sex education. Provisions have been made for parents to withdraw their children from all or part of the lessons on these subjects. Unfortunately, many Muslim parents are either unaware of this provision or lack confidence to ask head teachers for their children's withdrawal from these lessons, even if they do not like them. This passivity or inability can prove harmful for the future of Muslim children.[1]

The step to promote pupils' spiritual, moral, social and cultural development through RE, PSHE (Personal, Social and Health Education) and Citizenship by successive governments in Britain is taken positively by Muslim educationalists. At the same time, the opportunity to learn and develop a wide range of skills, such as, communication, social and problem-solving skills on the one hand and thinking skills on the other, in the beginning of their life in the primary school, is welcomed by all.

However, as the ethos and environment in Western multi-cultural education is broadly Christian, this can easily dilute the identity of non-Christian children. The demands of the system and its proselytising nature make many of these minority groups vulnerable. The Muslim community, with deep-rooted religious values, finds this especially daunting. As Islam is at the core of Muslim life, Muslim educationalists and social leaders need to assert our views on interaction, not assimilation into the melting pot of

Western culture. Most importantly, Muslim parents need to be extra vigilant in enthusing their children with Islam in every sphere of life from the very beginning.

CHOOSING A SCHOOL

By the time children become three Muslim parents start agonising about their formal education. Some Muslim parents help setting up nurseries on their own or with the help of similarly minded parents, in order to prepare their children with the basic skills of literacy, numeracy and sociability before they join the primary schools. There is strong evidence that children who attend pre-school nurseries have advantages over others. There are many Muslim mothers who could be motivated to run such nurseries for their young ones. In this way their energy could be harnessed for the benefit of the ummah. Young Muslim women with professional skills can contribute enormously if they seek relevant qualifications to set up toddler- and play-groups and nursery schools. If properly started and run, they could easily get public funding.

The Education Act 1944 in Britain gives parents the right to educate their children at home if they can fulfil certain criteria. Some groups, like the Travellers, have used this right to educate their children at home and found home-based schools beneficial to their needs. However, this needs consistent parental motivation over many years. In reality, it is largely groups of dedicated Muslim parents who could choose this after the children reach a certain age, although it is certainly a viable option for younger children.

Those who are not that fortunate enough to live in the heart of a Muslim community in the West in order to start a joint venture should spend extra time preparing their children with the basic Islamic moorings before they enter the doors of their local primary schools. Parents must take this burden on themselves in order to give their young ones the necessary confidence to start their schooling. They should try to expand their children's knowledge and interests in the world by involving them in indoor and outdoor activities.

Well-off and practising Muslims desperately look for independent Muslim schools and in many Western countries they are now available in some of the big cities. Others who are affluent and specifically look for academic excellence buy good education for their children by sending them to respectable private schools. But the majority of Muslim parents have no choice but to send their children to state-run schools. They are the people who need to be extra vigilant about the standards of education and the Islamic futures of their children. Parents must remember that about seven hours each weekday for thirty-nine weeks a year their children are in the hands of school teachers, many of whom may be secularists or proponents of permissive lifestyles. This is a gamble with the future of young Muslims and the options are limited.

Over the past few decades Muslim parents, especially in Britain, have been struggling to establish private schools to educate their children within Islam. There are now new breeds of school that try to follow a curriculum consisting of some aspects of Islam as well as the core curriculum subjects of the land. Unfortunately, these schools are generally under-funded and not equipped with proper human and material resources. Many of them lack qualified teachers because of the lower salaries and lack of facilities compared to the state-funded schools. But the enviable commitment of the management team and teaching staff to education and the enthusiasm of the parents have made this venture a success in most countries. As a result of the concerted efforts of Muslim educationalists private Muslim schools are now in the forefront of alternative education in many Western countries. In spite of handicaps, they generally out-perform state-run schools in the league table of results.

Many state-run schools, especially in inner city areas, are known for under-achievement and disciplinary problems. With social deprivation comes disaffection, and children do not generally find motivation in going through the rigours of the curriculum. Low teacher-expectation and lack of proper resources make things worse in those schools. The numerous social ills that abound in permissive societies also influence the young ones directly in their early years. As the choice for ordinary Muslims is limited, this leads to their educational disadvantage. The vicious circle of educational under-achievement and economic impoverishment in Britain has put the Bangladeshi and Pakistani communities at the bottom of the league table in terms of employment and social status. On top of this, racial and religious prejudice adds to their social exclusion.

Western people have choices in education. In some countries, e.g., Britain, there are thousands of Christian denominational schools - Church of England, Catholic, and others - which are funded by the government but run according to the ethos of Christianity. With a small population, the Jews have a few dozen of their own schools. After a long drawn-out struggle, British Muslims have, in the end, got funding for three schools, two primary and one secondary. In spite of this tiny number, Muslim denominational schools are coming under criticism for 'promoting segregation' in the society. This insensitivity to Islam is unfortunate when only Muslims are targeted. In fact, ordinary Muslims find their dream coming true when their children get accepted by these schools, which accommodate the values of Islam and good discipline. Many Muslim parents, fearing the negative ethos of state-run schools, desperately look for these denominational schools to secure their children's futures.

It is a historical fact that private schools have proved bastions of capitalist and the elitist societies of Western countries over the centuries. They are expensive, but they generally provide quality education in return. It has been observed that Britain's 80-90% most successful people in top corporate and management jobs, received their education in these private schools, which constitute only 7-8% of all schools in the country. These schools have high teacher-pupils ratios, strong discipline, high teacher-expectation and an enviable quality of teaching and material resources. It is no surprise that, like other rich people in the country, the wealthy and ambitious sections of the Muslim community are tempted to educate their sons and daughters in these prestigious schools. However, these elitist schools are not risk-free. In recent years, there have been reports that some of these in Britain have been undergoing drug and other problems.

Muslim parents, who send their children to private schools, Muslim or secular, are generally confident about their educational qualities. Their children start schooling with an advantage over others. On the contrary, for the majority of Muslims who send their children to state-run schools life is hard indeed. They need to be extra vigilant about the educational and social development of their young ones. This chapter is focused on the needs of the vast majority of Muslim parents who struggle to educate their children in state schools. In reality, whether in the state or private sectors, education of young people and bringing them up in the Islamic ethos are becoming more challenging.

Schools can never replace homes. Whichever school may be chosen for the children, Muslim parents cannot shy away from their responsibility in steering the way for their educational, social and spiritual development until they mature. Schools are education-providers and Muslim parents must learn how to use their rights to get the most out of them. They need to master the art of communication with the schools about the educational achievements of their children and put the schools in the dock, if necessary, on their rights. However, they must remember that their children's Islamic upbringing is their own responsibility and they cannot expect this from secular establishments. As such, parents themselves need to acquire the basic understanding of Islam in the modern context so that they can equip their children with its broader message.

Academic achievement should not be the only criteria in choosing a school. The overall environment or 'culture' of a school is important. Its racial and religious mix, the attitudes of the head teacher and other teaching and non-teaching staff, and the local catchment area, all contribute to a good school. In choosing a school, parents should ask themselves the following basic questions;

- How do the head teacher and other staff receive you?
- What is the catchment area like?
- What is its image in the area?
- How good are its extra-curricular activities?
- Do you feel confident that your child will flourish in the school?

SCHOOL EXPOSURE

Starting school is an exciting experience for young children and a challenging responsibility for parents. It is the beginning of independent lives in the wider world for children. Those who had the advantage of sending their children to pre-school nurseries or playgroups before the statutory age have already passed a phase in that challenge. Their children should have already learnt something about coping in the classroom. They now learn to listen and are able to respond to adults who are not their parents. School introduces them to a wide circle of friends and learning opportunities. The fact that their beloved young ones are going to be exposed to a host of life experiences should convince parents to plan and prepare for their new journeys in life. Evidently, conscientious parents are well aware of the challenge and they make their home environment a learning one so that their children can cope adequately with the new challenges in school.

Schools expose children to the outside world through formalised education. For the first time in their lives children pass through assessments and tests. Their learning curve suddenly takes a different shape. What do children learn at this age? In the task-centred education philosophy of the developed world children are treated as tools, albeit the most important ones. Their unique position as emissaries of Allah is hardly understood. The full might of the educational establishment is geared to make them good citizens of the country. In order to counteract all the influences brought upon them, Muslim parents must continuously interact with them so that they learn what is going on in their world. They should question, help and guide and continuously endeavour to build holistic characters in them. They need to share the experiences of school life with their children. They need to cultivate their potential and attempt to harness them. However, it is not possible without going through the children's learning process with an open and broad outlook, a sensitive approach and conscientious attitudes.

The first few days, especially the first day, of children's primary school can be daunting for them and full of anxiety for the parents if the children have not already attended nursery schools. One of the parents might have to stay with them for some time at the school. Children may not want to leave their parent at all. They may come home in the afternoon promising they will never go to school again. It may also be difficult for parents to part with their beloved ones for the first time in their lives. But this is the nature of life. All children pass this phase quickly.

As children progress through each year in their schools their characters gradually become more manifest and distinct. Each day they bring new experiences and new challenges. After a long day in school many children are still energetic and they look for something to do at home. Can the parents accommodate their demand and engage them in meaningful pursuits? If not, they will release their energy in vain activities or engage with the TV or video and computer games till they become bored. Children might need to watch TV for a while, but addiction to it can ruin them.

By the time children enter junior-school age, i.e., eight in Britain, they begin to show more independence. Nine-year olds are capable of looking at their own selves critically and they show greater self-confidence. They may insist on going to school on their own and can become very aware of how they are viewed by their peer group. They also become conscious of their family and feel responsible for their younger siblings. If any of their brothers or sisters behaves in a silly way they feel embarrassed. Children at this age generally show interest in hobbies, such as reading and stamp collection. If that is the case, parents need to encourage them to do things that are wholesome and innocent and possibly good for their future careers.

At about the age of nine and ten the characteristic features of boys and girls start to manifest. They usually prefer to play with children of the same sex and are interested in different activities. Boys and girls generally become lively and boisterous youngsters. They become more self-conscious and are able to make careful observations, prefer to talk about themselves and express their views.

QUALITY TIME WITH CHILDREN

Throughout the primary-school age of children, parents also learn and mature. From the continuous experience of dealing with them they get more confidence in rearing them. This on-the-job training, the trial and error, gives them an altruistic pleasure in life. Rearing children in the primary school years is as demanding as pre-school years, probably more, because the nature of the demands are different. As children spend about one third of their non-sleeping hours in school they learn many things and bring them home. Muslim parents need to spend sufficient time to check whether they learn something alien to Islam and moral decency. In that case, they need psychologically to screen them out from their minds with sensitivity.

It is a big job, as all parents have to earn their livelihoods and some are additionally engaged in various other works. When both parents have to work, it can bring chaos in the morning and evening. To deal with this effectively a good timetable is important. Children's homework, dinner and sleep time have to be planned, in consultation with them, and maintained strongly.

As mentioned earlier, Muslim parents must give preference to the akhirah over this world if they want to raise their children in Islam. No matter how busy they are in their livelihoods and social work, they must invest quality time for their education and Islamic upbringing. What does quality time mean? Everybody would agree that it means spending such time, often one-to-one, with children that is meaningful, in terms of action as well as outcome. Watching something together, telling a bedtime story, taking them out in the park, talking, chatting, laughing over family and other affairs, helping in school work - all help. They make a bond in relationship and fill the gaps in any understanding or perception. Parents should have a workable plan and they should stick to it. Failure to do this could mean crippling a young life. Unfortunately, there are many Muslims who, because of their odd jobs or busy schedules, ignore the demands of their children in their formative period - fathers spend most of their time outside, leaving mothers busy in the kitchen or with household work. The result can be ominous. Children grow on their own, watching TV, playing video games or hanging around outside. As a result, parents gradually lose touch with them and lose their grip on them.

There are some fathers who do not even take time to see their children or interact with them for days and weeks. They come home at night and find them asleep. How could these children grow up in Islam or gain education for life? This is the path of destruction and family disintegration. The under-achievement of the children of Bangladeshi and Pakistani origin in Britain is understood to be linked with this general parental indifference to children.

On the other hand, there are some career-minded parents who prefer to remain busy with their careers or earning more and more money, at the cost of their own lives and their children's futures. Many fathers get up very early, leave for work and come home late and very tired. They just want to eat something and go to bed so they can repeat the same routine day in, day out. Fathers who rarely see their children have little to contribute to their upbringing. Some might send their children to expensive private schools, but, can money alone buy education and a happy future? It is true that good schools can probably give good academic results, but, good degrees are not the only criteria for success in life. Good schools in the developed countries have not been able to produce good human beings. Muslim parents having a minimal understanding of Islam and the world should have second thoughts on this.

Parental time can only be effective if parents try to infuse in their children the importance of human life and a sense of time-keeping. They should help their young ones to discipline themselves from the start. As children grow up to junior school age, from the age of eight in Britain, parents need to help them in preparing their timetables and consistently maintaining them. Inculcation of this sense of time is one of the best gifts parents can give their children in their early life. The primary school children's life should have:

- Some time for study, reading books and home work
- Play and games (indoor and outdoor)
- Circles of friends to whom they can relate
- Free time or personal space
- Innocent entertainment with TV and computer
- Arabic learning and Qur'an recitation
- Some household involvement helping parents, mainly as a learning process
- Involvement with mosque and mosque-related activities

PARENTAL RIGHTS IN SCHOOLS

Education cannot be left to teachers alone. Muslim parents should not only invest their time in their children, they should also assert their parental rights on the schools of their children. It is an individual responsibility on a Muslim parent as well as a collective responsibility of the Muslim community. Parents are the customers of schools, and schools make every effort to satisfy their customers' needs. The good thing is the recognition of the increasing rights of parents that are mentioned in the 'Parents Charter' in many Western countries. Parents can visit their children's school, talk to the class teachers and head teachers on issues of education and the welfare of their children. They can talk on the broader educational, pastoral and social issues of the school. Parents can also become school governors and take part in the decision-making process. In Britain, Local Management of Schools (LMS) has given real power to school governing bodies. Muslims can play an effective role at the Local Education Authority (LEA) level and, even, at the national level.

However, in order to make effective contributions in all these bodies parents must learn the tools of the trade. They must be familiar with the educational issues of the day, the school curriculum and a host of other issues relevant to the education world. At the same time, they must be pro-active and articulate in expressing their views in the relevant forums. Muslim have been, so far, only raising their voices in protest on some issues. While that is important where necessary, they should now come up with their positive contribution as governors and members of various statutory bodies, not only to help the Muslim community but also to show the way of a distinct Islamic value system in education. There is no shortcut to this. They have to master skills to do this. Over the decades, Muslim parents have been on the periphery because of their lack of confidence and indifference. Unless they take up the challenge now they will face further hardships.

ISSUES IN PRIMARY SCHOOL

Most children in primary school age experience some common difficulties in their day-to-day life. They could be either home-based or related to school. Then there are important issues that raise questions in young minds. Conscientious parents can identify them in the beginning and deal with these problems with compassion and sensitivity.

• School Phobia

Fear of new things is apparently inherent in human nature. Children have common fears in childhood. Sometimes these fears are short-lived, but, at times, they can create serious worries in parents. Some children refuse to go to school for no apparent reason. Parents need to ascertain whether this is because of fear or phobia and whether this is due to some physical or emotional reason. This may prove difficult to discover, as many children cannot even properly express themselves at an early age. Whatever the reasons, parents should try to empathise with them and refrain from sending them to school forcibly. They should rather try to identify the cause and persuade them to attend school. Children who refuse to go to school at an early stage most often suffer from anxiety and the main source of anxiety is the fear of separation from their mothers. Older children can often make vague complaints, which need to be tackled.

Children are often loud, noisy and boisterous, especially in the playground. Some are hyperactive, others are loners. All these factors, and in addition the sociocultural make-up of pupils, can make some of them aggressive. This can give rise to bullying. Bullying can be carried out by an individual or a group of children on vulnerable children, who are unable or afraid to defend themselves. It can be verbal, psychological or even physical. Children being bullied may be unwilling both to go to school and to talk to their parents. If it ever comes to the attention of the parents they need to take this up with the school. They should also teach their children how to challenge it by becoming more assertive.

•Alien Cultural Celebrations

Christmas, Valentine's day, Halloween parties and other similar celebrations in primary schools may be presented as neutral innocent fun, but are known to be rooted in paganism. Among them are also Christmas and the white bearded Santa Claus about which there is great hype during November and December in the Western world. They have also been highly commercialised and have little religious meaning in them. The fact that Santa, Father Christmas, does not really exist has been instrumental in raising questions about the integrity of this hype. Children in nursery and primary schools are asked to participate in numerous Christmas programmes. The whole month of December, before the school breaks in the third week, is geared to enjoy and in some cases promote the myth of Father Christmas.

It puts psychological pressure on young non-Christian children, as they have to conform to the hype. On occasions, everyone in the class, including Muslims, is involved in various functions tinted with Christianity. Ceremonial Christmas Trees, the cakes and parties can be overwhelming for them. Although most Western countries take pride in being multi-faith, these programmes are presented to pupils as if they are value-free and for everybody. The lack of cultural and religious sensitivity puts non-Christian children in disarray. The season is so long that even practising Muslim parents feel embarrassed to withdraw their children from school.

Whatever the school or other parents might think, Muslim parents should politely talk to the teacher about this so that their children do not feel under pressure to take part in any of these celebrations. As they are essentially Christian celebrations and Muslims do respect other religions, schools also should happily waive young Muslim children from participating in them.

• Self-esteem

Self-esteem and the feeling of self-worth is vital in everybody's lives. It gives rise to drive which is essential for success. Lack or loss of self-esteem can make children ineffective in their lives. As they pass through their primary school phase, they develop varieties of personal and social skills, which are drawn from within their school, peer-group, society and families. When they succeed in managing the demands of day-to-day life, they feel proud.

This enhances their self-esteem. Parents are in a unique position to contribute to the development of children's positive self-image. Every time a parent or an adult praises them, cuddles, smiles at and recognises their achievement their self-esteem is enhanced. On the other hand, a negative or dismissive and uncomplimentary remark or look reduces their self-esteem. Abundant, explicit and loving approval of children makes them self-confident.

Some young children can be very shy and this can be taken as their lack of self-esteem. Shyness has two aspects - modesty and self-centredness. Modesty is not only acceptable in Islam, but strongly encouraged. On the other hand, self-centredness is the opposite of self-confidence. A Muslim can never be self-centred. Young children lacking in self-esteem also suffer from the 'dependency syndrome.' They need to achieve gradual independence of their parents as they grow. It is essential for parents to make sure their children are not dependent on them for long.

• Frustration

Children want to be loved and accepted all the time. They measure this by the behaviour of their beloved ones. If, for some reason, they feel their parents or teachers do not value them, they feel rejected. Fathers and mothers who do not get on well with each other and are depressed put tremendous pressure on their children. The children may wrongly suspect that they are the cause of all this and they can feel guilty. Teachers who do not have high expectations of the children also add to that. Insecure relationships with parents or teachers may be their main source of frustration. They may 'act out' and express themselves through misbehaviour, breaking rules and adopting other techniques for seeking attention. On the contrary, some children may decide to 'act in' through social withdrawal, depression and losing interest in childlike activities. The reaction could be mild or even severe. While acting-out, children draw attention from all, but acting-in children suffer in silence, on their own.

• The Challenge with a Gifted or Talented Child

As children grow, their natural abilities becomes clearer. Are they gifted or talented? Do they feel bored in normal work and do they always need extra work? Parents might feel thrilled about having gifted or talented children, but raising them can be very demanding. Not all gifted or talented children are socially and intellectually mature. Herein lies the difficulty. In the temptation to achieve brilliant results for their children at an early age many parents forget their emotional and psychological needs. They forget their role of preparing them socially and intellectually, in a holistic way. Children may be very intelligent, but that does not mean that they should be pushed hard to achieve miracles. If Allah blesses some parents with gifted children, they should plan how best this gift can be utilised for their own benefit and the benefit of others.

Over-ambition or putting pressure on children to achieve marvels can cost their childhoods. Success in a Muslim life is not confined to academic brilliance alone, it depends on whether they can explore their potential and how they use them for the benefit of their community and human beings in general. The recent story in Britain of a 15-year old Oxford University student, named Sufiah Yusof, is illuminating. The way she fled university and hid herself 'to find space' in her life shows that academic brilliance is not enough to produce intellectual maturity and social responsibility. A big educational debate thus arose as to whether under student-age children attending universities helps them at all. Educational experts from all spectra now agree that children should not be forced to lose their childhoods, no matter how intelligent they are.

• The Challenge with Learning Difficulties

On the other hand, do your children need special education in school for some cognitive or other difficulty? Do they have any physical or emotional problems that hampers their learning?

Conscious parents should be able to understand their children and address the issues before it is too late. Nursery or Primary teachers can also identify difficulties. Over the last few decades, educational systems in most Western countries have successfully addressed the needs of children with learning difficulties. Teachers are now more equipped in terms of the pastoral aspects of education. It has become evident through research that at least one in every five children in Britain will have some form of learning difficulty. They need to be addressed with professional efficiency and sensitivity Children can face these difficulties for the following reasons:[2]

- Sensory and Physical Impairments - Learning has a positive relationship with sound health. A wide range of the physical conditions of a child, including hearing or visual impairment, naturally affect his learning.

- Cognitive Difficulties - The largest group of children are those who are slow learners. There is a positive link between a child's general level of language development and intellectual ability. Children who find it hard to learn to read have also expressive or receptive language difficulties.

- Emotional and Behavioural Difficulties (EBD) - The term is used in relation to children who have difficulty controlling their behaviour and emotions. An unhappy child will himself have difficulty in coping in the classroom. He gradually develops low self-esteem and as a result cannot cope with the demands of the curriculum.

- Speech and Language Difficulties - They may arise from an inability to cope with the structure of language or with the way language is used to communicate. A child may exhibit problems with receptive language (processing the language he hears) and/or expressive language (verbalising his thoughts and feelings)

- Social Aspects - Family and social environment are fundamentally important for the development of a child. When he grows up in a positive environment in which he can express himself openly he feels comfortable and learns quickly. In inappropriate family and/or social modelling the child grows up with EBD and can enter into adolescence disaffected.

Children need assurance from and confidence in their parents. Having Special Educational Needs (SEN) does not mean that they are unfortunate or incapable. In Allah's design, every human being is different but important. All are subject to being tested according to their abilities. Every human being has been created with distinct strengths and weaknesses. Should a child display some of the features of SEN requirements, parents should push for a proper assessment by experts and ask the school for appropriate provision. Teachers and educational psychologists have now adopted remedial services within mainstream school education. In no way should parents undermine their children or compare them with other siblings or friends. Lack of sensitivity can have a devastating effect on their confidence.

• Unpleasant and Rude Language

Successful indeed are the believers who are humble in their prayers and who shun vain conversation. (Qur'an 23:1-3)

Language is the main means of communication with other human beings. It manifests one's character. The language that we use tells what kind of people we are. The tongue is the root of expressing oneself. It can bring people nearer to each other and closer to Allah. On the other hand, it can create hatred among people and drive them away from each other and far from Allah. Muslims put tremendous emphasis on human decency, in language and behaviour. Language must be meaningful and free from obscenity and vulgarity. Cultured and civilised human beings are refined in their language and manners. Vulgarities can lead to disastrous consequences. Language is the mirror of civility and culture. Development of a responsible individual who believes in Allah and the formation of a responsible society that enjoins right action need wholesome education, the cultivation of language being in the forefront. Nations put languages on their priority list and, as they decline, vulgarity in language creeps in.

We all should speak in the way that we ourselves would like to hear from others. Good and decent language is an essential ingredient of a happy family and of social cohesion. Unfortunately, the influence of the modern value-less culture is taking its toll. The language, attitudes and manners of many 'celebrities,' especially from Hollywood, are having tremendous impact on the younger generation everywhere. The f*** word and other sexually explicit or abusive words are now very common in the Western entertainment industry. They spread rapidly through the screen and other media. Children learn them in the street and from their peers at school. Street-wise vulgar language among schoolchildren is now widespread, especially in inner cities. When Muslim parents suddenly discover that their innocent children are uttering words or behaving in a way alien to what they have been teaching them so far, they are taken aback. In the beginning, children probably do not mean it, but, unless addressed properly and in time, it can turn sour in the end.

Muslim parents should not compromise on some basic principles of Islam and Islamic manners with their children. Parents' strong views on language work as a deterrent to their children using unacceptable language. No matter how frustrated or angry a Muslim may be, and for whatever reasons, they must learn to control their tongue. From the very beginning, parents should also watch with whom their children hang out.

SUMMARY OF GUIDELINES

Allah has given parents authority over their children. It needs to be used sincerely and conscientiously. Here are a few helpful tips[3] on how to use this authority for wholesome growth.

Parents should:

- make an early start in training their children and giving them the understanding of Islam and the world, before it is too late. They should be told about the history of Islam and pioneering Muslims so that they can visualise them and take them as role models. Stories from the Qur'an and Ahadith have tremendous influence on young minds and once the foundation is laid, they are less likely to slip away from Islamic moorings.

- encourage children to practise Islam. According to the Prophet Muhammad ﷺ's instructions, parents should begin teaching the children prayer at the age of seven. By ten, they should be disciplined for failure to do so.

- understand the psychology of young children in order to deal with them effectively. Simple observation and common sense are important.

- allow them meaningful fun. Children like to enjoy themselves. Parents should direct them to sensible enjoyment, otherwise they will be bored and might refuse to work. The Prophet Muhammad ﷺ asked Muslims to treat children as they are.

- establish a good pattern of parenting so that children know their boundaries. Parenting that lacks discipline is bound to create confusion in the children.

- watch their moods and be consistent in dealing with their words and actions so that the children feel comfortable. Constantly changing the rules or moving the goal-posts confuses children. Intelligent children test their parents to see how consistent they are. Consistency does not mean being rigidity even if rules need to be changed. However, if rules are changed, this must be explained to the children.

- refrain from giving orders to children. If we want children to do something we should use convincing methods. Explanations are sometimes necessary. Parents should try to use persuasion so that the children do things on their own accord.

- be in control of children. New to life as they are, children need guidance from experienced people. As such, appropriate control is essential for their benefit. However, attempting too much to control may be counterproductive.

- keep promises, even if difficult or costly. Breaking promises can be disheartening to children as they may take it as lying. Lying is forbidden in Islam and it is disastrous.

- use moderation in behaviour towards children. Too much liberty may spoil them and, on the other hand, too much rigidity may make them rebellious. Islam is moderation in life and children should not grow up in extremes.

- be forthright in action. Efforts to hide from children can have disastrous effects. They can gradually lose confidence in parents.

- speak simply and clearly so that the children learn to do the same. Straightforward and simple language encourages children to become positive.

- listen to children when they talk. Interrupting them encourages them to do the same when their parents or elders talk.

- arrange family sessions on important issues regularly. Through engagement in wholesome discussion parents can create interest in the children. Storytelling and other techniques can be used to further their conviction in Islam.

- accept mistakes. Children should know that no human being, including their parents, is perfect. When parents accept their mistakes this gives them confidence in their justice and they will not view them as unfair.

- be sensitive to children's feelings. Children have good and bad times and as such they need space. Parents should show their interest in them by sensitively asking about their day at school.

- involve them in wholesome activities, such as, easy household work, so that they feel the sense of belonging at home. It also increases their self-esteem and confidence.

- treat children equally (Ahmad, Abu Dawud and an-Nasa'i). It is cruel to show love and attention to one child and indifference to another. This creates jealousy and hatred among siblings.

- be pro-active in dealing with sensitive issues. When children grow, especially towards the end of their primary school life, fathers and mothers should divide their attention between their sons and daughters respectively in order to educate them in sensitive issues such as sex.

- discuss together the strategy of training and disciplining the children and agree to speak with one voice. Children must not be given the impression that one parent is softer or stricter than the other. If this is the case, they will play parents against each other. Should any disagreement arise on any issue, the parents need to discuss them privately, not in front of the children.

- reward children for being good. This gives them inner happiness and encourages them to keep on doing good things. It also gives them confidence that they are valued. However, parents must be careful that they do not bribe their children and spoil them.

- discipline but do not punish them. On the other hand, if children do something that does not befit them, discipline should be applied. Justice must be maintained while disciplining children, and both parents should be involved in the process. Parents who have a well balanced policy of discipline know when and how they should implement it. Unless something is serious, the natural sequence of disciplining is – a) showing disapproval, b) giving a caution, c) withholding privileges, and d) subjecting them to mild physical punishment. The last option is controversial in the West. Mild beating of children is allowed but only for the purpose of teaching courtesy and with love and mercy. Specific parts of the body should not be hurt.

- teach children to apologise and accept their apologies. This develops their conscience. Once they apologise, parents should readily accept their apologies without going into details. Children should also be taught to ask forgiveness from Allah.

- maintain good relationships with their teachers in order to learn how the children are doing academically and socially. Children, whose parents do show interest in talking to teachers, are better looked after in school.

11. The World of Schooling (Secondary)

CHOOSING A SECONDARY SCHOOL

By the time children finish their primary school - at eleven years of age in Britain - they have begun to grow physically and mentally to a level such that they can travel on their own. They have also learnt sufficient social and organisational skills. The parents have also gained the experience of looking after their children during the primary years, which needs further polishing. Children become conscious about themselves, their bodies and personalities, their place in the family and in the world. Depending on their maturity and sense of responsibility, they gradually come to terms with the world of friends and their peer group. They learn to deal with the opposite sex, teachers and other people. They think of their careers, however vaguely it is at that stage. They try to become adult human beings, although they still need guidance from experienced people, especially their parents and near ones.

Making the right choice of secondary school is one of the most important decisions for children and a daunting one for parents. After the security of the primary years the transition to secondary schooling is a time of anxiety and uncertainty. However, most children take it as an exciting experience in their lives. Secondary schools are different from primary ones, in terms of size, environment, teaching styles and pastoral demand. They offer specialist curricula in subjects like art and design, technology and modern languages. Unlike primary schools, curriculum subjects in secondary schools are taught by subject teachers. This puts extra demands on children to learn faster. Instead of working in one classroom with one teacher, they move across the school to different subject rooms to experience the teaching of various teachers.

While primary school gives children their solid foundation in education, secondary school prepares them for their roles in the society, with the first national examination in their lives that counts towards their academic careers. As secondary education is vital for children's lives, conscientious parents always want to choose the best possible schools for them. Some parents even move to different areas to have access to a better school, if they are convinced that schools in their locality are not good enough.

Choosing a good school can be very difficult for Muslim parents as they look both for academic excellence and social skills. However, the crucial point is the nature of the school, e.g., whether it is single-sex or mixed. Fulfilling multiple demands is most often impossible, unless a family is lucky to live within travelling distance of their desired school and the children are also bright enough to pass in the admission test, if any. Those who are prosperous enough to send their children to private schools, which are mostly single-sex, do not have to worry too much about their academic performance. Their main emphasis is about looking after their Islamic roots and growth, but for most Muslim parents, the challenge is double-edged - good academic performance and maintaining an Islamic ethos for their children.

Secondary schools generally publish their prospectus in which they show how their school is performing, with figures on examination passes and attendance rates. They also arrange for open days or evenings for parents so that they can learn at first-hand how the schools are. Primary schools also provide valuable information about nearby secondary schools. Parents can learn about the ethos and attitudes of a particular school through visiting and talking to pupils, teachers and other parents. There are choices available and Muslim parents need to take advice from others if necessary. The choice has to be made wisely and in good time.

Good schools are those with an emphasis on academic progress, a prompt start to lessons and a good relationship between teachers and pupils. Every child is unique. A studious child does better in a school that emphasises academic achievement, but a child with less academic interest may thrive in a school that offers a mixture of academic and non-academic subjects. What makes secondary education enjoyable and a learning process is its inclusive nature, positive ethos and the interest shown in the children. Good schools cater for all types of pupils so that the talented do not become bored and frustrated and, at the same time, under-achievers do not become distressed.

Proper information is important for parents to decide about a secondary school. The following checklist, though not exhaustive, may prove helpful in this regard;

- Is the school mixed or single-sex?
- What extra-curricular facilities does it have?
- What is the level of academic achievement of the school?
- Where do the pupils normally go when they finish school?
- What is the catchment area like? Is the area safe and socially stable?
- Is bullying a concern in the school and how do staff deal with bullying?
- Does it have a written behaviour policy and is it followed conscientiously?
- Are parents welcome in the school and can they meet teachers easily?
- What is the truancy rate? How does the school deal with truants?
- What are the fixed-term (occasional) and permanent exclusion rates?
- What are the children's and parents' attitudes toward the school?

- How is the relationship between teachers and children?
- What is the homework policy of the school?
- How are the special needs facilities?
- Is the school tidy and clean?

A SINGLE-SEX OR MIXED SCHOOL?

This issue is very alive, especially in post-modern permissive societies of the West. In an apparent zeal to involve women in all spheres and empower them, there are those who want to tear down the barrier between the sexes. To them, gender should not be a taboo and it should be taken easily by the society. According to them, boys and girls should grow up and learn about their life together, so that they know each other well. Free mixing is not only encouraged, but also taken as an endeavour for which they proselytise. Anyone not conforming to this idea is considered out-dated.

In contrast, there is an extreme opposite view that boys and girls should never go near each other. According to them, woman's place is in the home or more specifically in the kitchen, only to cook for and serve family members. Woman's education is also seen cynically as if it were a useless exercise. In the name of religion and culture, many women lose their natural human right to be educated. Islam treads a middle way. Education is vital in Islam, and seeking knowledge is obligatory for both male and female.

However, the issue of single-sex as opposed to mixed schools is an educational as well as a social issue. From an educational point of view, many Western researchers have found that boys and girls are better off in single-sex schools. They provide better psychological environments for young people in that they remain free from the pull of the opposite sex. Irrespective of religious and social views, they recommend single-sex schools for better educational achievement. As a result of these research findings, and, of course, due to parental demands, some mixed schools even arrange separate single-sex tutorial groups for better learning and discipline. This is bearing fruit in many otherwise difficult schools in the country.

The issue is at the religious root in Islam. Islam has the basic requirement of young men and women maintaining the purity of their sexual lives from the very beginning. As the sexual urge is strong during puberty and attraction to the opposite sex is a natural physiological and emotional phenomenon, Muslim adolescents are specifically asked to maintain a safe distance from the opposite sex for their own benefit. Boys and girls have different and complementary roles in life and their needs are also different. In societies where sensuality is nurtured by others, restraining this powerful urge is a major jihad (struggle) indeed. Young men and women can easily become impulsive and succumb to their sexual urges. The high number of teenage pregnancies in Western countries, in spite of a campaign for 'safer sex,' is frightening for parents.

Men are, by nature, aggressive sexual partners. As such, girls generally lose out in the mixed school environment. They perform better in girls' schools. The overall trend of girls out-performing boys at GCSE and 'A' levels in Britain has also recently been a matter of intense social debate.

Choosing a suitable single-sex secondary school is all the more important at a time when they can easily be driven by the impulses of adolescence. Having an attraction towards the opposite sex, at a time when they need seriously to focus on building their life foundations, is a psychological pressure upon them. Boys and girls mature at different rates and they tend to have somewhat different educational interests. Arguably single-sex schools cater best for their needs and provide appropriate role models for the boys and girls. Boys and girls teasing each other in sexually explicit languages in some mixed schools and the provocative scenes of upper-school (years 10 and 11) boys and girls hugging and often kissing each other in school corners or at the far end of the playground, are alarming indeed for Muslim parents. Unfortunately, most teachers in the West consider this behaviour part of adolescence and do not find anything wrong in it.

Britain has still a good number of single-sex schools. Many religious denominational (voluntary-aided) schools, mostly funded by the government, are single-sex. After a long-drawn out battle, Muslims have only one such girls' secondary school, in Bradford. Unfortunately, many single-sex schools are becoming mixed apparently for 'economic' reasons, but in fact because of a powerful social trend initiated by lobbying and pressure. As a result, Muslims are finding that their choices in educating their children according to their wishes are further limited. Establishment of a private, single-sex, secondary school is an expensive business. Although a few have emerged in the Muslim community they are impoverished and can only cater for a tiny minority. In this situation, Muslim parents need to be pragmatic and take extra care if their sons or daughters end up in mixed schools. They should try their best and rely on Allah.

THE CASE FOR MUSLIM DENOMINATIONAL SCHOOLS[4]

Even single-sex schools within a purely secular setup have their problems. As the environment of these schools is ripe for permissive values, and teaching and other staff are mixed, they can lead to an unhealthy life and double standards in a Muslim child. That is why Muslim parents are not the only people to insist on the right to send their children to denominational schools. Many Christian and Jewish parents feel just as strongly about it. They have many schools of their own that are funded by the government. Muslims have the same right to establish their denominational schools with public money.

As mentioned in the previous chapter, Muslims in Britain have been selectively accused of encouraging 'ghetto' schools for their children. The deliberate misunderstanding of public-funded Muslim schools, although only three at present, also stems from the 'sexism' falsely perceived in them. In Britain, the national curriculum is mandatory for any state-funded school. In this respect, Muslim schools are no different from others, as the national curriculum will always be in place. It is, therefore, an exaggeration to think that Muslim schools will teach their boys and girls differently from the mainstream syllabus. Of course, their main focus is to instil Islamic values, so that Muslim children can comfortably relate to the wider society with confidence and contribute to its progress. The complaint about ghettoisation and sexism is probably based on a lack of knowledge about Islam and also on malpractices in some quarters of contemporary Muslim society, many of which are cultural and rooted in ignorance having nothing to do with Islam. It is unfair to criticise a world-religion and a community on the basis of misinformation.

If Muslims are to be accused, the same accusations can even more so be levelled at others. The concept of separate schooling in Britain was not invented by Muslims. Over the centuries, much of education here has been based on 'separateness,' such as social class (private schools), religion (religious denominational) and ability (grammar). The history of comprehensive education is not that old and it has not abolished the above mentioned schools.

Religious denominational schools may show some insularity in their nature, but they should be seen in the social context. Minority communities struggling to maintain their traditions need confidence and security in their early stages. Once that confidence is achieved, natural interaction then leads to wholesome integration. The word 'assimilation' has different meanings to different people. When this is used by the far right in the political and educational establishment it inevitably frightens minority communities. Religious communities can only survive and contribute in a pluralist society if their children are well anchored in their religious and cultural tradition. Integration should be on equal terms and minority children must secure their own identities first, or else integration will merely mean absorption.

The educational and social argument for Muslims having their own voluntary-aided schools is compelling. Fairness demands that, as citizens of the country, Muslims have the same rights as others. A genuinely pluralist society feels proud of its diverse nature. Muslim communities, with their distinctive characteristics, have added a new flavour to Western countries. We need to be included on a par with others. The fact that under-resourced Muslim private schools are performing better than state schools should be enough to give them credit.

Needless to say, Muslims should play a positive and effective role in their struggle to educate children within Islam. They need to show their enthusiasm, commitment and professional skills and integrity to assert themselves for their rights. They should value the importance of inclusive education in its widest sense, promote equality and encourage creativity. In other words, they must not fail themselves. With three Muslim schools getting state funds in Britain and some European countries already endorsing a similar principle, Muslims have now a bigger challenge to show that we are genuinely in the mainstream.

School Curriculum and Life Skills

It is generally acknowledged that the curriculum in Western education is broad and caters for social, economic and cultural demands. Western countries are broadly successful in fitting school education to their national demands. Secondary schools serve as a link between the formative period of the children's life in primary school to higher education and the world of work. Children are prepared for the demands of the nation. As they pass through the stormy phase of adolescence in secondary schools, their social and moral development is addressed, but unfortunately in broadly secular perspectives.

In Britain, the National Curriculum makes sure that schools provide the learning and knowledge, understanding, skills and attitudes necessary for pupils' self-fulfilment and development as active and responsible citizens in their highly limited and materialist view of existence. The National Curriculum has three main aspects.

• Academic Aspect

English, Maths and Science continue to remain the core subjects in secondary schools. The balanced curriculum with other Foundation subjects, such as, ICT (Information and Communication Technology), D & T (Design and Technology), History, Geography, Art and Design, Music and Physical Education is followed on the basis of two key stages, Key Stage 3 (age group 11-14) and Key Stage 4 (age group 14-16). There is a national test at fourteen and the most important one, GCSE, at sixteen. Each child has to choose a Modern Foreign Language from the age of eleven. A new subject, Citizenship, is going to start for all secondary school children from August 2002. Teachers follow programmes of study that tell the syllabus for the pupils. To ascertain the knowledge, skills and understanding of pupils of different abilities and maturity by the end of each key stage an 'Attainment Target' is set. Under the Education Act 1996, all schools should also teach their children RE (Religious Education) and sex education. Provisions are still there for parents to withdraw their children from all or part of the lessons on these subjects, but, it depends on how informed or confident Muslim parents are on this right.[5]

• Social, Moral and Spiritual Dimension

Section 351 of the Education Act 1996 in Britain requires that all government funded schools provide a balanced and broadly based curriculum that promotes the spiritual, moral, cultural, mental and physical development of pupils.[6]

The step towards promoting pupils' spiritual, moral, social and cultural development through RE, PSHE (Personal, Social and Health Education) and Citizenship by successive governments in Britain has been taken positively by Muslim educationalists. At the same time, the opportunity to learn and develop a wide range of skills, such as communication, problem solving skills and thinking skills at the beginning of their life, is hailed by all.

It is, however, unfortunate that even morality and spirituality in the modern West are tinged with the concept of material gain, where the genie of commercialisation is now running amok. There is very little room for transcendental values, and the concept of accountability to the one 'Mighty Creator' is absent. The urge for individual material self-fulfilment has taken over the modern mind. Education in Western countries is now predominantly task-centred, and a child is no more considered the emissary of Allah on earth. With the little bit of religious education, PSHE or the coming Citizenship education, the question of human beings' role on earth remains unanswered. With materialistic ideas and permissive practices powerful celebrities and megastars wield tremendous influence in moulding the character of the young people. On top of this, many teachers teaching these subjects themselves consider all religions dogmatic and linked to irrational fanaticism.[7]

• Extra-Curricular Activities

Good schools provide young people with life skills, often through extra-curricular activities. Drama, debate, essay or poetry competitions and trips are just a few, in which children can participate informally and speak their minds. They enhance their confidence and equip them with some of the necessary skills to succeed in life. Muslim parents should encourage their children to take active part in available activities, without jeopardising their study and Islamic Adab.

THE ISLAMIC PERSPECTIVE

With all the positive aspects of education in the West, Muslim parents are worried about their children's Islamic upbringing. The situation is not a satisfactory one. Allah expects from Muslims a clear understanding of the human's role on earth. Education is vital in this. With the pure concept of Tawhid (the Oneness of Allah), Islam's unique message on the purpose of man on earth and his ultimate accountability to Allah in the Hereafter, Muslims have strong views on man's moral integrity, sexual moderation, our responsibility to one another and, above all, obedience to Allah. In spite of the religious presence in the West, all these are losing importance for modern human beings. Here, from the beginning of adolescence in Secondary schools, wrong action is accommodated, chastity is chastised and spirituality is ignored. Young children are overwhelmed by the value-less ideas on life. Teaching sex to children, as young as eight, in an insensitive manner is a heavy burden on them. Overall, the ethos and environment of schools is a recipe for a self-indulgent lifestyle and materialistic thinking.

Islam is by no means an insular way of life. As such it has the widest accommodative power of any life-transaction anywhere in the world and at any time in history. It has a frame of reference based on human decency and transcendental values. Islam is ever modern. It does not have to compromise to accept and digest elements of modern creativity and innovation. It is a religion for practical people living on earth, in the East or West. Muslims are also known as a universal community or ummah. It is true that Muslims have not succeeded yet in implementing their cherished values, even in their own denominational schools. It is also understandable that social pressure tends to override and dictate minority values and cultures. But, Muslim parents can definitely contribute in re-igniting the natural urge of human beings' spiritual quest.

SECONDARY CHALLENGES

Once the hurdle for secondary admission is over, Muslim parents should start a new phase in their parenting. In the beginning, they are naturally worried about how their children settle in the new school environment. As they did in primary years, some of them probably accompany their children to the school gate. Gradually, they become used to the new arrangement. The first three months in the transition from their primary to secondary are crucial for the children to settle. Children are normally quick in making new friends and, depending on the school environment, also quickly fit in the system.

However, things might not be that smooth for some, especially in schools that have pupils of diverse ethnic and cultural background. Pro-active and assertive children easily take their position in the new setup, but, quiet, lonely and shy children will take time. Some, especially those who are too dependent on their parents, may face difficulties in adjusting, as teachers generally expect secondary children to be more independent. Parents, school and the children themselves have all to play their part in integrating such children in the school. The challenges are many: educational, social and, of course, very much related with the world of adolescence.

• Bullying and the Broader Issue of Safety

'Bullying' was widespread in England in 1977.[8] It means deliberately hurting someone, often repeatedly over a period of time, when the victims find it difficult to defend themselves. The scourge of bullying can be:

- physical - hitting, kicking, taking belongings, etc.
- verbal - name calling, and insulting and offensive remarks, etc.
- indirect - spreading nasty stories, excluding others from social groups, making a child the subject of malicious remarks, etc.

Stories of pupils physically and mentally traumatised by bullying are common in schools. The fear of bullying is experienced by a significant section of the pupil population. It is an acute fear for first year pupils in secondary schools. Good schools have strong anti-bullying policies and monitoring mechanisms. Schools, consistently showing zero tolerance to bullying, succeed in creating an ethos of mutual understanding and respect. However, success depends on every member of the school community, including the victims themselves.

A bully generally targets someone who is seen to be different, generally vulnerable and docile. Children from a minority group can be targets. Muslim children can be picked on for their ethnic and cultural features. Muslim girls who wear head-scarves can be targeted. Parents should take extra care to educate their children on how to challenge bullying. Parents should encourage their children to make friends, interact with others, become assertive and challenging if they encounter a bully.

• Discipline

The desire for freedom is in human nature. Human beings are born free, but civilisations have invented rules and laws to chain them, sometimes for their own benefit and sometimes for the benefit of the state and those with control within it. As children grow and step into secondary schools, they start getting their first taste of the illusory freedom that this society claims to offer its citizens. They travel by themselves, organise their own work and, in many British upper schools, are allowed to go out of school during the lunch-break. Teachers also tend to give them some freedom and space in order to inculcate creativity, innovation, enterprise and motivation in them. This freedom in the school years appears to have given Western countries the edge over others. Western parents also give lot of freedom to their children at home and in society. They expect their children to grow up socially and intellectually so that at sixteen they largely know how to run their own affairs. Many children leave home at this age to live independently. While this apparently prepares them to face the challenges of life, it has also given rise to extreme selfishness and eroded the family bonding and social fabric. The rise in the 'couldn't care less' attitude is engulfing modern society.

Freedom without responsibility is dangerous. For any civilised society they are intertwined. Freedom brings choice, but one has to learn the consequences of choice. In Islam, accountability to the Creator, one's own self and others is the perimeter of freedom. This makes freedom meaningful and saves human beings from chaos. Needless to say, while their version of freedom has given an apparent creativity to the West, unlimited sexual freedom in recent decades has created a social crisis. Rampant adultery, fornication, homosexuality and moral self-indulgence are weakening the social fabric. The standards of sexual decency have changed to such an extent that nobody now dares to go against the current. Individuals conform to the changed values of society to avoid social isolation. Virginity and chastity, valued so highly by men and women only a few decades ago, are becoming synonymous with backwardness.

The unlicensed and quite illusory freedom in a society has its impact on its school life. With 'individualism' being the ethos, many young secondary children grow up with 'I don't care' or 'so what' attitudes. Class discipline is now the most difficult aspect of teaching in secondary schools. Many teachers leave their profession because of the stress caused by children who give little respect to teachers or the system. Fear of the chaos in classrooms is causing concern over teacher recruitment. Teachers in many inner-city schools are, in effect, engaged in 'child-minding,' instead of teaching the curriculum. Disproportionate numbers of teachers seek advice on stress management from their unions and help-lines. This generally becomes worse in mixed schools where many upper school boys and girls behave openly in an unbecoming manner, not only in the corridors or in the corners of the playground, but sometimes in classrooms as well.

Schools are not isolated islands in a society. Young people's lives are dictated by the wider social norms, e.g., TV programmes, printed media, parental lifestyles and other factors. The challenges young people face in their lives are multi-faceted, e.g.:

- Personal Factors - low self-esteem, learning difficulties, emotional and behavioural difficulties.
- Family Influences - poor parenting, economic deprivation, family conflicts.
- School Environments - the curriculum, peer pressure, the *hidden curriculum,* low teacher expectation.

- Social Factors - race and culture, social deprivation, unemployment, media imagery.
- Social Trends - moral permissiveness, sexual promiscuity, and the ideological maze.

Like everyone in the society, young people at school look for recognition and a sense of worth. Those who are disadvantaged and feel strongly so, tend to express themselves in unconventional ways. Gang-fights, drug abuse and petty crimes are some of the outlets and anti-social practices they adopt to vent their frustration and anger against the system. With negative role models abounding, many of them follow social trends that clash with the interests of the wider society. New technological gadgets, with their value-less promotions, often make them the worse tools of self-indulgence.

Young people always want to be special. They crave to be recognised and noticed. They want to be in the forefront of any social change. An example of this is the recent explosion in mobile phone use which has enabled young people to show their worth in school campus. Surveys have shown that mobile phone use has become a symbol of dignity and, like many other trends, has become a part of youth culture, thus illustrating the counter truth that youth culture is entirely a creation of marketing man intent on selling gadgets and consumer items. Even in run-down inner city areas of Britain, where three-quarters of the school intake eat 'free school dinners', secondary schools are struggling to cope with this nuisance. Teachers are often interrupted by the sudden ringing noise and find a boy or girl talking on the mobile, even in classrooms! This is in spite of schools' strong rules on discipline. I once asked a year ten year old boy of a secondary school about this, as I saw him talking on the mobile phone in the classroom. His frank answer was, 'I was talking to my girlfriend, sir.' This is probably one of the worst cases, but a serious flaw in youth culture is showing us a warning sign of an alarming future.

Given this laxity in youth culture, can Muslim parents afford to take a back seat in the affairs of their children, especially in their transition to adulthood? There is a sense of urgency in some quarters of the Muslim community to educate their children in Islam in an Islamic environment. Unfortunately, for decades, Muslims have generally displayed the 'ostrich syndrome' on the education of their children in the West by simply resorting to 'additional' Qur'an or community language teaching at home or in the mosque. Some years ago, a prominent orthodox Jew commented to one of his Muslim friends, 'I don't understand why Muslims are so apathetic about their children's education in the West!'

Now, fortunately, most Muslims parents do realise the dangers looming ahead, but, many do not know how to counter them. We have to help each other. There is no room for complacency, indifference and ignorance. We should help each other in inculcating motivation in our children and in strenuously trying to create in them a sense of discipline and responsibility reflected in their behaviour at home, in schools and on the streets. Discipline has to be ingrained in the nature of young children. In a sound family environment children grow to be active rather than reactive, positive rather than pessimistic and collaborative rather than individualistic. They try hard to create a decent environment in their schools as well.

Parents have to remember that unnecessary coercion does not help in implementing discipline. Forced discipline often brings a negative outcome, in spite of the good intentions. Young people, especially in the West, want to know the reason for any action. Too much control with only do's and don'ts leads at best to docility and passivity and at worst rebellion. In order to be effective in discipline, parents must avoid head-on confrontations with children. Clarity, integrity and justice are effective tools for success and are essential in dealing with a young person. Father and mother need to do a lot of background work and need to act in unison to deal with their children. Inconsistency between two parents is disastrous and smart children can easily take advantage of that.

• Dealing with the Opposite Sex

The issue of se' becomes important at secondary school, as the pupils pass through the juncture of adolescence. The sex drive is natural. It is essential in the divine wisdom of Allah on earth, but needs restraint and careful use. The attitude toward sex has often influenced the direction of human destiny. Civilisations rise due to the hard work of the founders, but in their decline sexual indulgence often plays havoc destroying them from within. Once sexual profligacy permeates the social fabric of any nation, it collapses. It seems that the West is passing through a phase where sex has become a commodity and as a consequence the sex industry has become enormously profitable. Since the Second World War the so-called sexual revolution has brought unparalleled changes, where young people are at the receiving end due to the easy availability of pornographic material, contraceptives and transient partners. There is strong social pressure on young people to conform to an self-indulgent lifestyle. The style and content of sex-education, even in the school environment, are considered provocative by many conscientious parents.

Sex cannot be a matter for neglect. As children grow, the issue of gender will naturally come in their lives, but, with the present hype surrounding sexuality they are utterly confused by the explicit display of sex everywhere, even before their adolescence. The innocent view of childhood of mothers and sisters is shattered by the vulgar display of women's bodies around them. As the natural attraction between a boy and a girl in secondary years is too tempting to ignore, many of them succumb to the pressure and engage in sexual acts. In societies where definitions of adultery and fornication have been altered, and sexual experiences are tacitly encouraged, it is difficult for young people to maintain sexual purity. Young Muslims need to follow the example of Yusuf عليه السلام in Egypt, who although tempted by the seductions around him was more inclined to the love of his Lord and preferred prison to temporary sexual indulgence.

Muslim children going to mixed secondary schools undergo tremendous psychological and social pressure from their peers and, unless reared within a proper Islamic ethos, may end up giving in to the self-indulgent lifestyle. Parents and the Muslim community together should adopt a multi-prong safeguard mechanism in order to bring their children out unscathed from this danger. Children need to be strengthened with knowledge and taqwa so that they grow with the necessary immunity. They need to be given a decent alternative environment in which to channel their youthful energy.

Islam has its decent way of educating young people about sex and the male-female relationship. It promotes courtesy in the behaviour between a man and woman. This is all the more important with young people who are naturally driven by impulsive passion in their early and not-so-mature adolescent lives. The sense of respect for each other, responsibility in life and accountability to Allah, are the guiding principles when young males and females need to deal with each other. The requirement of chastity and virginity are of fundamental importance, and are enshrined in Shari'ah. Islam is stubborn on this and Muslim children learn this from childhood. As Islam prescribes rooting out the cause of evil, rather than fighting for the cure, physical proximity, intimate closeness and physical contact among secondary boys and girls, that can create sexual attraction between them, is forbidden for their own benefit.

Parents must be open about this issue with their children. Within the limits of decency and in all sincerity, they should discuss the Islamic requirements of a wholesome approach toward dealing with the opposite sex with their children and the pitfalls of society. They need to take the lead in teaching about the roles and responsibilities of man and woman before school, TV or some other agency take this on board and present them with unacceptable views. It would be impractical to advise young people to remain aloof from the opposite sex. What they need is guidance in self-control to attain spiritual heights even though living in the world of Jahiliyyah. In-built *taqwa* (consciousness of the presence of Allah and the resulting avoidance of wrong action and engagement in right action) is the only way to sail through this difficult period.

• The Issue of Identity

The understanding of one's identity receives importance in secondary school when children's vision of the world starts becoming wider. As they grow in physical and intellectual maturity, they gradually come to terms with their roots. Depending on the parental upbringing, they start seeing the world through their own eyes. The dream life of childhood gradually disappears and they learn how to confront a 'real world' torn apart by religious, cultural and ethnic differences. Where do they fit in that world? How do they relate to their friends from other communities, who may possess very different attitudes toward life? One thing about which Muslim parents must be cautious is their children growing up with insular and selfishly individualistic attitudes. As a community of purpose and divine mission Muslims should, by nature, be sociable, hospitable and open-minded. The essence of Islam is to serve humanity and, as such, ghettoisation or cantonisation of the Muslim community is a big folly that can lead to danger in the future.

Muslims are still at the receiving end in many Western countries, as Islamophobic and xenophobic hatred from some quarters of the establishment, especially the media, still abound. The heightened passion against Muslims as a result of terrorist attacks on the US has made our lives in the West more difficult. Muslim children can experience negative stereotyping from schools, the media and in day-to-day life. As such, many of them may feel vulnerable. Some even feel embarrassed to identify themselves as Muslims. This social stigma can induce many young Muslims to lead double lives. Some may even alter their names or accept their alteration by teachers or their peer group in order to feel accepted. This is the recipe for their low self-esteem, leading to under-achievement.

Muslim parents must observe their children, day in and day out, as to whether the young ones develop impoverished self-confidence. A news item was distributed on the internet that a seven-year old Muslim child in Canada once came home from school and mentioned to his mother, 'Mum, I have told them, I am a Muslim, but not a terrorist.' In a world full of antagonism against Muslims, this psychological damage haunts Muslim children. It is imperative that Muslim parents become extra caring towards their children in order to empathise with them and share some of their burden, so that they grow with a 'self at rest and at peace' (Qur'an 89:28).

• The Black-hole of the 'Pastime'

The modern entertainment industry is enormously wealthy and employs a huge number of people. With Hollywood and Disney's vast empire, they are taking over children's imaginations, and also their free time. The films produced by these companies, often find a way of entertaining children whatever time of day. Action thrillers and romances - all manage to lure these susceptible and vulnerable children into spending their (and their parents') money on watching them, buying them, and also buying their associated merchandise. Children think that if they don't watch the major celebrities, people will think that there is something wrong with them.

It is not only the Western industry that grabs young people's attention, the Eastern amusement industry also plays a major part in the lives of young Asians everywhere. With Bollywood producing more than three hundred films a year, it is difficult for young Asians to keep away from modern 'Eastern', mythology-tinted, Indian entertainment. To Muslims of Eastern origin this is probably worse than even the Western version. As the characters have some similarity to their own, some Indian film stars are idolised by many Asian youngsters, including Muslims.

It is not only films that fill up young children's timetables, but computer and video games, the 'terrible virus' - the TV - also manage to pull the young people into the black hole of 'passing or killing the time'. The post-war West, Japan and some Far-Eastern countries produce the majority of these products. In a competition to hit the market, old consoles such as the Mega Drive, Nintendo and Gameboys, are replaced by the more high tech, powerful new consoles that find their places within the homes of almost all young children in the West. Play Stations, N64's and Dreamcasts now grace their living rooms, taking away their free time and engaging their brains in very impure fantasy. The computer-generated virtual world becomes their reality and many children fail to comprehend the complexities of real life. Even the concepts of life and death lose seriousness in their virtual reality.

What is the effect of these? Research has shown that TV, video- and computer-games make children more aggressive. The effects of exposure to media violence was acknowledged at the James Bulger trial in Britain in which the judge commented that the killers' exposure to violent videos could have played a part in the two year-old's death.

And of course there is the music industry that seduces the ear and mind. The often sexually explicit, often meaningless, message of the music engages the whole personalities of our young people. This sometimes creates public nuisance as well. It is not surprising that video shops are mushrooming on almost every street corner in the West. It is probably true that human beings cannot live without some music, but what sort of music do we need?

Music is a part of human culture. It is as old as human beings themselves. Music has a power to speak. Mothers sing their children to sleep, armies march to the sound of drums and creatures (e.g., birds) sing to express their happiness and to praise Allah. The melodious recitation of the Qur'an can creates joyous and also fearful feelings among believers. All children respond naturally to rhythm and melody. Scientists have found that certain parts of the brain play important roles in the perception and production of music. Some children are born musically gifted.[9]

Unfortunately, present day Muslims have so far failed to provide a wholesome alternative, including music, for their young people. Some Muslims tend to appear dry, monotonous and uninspiring, even in entertainment programmes. It is true that Islam has specific guidelines for refreshing the human heart, and Muslims never lacked for lighter moments and uplifting experiences. 'Entertain the hearts in between hours, for if the hearts get tired they become blind' (*Sunan ad-Daylami*).

Life, of course, is a serious business. The effect of uncontrolled exposure to amoral, or often immoral, forms of entertainment may lead children toward moral laxity. The juvenile delinquents that abound in industrialised countries get their inspiration from aggressive and sometimes perverted video- and computer-games. Social thinkers are worried at the increasing trend of young people resorting to violence for no apparent reason.

Can Muslim parents insulate their children from these pastimes? In reality, we cannot. We cannot ignore the demands from our youngsters to buy something for their amusement, even if we prefer not to, because otherwise our children would be outcasts among their friends at school. However, parents must use their judgement on what to buy and set some rules regarding their use. This may sound compromising to some Muslims, but it is a fundamental insight of Islam that one must sometimes choose between two evils and choose the lesser of the two.

PREPARING A SOLID FOUNDATION FOR LIFE

Children's educational achievement is important. Parents should make sure that they do not fall behind in their homework. We should also occasionally check their class-work and ask about their experiences at school. At the same time, their social and intellectual development should not be ignored. All these should supplement their ultimate purpose of life, i.e., their role as emissaries of Allah on earth as conscientious Muslims. We should observe their social development, how they talk and behave with elders, siblings and friends. Parents should have reasonable information about their children's friends and their backgrounds. At the same time, their spiritual development should be given prime importance. Life is a complex whole. Everything around children contributes to their lives. Well-disciplined family life and sensible pro-active parents cause them to blossom to their full potential.

It is widely acknowledged that good literacy, numeracy and communication skills put people at an advantage. Without these skills children find it difficult to grasp the wider curriculum and soon lose their self-esteem. As they grow older their self-confidence falls and by the time they leave school they start feeling that the world is smaller for them in terms of the job market and social recognition. Some of them end up becoming burdens on society.

During the period of adolescent turmoil, parents need to be more sensitive and persuasive but remain firm in dealing with them. They must only enthuse their children and inject the values of Islam. Success depends on the self-initiated responsibility of the recipient. From a direct role of helping, as in the primary years, parents should gradually switch to the role of advising and guiding. They can be catalysts of change in their children's challenging lives in the coming years. The onus is on parents to prove that they are their best friends and allies. In order to create this dynamic and warm relationship parents must maintain excellent communications with their children so that they do not hesitate to open themselves to their parents. Parents should not, in any case, lose their confidence in their children or lose their tempers at them. That would simply lead to breakdown of communications inviting disastrous consequences.

• Academic Achievement

Secondary schools prepare children for higher education or the world of work. Muslim parents need to make sure their children make the most of this period. They should always keep their eyes and ears open so that they can help them out emotionally, socially and academically, if that is possible, or identify any problems that may arise. It does not matter if the parents are unable to help their children in academic subjects, in fact many parents cannot, but children must feel that their parents care about their educational achievements. Caring parents ask their children almost everyday about how they are doing with their class and homework or whether they are facing any difficulties at school. Parents need to look out for the following:

- Do they go to school willingly?
- Are they facing any problems with their class/homework?
- Are they getting on well at school?
- Do they come home straightaway after school?
- Are they happy everyday or do they suddenly become quiet?
- Are they getting on well socially?

Children need a good routine and a balanced timetable for their study at home. They should be encouraged to make their own so that they feel comfortable to follow it at home. There should be two timetables, however informal - one for school-days and the other for weekends and holidays. Parents could contribute in producing them. Once they are agreed, they should earnestly and consistently try to follow them. The routine should cater for the following:

- Subject study and homework (more in the weekdays)
- Socialisation with friends (more in the holidays)
- Free time or personal space (everyday, but more in the holidays)
- Using computers for knowledge and schoolwork (as and when necessary)
- Arabic learning and Qur'an recitation (everyday, but more in the holidays)
- Youth activities, i.e., games/sports, in mosques or Muslim youth centres (more in the holidays)
- Newspaper reading, watching TV for news and innocent entertainment (regularly)

It is always a good practice to remain ahead of the class or, at least, be apace with them. Homework and course-work form essential parts of school education. They show how children work independently with the help of additional texts or information from other sources, such as reference books, the Internet, newspapers, etc. Many schools have homework clubs for pupils who otherwise find difficulty in doing them at home. Parents need to encourage their children to do homework or course-work on their own, even if they could help them directly, so that they become self-reliant.

Exams are not the end of the world, but they are important in formal education. There are two national exams for secondary school children in Britain and the most important of them, the GCSE, is demanding. All exams are stressful and worrying. Whenever children face an exam, parental support and love is vital. They should encourage their children to prepare well for major exams, especially the GCSE and 'A' level, and help them in making and following a routine before and during the exam. Parents should not push them too hard, making demands that they should get the same or better results than someone else. In any case, exams should not bring too much anxiety. Parents must make sure that their children have enough exercise and leisure time. Muslims definitely try hard, but they believe that the result is from Allah.

In order to achieve good grades and succeed academically children have to acquire the necessary learning skills. Learning is a life-long endeavour. If necessary, extra tutoring should be arranged on subjects the children feel important. The following skills are all important in their own context. An individual learner, depending on his interest and capability, should try to maximise his learning through the combination of these skills. A good learner always uses the mixture of these:

- Rote learning - There is generally no cognitive demand in this learning and it has little context. But it is important for memorising some text, such as, remembering quotations, formulas and Qur'anic references.

- Factual learning - There is little cognitive demand in this learning. But, it has context. It is important for very relevant, down-to-earth learning, such as scientific facts.
- Conceptual or abstract learning - There is cognitive demand in this learning but it has little context. This is important in Art and some other subject areas.
- Critical learning - This has cognitive demand and context. It is important for any creative subject, such as poems.

However, learning is accelerated by the conscious use of the intellect and contextualising the topic. Children should be encouraged to improve their understanding through the age-old techniques used by Muslim scholars, e.g., dynamic utilisation of brainpower and constant supplication for its increase in the words of the Qur'an, 'my Lord, increase me in knowledge' (Qur'an 20:114).

• Physical and Mental Fitness

Children should be guided to consume healthy food with sufficient nutrition, take regular exercise and engage in intelligent games. A happy life depends on balanced physical and mental growth. The maxim 'health is wealth' is a universal one. In the days of cultural and psychological indoctrination, young children could easily be glued to TV or computer. These black boxes could insulate their mind from the broader world. They are probably the main causes of the physical and mental ill health of modern human beings. In addition to making children physically inactive, they can make them dull and socially passive for the whole of their lives.

Human beings are superior in intelligence so that they can run the affairs of the planet earth. All humans, unless brain damaged, have different forms of intelligence, e.g.[10]:

- Personal intelligence - makes one aware of oneself, one's thoughts and needs.

- Physical intelligence - helps one to learn through the body and develop physical skills.
- Social intelligence - makes one aware of others and relating well to them.
- Visual intelligence - helps one learn through seeing and being aware of shapes and space.
- Linguistic intelligence - helps one to learn, speak, read and write through language.
- Mathematical intelligence - helps one to understand numbers and become logical in thinking.
- Scientific intelligence - helps one to learn about the world and being curious to find out more.
- Musical intelligence - helps one to learn through listening and being aware of sounds.
- Philosophical intelligence - makes one think and ask questions about the meaning of life.

Children are born with some of these natural skills, and some may be gifted with a particular one in abundance. Parents and teachers need to explore this in their children and help them in excelling in specific skills. The best mentor of the children tries to inculcate in them the thinking skills which sharpens their:

- Information processing skills
- Reasoning skills
- Enquiry skills
- Creative thinking
- Evaluation skills

The best educator of young people encourages them to inculcate this power of thinking. In an environment where this power is suppressed dogmatism creeps in and makes them stagnant. The best parents are those who possess this liberating view of the intellect and encourage their children to think. The success of early Muslims lay in this creative engagement of their brain in creating new frontiers of human endeavour. Islam linked this power of thinking with the self-awareness of the sense of responsibility and through the knowledge of accountability to Allah. As a result, Muslims succeeded in creating a civilisation, rich in creativity and deep in spirituality. In contrast, while the European Renaissance liberated human beings from the clutches of dogmatism, it de-linked them from this accountability. Thus, Europe became lost in the wilderness of secular materialism.

• Personal, Social and Life Skills

Education can be for success in life and parents can provide the best of it to their children, but education is not only getting good grades in public examinations and good degrees in universities. It includes providing young people with the opportunity to develop and explore their talents and interests, engaging in jobs or careers that interest them and lead to work for the benefit of humanity. The Muslim ummah needs people of knowledge and understanding who can challenge the stagnation and apathy of the past few hundred years and engage, with all sense of urgency, in the recreation of a civilisational paradigm based on human beings' vicegerency on earth.

The struggle for children's academic excellence should be taken hand in hand with their continuous fight to achieve personal, social, intellectual and spiritual development. Learning to become responsible and gradually independent in life receives a new impetus in secondary school. Homework, visits arranged by the school, extracurricular activities - all are the tools of disseminating these skills. Parents should encourage their children to actively participate in them. Along with this, they should help them in becoming full members of the community.

Personal skill is about understanding oneself and one's self-worth with a view to attaining self-control and behaving in a dignified manner. Maxims such as, 'know thyself' or 'those who know themselves, know their Lord' have guided human beings through the ages in exploring their selves, although certainly the latter leads beyond the self and to knowledge of Allah. This helps children to become more mindful and conscious without becoming self-centred or arrogant. How children think of themselves and what they think of their appearance, personality and talents are important for their balanced growth. These give them self-respect. Parental guidelines can save children from the pitfalls of over-confidence or low self-esteem. They should talk about this with their children and involve them in such projects from which they learn how to reflect on and evaluate their achievements and short-comings and identify ways to deal with them. Conscious aware-ness of one's responsibility is a key to success.

Social skills are about understanding others and acting wisely in human relations. Children naturally learn this through their relationships with parents and others. Humans are social beings. 'Only beasts or saints are happy living entirely alone,' commented the Greek philosopher Aristotle long ago. 'People skill' or the ability to form good relationships with others is at the heart of social change, which Muslims are required to attain. This can be done through talking with others, showing them respect with good manners, showing sensitivity to and empathy with others and working together. Social skills help children make friends, rec-ognise differing values and live together peacefully. Life skills are about acquiring the 'know how' of living decently, without being irritating to or a burden on others. All these skills are to be earned by conscious effort.

• Spiritual Attainment

The modern world has unfortunately become spiritually barren and the result is anxiety, disquiet, stress and tension which per-vade the human mind today. Peace and tranquillity are all but lost due to neglect of the soul. We know that the *ruh* (spirit) of the human being is from before time. It is an irony that over-whelming materialism has reduced us into 'intelligent animals,' with little left for our spirits. Modern people now feel pride in their spectacular material progress. Many 'mini gods' - whims, desires, technology, art and the like have occupied our lives. Consequently, we are suffering from a terrible spiritual thirst. To quench it many have resorted to unnatural practices, such as hedonistic rituals, that bring even more misery in their life.

Human beings' creation, survival and success are absolutely dependent on Allah, our Creator. He has given us some freedom so that we, when we return back to Him in the Day of Judgement, give full account of our lives on earth. Firm belief in this is at the root of spirituality. However, Muslims never make a show of spirituality. As it flourishes within us, it becomes embedded in our natures. Spirituality is reflected in the appearance, the expression and, in fact, the whole being. The spiritual height of the companions of the Prophet ﷺ is mentioned in the Qur'an – 'Their mark is on their faces, the traces of prostration.' (Qur'an 48:29).

In the midst of a spiritual desert, Muslim parents have an obligation to create an oasis for their children and equip them with love and loyalty to Allah and His Messenger ﷺ. Spiritual happiness brings peace and tranquillity. It is true that the challenge to inculcate deep love for Allah in children in these modern times is daunting, but children, by nature, are adventurous and explorative. If they are properly guided into the world of infinite joy in spiritual solace, they will love it.

• Enthusiasm for the deen

Post-pubescent young Muslims have an obligation to follow the compulsory Islamic rites and abide by many Islamic rules, and indeed they are obliged to learn the prayer and seven and are beaten for not doing it at ten years old. This is a big test for secondary school age children, especially in the GCSE years, who need to observe their practices in school hours. One of them is the mid-day (Dhuhr) prayer in all seasons. Muslims cannot escape this for any reason. Schools in most Western countries are generally accommodative of the religious rights of minorities and head teachers generally comply with the request from Muslim students. This is in tune with the equal opportunities policy on racial and religious harmony. There may be some die-hard secularist head teachers who either procrastinate or refuse to provide this basic need to the Muslim children, but they are an insignificant minority.

The issue of headscarves for mature Muslim girls is also another misunderstood phenomenon. In their 'liberal' bigotry some believe that headscarves are tools of oppression. Some countries make an open fuss about this and tend to restrict or negate the rights of Muslims on the pretext of defending liberal values. To them, it is an ostentatious practice and thus unpalatable to their 'civilised norms.' In this situation, Muslim girls feel more vulnerable because of their distinct dress. One can only hope that ignorance and intolerance die out with time.

Muslim boys and girls are in a unique position to argue the case of their civil and religious rights with head teachers and, in that process, many of the misunderstandings can easily be removed. What matters in this endeavour is their conviction of Islam, their courteous manners and articulate persuasiveness. Islam is strong on its basic principles, and there is no compromise on them. It is important to understand that there is plenty of room for flexibility in secondary aspects of Islam. Muslim children have reasons to be proud of their deen and enthusiastic about it.

Muslim parents and community representatives should help their children sensitively in exercising these rights in their schools. As taxpayers they need to be more assertive.

PREPARING FOR LIFE AFTER SIXTEEN YEARS OF AGE

Secondary schools try to make sure that they equip their young people with some basic skills so that they do not become burdens on society, even if they fail to pursue higher education for whatever reason. In British upper schools, children are asked to choose their optional subjects for GCSE. Obviously, parents are involved in this decision-making process. This is an important phase of children's educational life. In GCSE years 10 and 11 they are advised by the school's Career Service what options are available for them when they finish their statutory education. The Education Authorities publish books on career choices. As children reach sixteen years of age they should have a fair idea of their own strengths and weaknesses. The opportunities for their lives are laid open before them so that they can take informed decisions well ahead.

Unless one decides to end education, there are two educational routes in Britain. One is the academic route, called 'A' level courses in schools or sixth-form colleges, for those who are academically brighter. The other, vocational, is for those who prefer specific careers without going through the rigours of academic life. Education after sixteen is not statutory, it depends on children's interest and ambition. It can be full-time or part-time, day or night courses, and subjects are as wide as possible. Many universities are now providing distance learning facilities for those who, for economic and other reasons, cannot afford to attend classes. Education after sixteen has its own challenges. As children grow up and learn to take responsibility for their lives, they start getting more freedom. Educational institutions rely on self-initiative in students. Parents also expect that their time and effort with their children have given fruit.

As children pass through adolescence, dependence on their parents gradually diminishes and the legacy of what they have learnt so far endures. However, support and guidance from the parents is still vital, especially in the family context in which Muslim parents never lose authority over their children. The attitudes to and orientation in life that have formed so far in the children face the test of reality. For some, these may drastically change due to environmental pressures. The fortunate, who have passed through a broader school curriculum and positive family upbringing, comfortably prepare to enter into adult life with confidence.

Life can be a hard reality and children must be taught to face it. Success kisses those who face the challenges of life head on.

There is no cutting corners in life. We all love our children and our love for them should be manifested in equipping them with real life experiences.

USEFUL TIPS

The following tips about secondary age children are helpful. They are not exhaustive. Muslim parents should use them with conscientiousness and sensitivity. We should:

- teach our children to be proud of Islam. This is absolutely important for their self-esteem and confidence. The pride must be embedded in their characters.
- teach our children modesty and humility. These excellent qualities are important social skills. They help create genuine friendship in life.
- try to be role models for their behaviour and action. Children tend to follow example, not merely what their parents say. When they find exemplary qualities in their parents they feel confident in following them.
- teach discipline and self-control. They are keys to survival and success in life.
- build a sound and lasting relationship with the children, on the basis of love and respect.
- watch their moods. There are ups and downs in human behaviour. Secondary school children are under academic and social pressures. Parents should observe them carefully and deal with them accordingly.
- give our children sufficient space and freedom. We should avoid poking our noses into their affairs.
- understand the psychology of our children in order to deal with them effectively. Simple observation and common-sense are needed.
- use moderation in behaviour towards our children. Too much liberty may spoil them and, on the other hand, too much rigidity may make them rebellious. Islam teaches moderation in life, and children should not grow up in extremes.

- be transparent in our actions. Efforts to hide from children can have disastrous effects, especially with adolescent children. They can gradually lose confidence in their parents.
- listen to children when they talk. Parents should give full attention when they talk. It is the Sunnah of the Prophet ﷺ. Interrupting them encourages them to do the same when their parents or elders talk.
- apologise for any mistakes. Children should know that few human beings, including their parents, come close to perfection. When parents apologise for a mistake this gives the children confidence in their sense of justice and they cannot view them as unfair. It is also a training for them.
- involve our children in various activities, such as, household work, so that they feel a sense of belonging at home. It also increases their self-esteem and confidence.
- be active in dealing with sensitive issues. This is vital, as they are already learning unpalatable things from outside the home. Fathers and mothers should divide their attention between their sons and daughters respectively for issues that is embarrassing but unavoidable in life, such as sex.
- recognise our children's worth and reward them for any good. This gives them inner happiness and encourages them to keep on doing good things. It also gives them assurance that they are valued. However, we must be careful that we do not bribe and spoil them.
- gradually encourage children to take responsibility for their own decisions. Undue dependence of secondary school children can be devastating for them.
- avoid making negative comments, even for fun, about children's choice, behaviour and actions. They have been shown to be demoralising to young people.
- avoid being drawn into sibling arguments. This can bring embarrassment, as they generally forget within a short time.

It is part of their growing process. Obviously, serious incidents should not be overlooked.

- avoid using language such as 'never do this!' We should instead use words like 'I would be happier if you didn't do it this or that way.'
- empathise with our children. We should avoid repeating the behaviour or comments that hurt them. Children are under tremendous pressure nowadays and we need to understand their perspectives.
- avoid passing on the stress of our job or of our lives to the children. There is no doubt that modern life is stressful, but children are not in a position to appreciate that. It rather lowers us in their eyes.
- keep family arguments away from the children. Parents must show the utmost tolerance and sensitivity among themselves. There may be arguments among adults in the family, but children should not be overburdened with them before they are in a position to understand them.
- discipline them with justice. Disciplining secondary school children needs sensitivity. While they must be disciplined for any wrongdoing, they should not be shamed, especially in front of younger siblings. Justice must be maintained and both parents should be involved in the process. Physical punishment should only be used in extreme situations and for the purpose of teaching only.
- avoid scolding children in front of their friends. Should any problem arise, parents should deal with it privately and later on when the situation calms down.
- maintain a good relationship with the children's school. In order to learn how they are doing academically and socially parents should create good links with their Form Tutor and Year Head. Research shows that parental interest in children's work and a parent's involvement in school not only raise their performance, but also aid their emotional development.

12. Home as a Castle for Young People

Children spend a significant part of their lives in school, something like 15,000 hours between the ages of five and sixteen. This has tremendous effect on the formative stages of their lives and, in fact, on their whole being. The school ethos, teachers and peers continuously influence them to conform to the established norms of society. If the norm is value-laden, it has a positive effect; but if it is value-less or value-neutral, it can have detrimental effects on them.

However, compared to their lives at home, this period is shorter. Schools are places for formal education but homes are the abode where children learn informally, hopefully within a relaxed atmosphere. Ideally, this should have an larger influence on them. The moment they open their eyes to the new world they find mother, father and other close relations and family friends. As they grow at home, their character is formed and moulded under the eyes of loving and caring people.

Formal education in schools may be an essential part of human civilisation, although serious and scholarly people have suggested that institutionalised schooling is detrimental[11]. A complementary relationship between home and school is crucially important for the balanced development of children. Educationalists throughout history have always given importance to children's home environment and recommended a strong link between home and school. Many schools in the West have started refocusing and becoming community based. Home liaison has become one of the most important and positive steps to improving school performance and improving children's behaviour. Through Parent Teacher Associations, parents' evening and other mechanisms, schools are building strong links with parents and this is paying dividends. Involvement of parents in school affairs is a significant development in Western education. Human beings are re-inventing their past, as this relationship has always been there in civilised societies. This is fully appreciated by Muslims, as Islam had always given prime importance to a secure home environment and emphasised a holistic approach to a child's education, involving family, community and school.

Home is often sweet, and a castle for many people, although there exist people for whom it is a nightmare. Home is a place to protect oneself and to keep away from evil. It can be a sanctuary in time of difficulty and strife. Home is the most important starter for building a society and a nation. As such, home ought to be a centre of joy and happiness, an abode of moral and spiritual training and a bastion of divine civilisation. It is only possible when the leaders of the house, the parents, provide positive leadership in the nourishment of virtues and prevention of vices.

"Allah has made your houses places of rest for you." (Qur'an: 16:80).

The Prophet Muhammad ﷺ said:

The likeness of a house in which Allah is remembered and the house in which Allah is not remembered, is that of the living and the dead, respectively.

Do not make your houses into graves. The shaytan flees from a house in which Surat al-Baqarah is recited. (*Sahih Muslim*)

THE MUSLIM HOME: AN OASIS IN THE DESERT

What should a Muslim home be like for school-going children? Ideally, both parents should make a long- and short-term plan or set goals for the wholesome development of their children. In Islam, parents are like shepherds who are under divine obligation to look after the physical, moral and spiritual development of their children till they become mature. This begins from the very basics, i.e., providing them with food, clothing and shelter on the one hand, and inculcating higher values of life on the other. A balanced diet, regular exercise, cleanliness and happy mind from the beginning of their lives are the ingredients to keep them fit and sound. Children ought to know their Lord and the basic rites of Islam and as much of the shari'ah and the

Sunnah as is needed to relate to Him, and this obligation falls on the parents before puberty. At the same time, the parents of the children ought to seek out the best education in all kinds of knowledge and sciences for their children since these a part of the basic equipment of a knowledgeable person today and are necessary even to survive in today's world.

• As a Centre of Learning

Knowledge (*'ilm*) is at the root of human beings' superiority over other creatures. Muslims were naturally pioneers in knowledge in our heyday. Unfortunately, for many Muslims it is no longer the case now. In the league table of modern secular education, Muslim countries are at the bottom while, more seriously, neglecting to teach even elementary knowledge of the deen and the shari'ah. This tells us one of the reason for our predicament in the world today. Concerned Muslim parents arrange for their children's knowledge of Islam, Muslim history and the contemporary world, from an early age. Parents who, for whatever reason, did not have the chance to acquire knowledge cannot evade their responsibilities on the pretext of their own inability. We should consult those who are knowledgeable and also try to educate ourselves through the numerous facilities available to adults. Nothing is too late. The akhirah is not waiting for us, for we must strive hard if we are to have a share in it. In these days of technology, technical knowledge is widespread and can be achieved relatively easily through various means, and there are people of considerable knowledge among us of the deen of Islam with whom we can advance our knowledge of the parts of the deen which are obligatory for us to know. 'Where there is a will there is a way.'

To develop an understanding of Islam and the world an Islamic library at home, however small, is essential. Qur'an, the works on the fiqh and the Sunnah, and other books, posters, audio/video cassettes and CD ROMs on Islam and Muslim life are now available everywhere in the world. Parents, of course, should keep an eye on the authenticity of the sources. Partial or extreme views on Islam can create confusion in children. Muslims are aware that, for observance of the deen, practising Muslims have more effect on others in disseminating knowledge than non-practising academics.

Children have strong capabilities for memorisation. Chapters from the Qur'an, the Sunnah, poems and Islamic songs (*nasheed*) are easily memorised by them. Given seriousness and a good environment, some can even memorise the whole Qur'an and become *Hafidh*. Children's voices are also adaptable to pronouncing different sounds. This is why they should be taught to recite Qur'an correctly from childhood so that its words are engraved on their hearts. Once this is ensured along with a concomitant knowledge of the practical Sunnah and the fiqh rulings of Islam on the rites of worship and ordinary situations, they are more likely to be stable in adolescence.

• As a Centre of Personal Development

Every human being ought to become Allah's emissary on earth. This noble position of human beings among the creation can only be achieved if we make utmost effort to develop ourselves physically, intellectually and spiritually. The concept of personal development in Islam is unique in that it encompasses one's comprehensive development as a human being. Islam deals with both the mundane and the highest. It does not ignore anything that is relevant to human life.

Islam's five pillars teach Muslims to become physically and spiritually active. Prayers of the day, especially the dawn prayer (*Fajr*), spark in us the process of inquiry and create in us the desire for reflection and meditation. It drives away the lethargy of our bodies and sterility of mind. Waking up in the latter part of a cold night for prayer or for fasting is too difficult to the slaves of the world, but, to Allah's slaves, even in their school years, it is enjoyable and rewarding. Through prayer we Muslims face our Lord directly. This one-to-one relationship of human beings and our Creator has given us unlimited strength of character and vigour to work for good causes on earth. Children who pray in their youth learn to spend their energy in the noblest of ways, instead of wasting it in vain gossip and meaningless work. The same is true of the other pillars of Islam as well as of Jihad (continuous struggle in the way of Allah and ultimately physical fighting and warfare), which helps us to attain physical fitness and spiritual heights.

Children, by nature, are physically and mentally restless. They always tend to be on the move and thinking. In their growth they tend to talk fast, work fast and most often think differently. Muslim parents who look for wholesome growth in their children at home always engage them in physical and intellectual work that satisfies their needs. They need often to be stretched, but not beyond their limits, to give them more confidence. They should be engaged in helping their mothers and fathers in household chores, e.g., hoovering the house, tidying rooms, shopping, washing cars and similar other work. At the same time, we should encourage them to become involved in swimming, games, sports and athletics. Such outdoor activities are important in preparing them to become confident members of society. If, for practical reasons, these physical activities are impossible they should have a minimum of physical and mental exercise at home, including breathing and stretching exercises, which sharpen the brains. The Prophet Muhammad ﷺ said:

> The strong believer is better and more beloved to Allah than the weak believer, but there is good in both. (*Sahih Muslim*)

QUALITY TIME WITH PARENTS

This was touched on in chapter ten. Earning a livelihood has become a struggle, and as such spending quality time with children is becoming increasingly difficult for parents. There are many fathers who seldom see their children. Odd jobs at night and over-stretched work schedules hinder their interactions with their loved ones, leaving mothers alone to struggle with household work and educate their children. Time is a precious commodity in modern life, and it has been estimated that working fathers generally spend very little time in a day with their children. What is the use of life if we burn up all our energy for mere earnings and find no time for building the future? We should make serious efforts to get out of this vicious circle.

It is essential that parents find time to sit together sometimes and discuss family issues of importance. Even if it is absolutely necessary for both parents to work full-time we must have plans for getting the whole family together on occasions to talk and play with the children. Children should also be made aware of the difficulties faced by their parents.

The Prophet Muhammad ﷺ has advised that those who have children should act like children with them. He used to line up three young sons of his uncle 'Abbas î and ask them to run towards him. They ran, jumped on him and he hugged and kissed them. He sometimes crawled on his hands and knees while Hasan and Hussein were riding on his back. All these can only be possible if parents, especially fathers, manage to spend quality time with the family.

Whatever you spend for the pleasure of Allah will be rewarded; even the mouthful of food you give to your wife. (*Sahih al-Bukhari* and *Muslim*)

Anyone spending for the family for the pleasure of Allah [then it] will be treated as sadaqah. (*Sahih al-Bukhari* and *Muslim*)

Earning a livelihood can be an act of worship, if one engages in it intending to seek out halal livelihood and to observe the shari'ah and the Sunnah in one's commercial transactions, and intending by that for oneself and one's family to have the strength to worship and remember Allah. Spending on the family is the best of spending. The above and other sayings of the Messenger of Allah ﷺ encourage Muslims to earn and spend on the family and others. Provision comes from Allah, and Muslims should be grateful for what they earn, and know that although one had to strive in earning that the provision is Allah's gift to us by His mercy. A Muslim's earnings are for a meaningful life, raising children in Islam and leaving successors committed to Islam when one dies.

ISLAMIC UPBRINGING AT HOME[12]

Children, by the end of primary school-life, are growing fast. Their secondary school years see visible physical, emotional and social changes, as they enter upon the threshold of puberty. The moment they cross the threshold, the Shari'ah rules become determining factors in their lives, i.e. they themselves become directly accountable to Allah for their conduct, an accountability which had belonged to their parents before. This life in transition is often rough and uncertain. For some, it can be very difficult. Parents, teachers and friends on one hand and home, school and the social environment, on the other, pull them in different directions. In this period, both father and mother should be actively engaged with their sons and daughters respectively so that they are not left alone or misled by confusing messages about life.

The way children are brought up determines how they cope in this rough but adventurous ride of life. In a caring, value-rich environment, where yet there is lot of freedom, within the broader ethos of Islam, they often come out successful. They generally grow up motivated to challenge the inherent difficulties of this phase. On the other hand, both the unusually rigid and the too liberal environment give them wrong signals and the transition becomes daunting. Parents who force their children and use frequent threats of punishment, or mention 'sin' too often, do not help. Of course, parents need to be strong in some basic Islamic requirements, e.g., prayer and Islamic Adab, but the technique in teaching or reprimanding is important. For any genuine learning, creating a positive environment is essential. We all need time to grasp a new idea or initiative. Although any rite is fully obligatory only after puberty, Muslim parents are asked to prepare their children from the early age, e.g., from the age of seven, for the prayer. The Prophet ﷺ has said:

> Command your children to pray at the age of seven. At the age of ten, punish them [for omitting it] and separate them in their beds. (*Abu Dawud* and *al-Hakim*)

The same is true of the headscarf for girls and fasting for children, which should be practised long before they enter into puberty because otherwise the sudden and rigorous implementation of Islamic practices may prove overwhelming to them. At the same time, Islamic practices should not be taught as only empty and meaningless rituals, they are for creating a close link between the slaves of Allah and their Creator.

It is a part of human nature to become accustomed to new things. The reason why some Muslim children rebel against Islamic practices at puberty is their sudden imposition without the necessary groundwork and sensitivity. The intention behind the persistent bombardment of advertisements in the media and on the streets is to make certain that the image of the products is imprinted in consumers' brains. As a result, all major companies in the world spend a significant proportion of their money on advertising their products. Parents also need steadfastness in guiding their children.

Children who are trained to practise Islam from an early age accept it as part of their normal daily routine. If, unfortunately, these do not become a part of their regular practice of Islam at the right age, parents are commanded to punish them. Physical punishment, such as smacking, is the last option and before one is compelled to use this parents should continuously seek help from Allah and supplicate for the guidance of their children. In spite of all efforts, children may go off track and disappoint their parents. Whatever, physical violence beyond the limits of simple beating for disobeying Allah must be avoided and the matter left in Allah's hands. Guidance is from Him alone. Even Nuh ﷺ could not save his own son from doom!

• Islamic Adab (Manners)

Teaching Islam in the family is at the core of maintaining or expanding the frontiers of Islam. The Messenger of Allah ﷺ was sent to humanity as a teacher and he guided human beings in all aspects of life. Acquiring knowledge is a fundamental part of life, and education starts from childhood at which time it is the responsibility of the parents.

> Abu Hafs 'Umar ibn Abi Salamah said, 'I was a child under the care of the Prophet ﷺ. While eating, my careless hand would move around in the plate. The Prophet ﷺ said, "My son, start in the name of Allah with the right hand and take the nearest food". From then onwards I used to eat the way he taught me.' (*Sahih al-Bukhari* and *Muslim*)

As manners and behaviour have a high place in Islam, children need to be taught how to behave with other human beings in whatever environment they are. The Islamic courtesy of greeting and responding, seeking permission to enter a house or room - are all part of Muslim culture that has made the ummah a community of distinct social etiquette. Children's manners reflect their family backgrounds, their character and future potential. It is important to understand that in the modern world fashions, often promoted by celebrities, guide young people's lives. They are geared toward an amoral, and often immoral, consumer culture that influences young minds. The way to survive in this global consumer culture is to link children with Allah by Islamic practice and modes of conduct.

Islamic *adab* is at the heart of Muslim social life. The Prophet Muhammad ﷺ was the epitome of excellent human behaviour even before he was commissioned as a prophet. He was the kindest of his people. He served his people with humility and persistently taught them how to be 'good' to others, without having the slightest desire of any worldly return. Emulating him to the best of one's ability is the most rewarding goal possible in a Muslim life.

How can Islamic manners be implanted among Muslim children in a world where arrogant pride in material progress and ignorance of spiritual worth are so extremely pronounced? The answer is that it is not that easy, but, with the Prophet Muhammad ﷺ as a role model, Muslims have the upper hand.

• Dealing with Egocentric Behaviour

The absence of a sound Muslim culture in the midst of the all-pervasive materialism of the West has adverse effects on the younger generation. Children raised in a sound Islamic environment can cope with the pull of society, but, in reality, many Muslim homes fail to provide them those strong roots. As a result, behavioural problems arise, especially in the secondary years, which Muslim parents find it difficult to tackle. Whatever the problem, parents should not give in by becoming judgemental about their children. Problems can be one-off, due to psychological reasons or external incident. They are quite different from those which are deliberate or which have patterns. Parents should categorise any problem on the basis of its

- severity
- frequency
- duration
- persistence

Dealing with problems depends on the context, the parent-child relationship and the intellectual maturity of the children. Should a problem arise in a child, it is most important for the parents not to lose their tempers and to avoid shouting and accusations. Natural justice and tolerance must prevail, if they want prevention or correction. Children should be helped to realise their own mistakes. In any case they should not be humiliated or denigrated in their sense of self-worth. Confident proud Muslim children will understand the consequences of their mistakes and themselves try to repair and rebuild.

Managing challenging behaviour from one's children needs more patience, as parents normally have very high expectations of them and if anything goes wrong in their behaviour we become upset. We often forget that 'to err is human' and have the tendency to look for perfection in our beloved ones, when we ourselves fail to maintain high standards. The following 5 Cs are important to remember when the unfortunate situation of our sons' or daughters' behavioural problems tend to frustrate us. What we need are the following:

- Calmness
- Confidence
- Consistency
- Clarity
- Control
- Communications
- Cleanliness (*Taharah*)

Islam is based on the five pillars and for all of them cleanliness is the starting point. New Muslims only start their journey in Islam by saying the *Shahadah* after taking a ghusl. *Taharah* (cleanliness) encompasses one's purity in preparation for acts of worship, personal hygiene, and keeping one's things and surroundings tidy. It emanates from one's feeling of aspiring to purity, as Allah, our Lord, is the Pure and loves purity and those who purify themselves. Cleanliness keeps us joyful and fit.

> The key to the Garden is prayer and the key to prayer is cleanliness. (*At-Tirmidhi*)

Physical and intellectual fitness are not only for our happy lives, but also for the life-long struggle of a believer. Muslims are asked to earn halal incomes and spend from it halal. We are commanded to eat clean food so that it nourishes our blood and our bodies. Allah has forbidden carrion, blood, pork, wine and things that are dedicated to anything other than Allah (Qur'an 2:173, 5:3, 5:90, 16:115) because they are intrinsically unclean.

Allah loves those who repent and loves those who purify themselves. (Qur'an 2:222)

Cleanliness is so important in Islam that an unclean person, in the sense of someone not in the clean state in preparedness for prayer, cannot touch the Qur'an.

It truly is a noble Qur'an, in a well-protected Book. No one may touch it except the purified. (Qur'an 56: 77-79)

Cleanliness and a clean environment are essential ingredients in Muslim life. According to the Prophet Muhammad ﷺ it is a part of iman. He was the symbol of cleanliness and he emphasised it so much that when he entered his house he would clean his teeth (with a *siwak*) first (*Sahih Muslim*).

In our Western societies where everything is well organised and the importance of general tidiness is properly emphasised, this notion of personal cleanliness is unfortunately absent. Islam's repetitive wudu, the requirement of the ghusl, cutting the nails and removing pubic hair and hair under the armpits - all maintain personal hygiene and lead to self-purification. Inculcating this sense of cleanliness and purification in the child, from the beginning of its life, is essential.

• *Haya* (Modesty)

Iman consists of more than sixty branches and modesty (*haya*) is a part of faith. (*Sahih al-Bukhari*)

Indecency disfigures everything and modesty (*haya*) enhances the charm of everything. (*At-Tirmidhi*)

Modesty is an essential ingredient of iman. Ever since human beings were created *haya* was embedded in our natures. Ancient human beings invented garments to cover themselves, as they realised that tree-leaves were neither convenient nor enough to do the job. A woman had to cover more of her body, as her beauty can be the source of temptation to men leading to her vulnerability in the midst of menfolk who are bestowed with a more assertive sexual libido. Allah has commanded Muslim men and women to be modest in their dress and also to lower their gaze when marriageable members of the opposite sex encounter one another (Qur'an 24:30-31).

The hadith that asks parents to separate children in their beds at the age of ten is important. In sexually permissive societies this can hardly be over-emphasised, as incest between family members is increasing rapidly. The lack of *haya* in homes, open immodest discussions of sexual matters, and the practice of family members sun-bathing and swimming semi-nude, and in some societies nude, together on the beach contribute to this.

Social norms in modern societies are changing to such an extent that aberrant sexual practices are no longer treated disapprovingly. There are now influential people in the higher echelons of society who not only feel proud to openly declare their unscrupulous sexual practices, but also try to impose their deviant views on others in the name of human rights and equal opportunities.

Mixed swimming and collective showers at school, the revealing dress of young women in public and bikini-clad or topless sunbathing - are all opposite to the ethos of *haya* in society. Sunbathing has its physical dangers as well. In addition to the promotion of lewdness and illicit sexual desire, it can cause skin cancer. Malignant melanoma, the deadliest form of skin cancer, kills thousands in the West. As the libertine sections of society ridicule modesty, chastity and virginity, Muslim parents have an uphill task in raising their children in innocence.

• The Ethos of Listening

Children are not yet adults. When they talk, they often repeat things unnecessarily and sometimes talk without any clear meaning. This is the way they learn how to communicate with others. Parents need to have patience in listening to them, as active listening is a skill. People have a tendency to talk more and listen less, but wise people are those who reflect on what Allah has given them in their physical beings: haven't we two ears and one mouth in order to listen more than talk? We parents need to talk to our children meaningfully and in a way they understand. The Messenger of Allah ﷺ was an active listener and meaningful speaker.

> A'ishah, may Allah be pleased with her, narrated that the Prophet ﷺ spoke clearly so that all those who listened to him would understand him. (*Abu Dawud*)

> Anas î related that the Prophet ﷺ used to repeat his words three times so that the meanings were understood fully. (*Sahih al-Bukhari*)

When children are listened to, it gives them confidence that their words have some weight to their parents. It also teaches them to listen when their parents talk. Active listening is the Sunnah of the Prophet ﷺ. When he listened to someone his whole being was involved in it. The ethos in which listening is valued trains children to value others and makes them more accommodative to people around them.

Listening involves conscious hearing with the intention of understanding what the speaker is saying. Active listening leads to meaningful action. Children are always in a hurry, and generally possess a shorter concentration span. In a home environment where parents practise this skill, Muslim children gradually acquire it and thus have more chance of success in life.

• Moderation

Parents should treat their children as they are and should not, in any way, overburden them beyond their abilities. We should not expect an immediate result from them. Too much rushing or too much pressure can bring frustration. Working with children is a long-term investment. To Muslims this is an investment in the *akhirah*. Allah does not overburden His slaves (Qur'an 2:286) and we Muslims are asked to follow the middle path in all affairs of life, including how we spend money, time and energy (Qur'an 17:29, 25:67). The Prophet Muhammad ﷺ has said:

A good manner of conduct, deliberation and moderation are a 24th or 25th part of Prophecy. (*Abu Dawud* and *at-Tirmidhi*)

Whenever the Messenger of Allah ﷺ was given the choice of one of two matters, he would choose the easier of the two, as long as it was not wrongful to do so, but if it was wrongful to do so he would not approach it. (*Sahih al-Bukhari*)

Because of a self-imposed sense of urgency some Muslim parents may exert too much pressure on their children to achieve miracles in their schooling or in their performance of religious duties. While stretching someone to his or her furthermost potential is appreciated, pressure does not help. It may even have adverse effects.

EVENING/WEEKEND ISLAMIC SCHOOL

Getting a basic understanding of Islam is a fundamental right of all children born in Muslim families. In some Muslim countries where 'religious' education is integrated with 'secular' education, Muslim children can learn about their deen and the world from the same institutions, however partial and biased that education is. Unfortunately, the situation is not that rosy in most Muslim countries, where secularism has fragmented human life. In Muslim minority countries of the West, only a few private Islamic schools are struggling to follow an integrated curriculum. State schools in the West have religious education from a secular perspective.

Muslim children going to Western schools have little chance to learn about the deen from an Islamic perspective. Unless their parents teach them Islam or send them to weekend and/or evening schools, where they can learn Qur'an, Arabic language and Islamic Studies in an Islamic environment and Muslim-friendly atmosphere, young Muslims are in danger of losing Islam. In fact, in recent decades many Muslim children have become confused about their roots. As Muslim communities are battling to keep their youngsters in the fold of Islam, many evening/weekend schools have sprung up to address the issues in localities where Muslims have a sizeable presence. The task is huge.

However, these schools are littered with obstacles. First, children attending a state school for the whole day come home tired and need rest to prepare for the next day. If they have work pressure from the school they find it difficult to cope with extra schooling in the evenings. The same may be true for the weekends, as they need some time and space for relaxation. Second, most of the evening/weekend schools are arranged in crammed spaces with little resources. Third, the way most of these schools are run by largely non-professional teachers, the youngsters dislike them. There cannot be any comparison between them and the resources and professionalism of state schools. Fourth, where in the West physical punishment is non-existent, many of these schools are still run by teachers having little knowledge of modern classroom management. With sticks in the teachers hands, there are no positive incentives attracting the children to learn. Children attend them, because of pressure from their parents.

Weekend School – A Success Story

Saturday Islamic School (SIS) in the East End of London is an innovative project by some professional teachers who, as parents of young children, thought it vital for the Muslim community there. These Muslim professionals, before starting the school a few years ago, carried out an informal survey of the existing evening/weekend schools and learnt a great lesson from them. From the very beginning they strongly maintained that children should not be overburdened with evening classes, as tired children can learn very little. They also left one day in the weekend absolutely free for the children to have their own time.

Being open-minded, they learnt from the experience of the well-resourced state schools and tried to include as much teaching resources as financially possible. In the beginning, they fortunately received some financial support from a local mosque, the historic East London Mosque. Gradually, they became self-sufficient because of the tuition fees from parents who paid gladly.

They recruited quality teachers with good Islamic and professional backgrounds and paid them reasonable salaries.

The subjects they teach are the Arabic language, Qur'an Study, Islamic history and Islamic studies. In only a few years the number of children has risen to about two hundred and a similar number is on the waiting list. They have sorted out the accommodation problem by creating a good link to a local secondary school, which has allowed the use of some rooms. Through their hard work, they have created a sense of belonging among the children who like the SIS more than their normal schools. They have produced a syllabus for all the subjects they teach and booklets for pupils and parents. They arrange internal training for the teachers to keep them abreast with knowledge of the profession and presentation techniques in modern classrooms. The attractive logo in the exercise book and bag gives pupils pride in their school.

Supplementary schools for teaching mother-tongues are also important. Parents of minority ethnic communities in many countries have been organising these schools, some with the aid of government grants. They are an important contribution to maintaining the linguistic and cultural roots of the children in pluralist societies. Muslim parents should play their role in this venture, as mother tongues are important tools for anchoring children. Most Muslim community languages are historically rich and carry the Islamic message by default.

CREATING A MUSLIM YOUTH CULTURE

Taking children to mosques and Islamic centres from a young age, properly the age when the children must learn the prayer and are able to maintain the adab of the mosque, opens the door to a wider world with people of different races and languages. Mosques have been the central institution for education and community purpose in Islamic history. Unfortunately, many mosques are today quiet and are even locked outside prayer times. Regeneration of the ummah will remain a dream if they are allowed to remain like this, as places of ritual prayer alone. Mosques must be brought back to play their full role, as was exemplified by the mosque of the Messenger of Allah ﷺ in Madinah. In addition to congregational prayers and Qur'an classes, the core groups organising mosques should organise a host of activities, e.g., sports, discussion groups and supplementary classes.

Mosques, weekend schools or community clubs can occasionally arrange for day trips and camps, for fun and learning so that children can grow together as Muslims. They also create opportunities to make friendship with others, which is very important for their social life. Children easily make and break friends and through this learn about themselves and the world around them. Parents can and should help their young ones to choose suitable friends.

At the same time, if time and economics permit, children should be taken to 'Umrah, when they are old enough to realise and appreciate the value of it, or to visit other historical Muslim places, e.g., Spain and Turkey, to give them wider perspectives on Islamic history. With careful planning this may not be impossible for many parents.

It is a part of parental responsibility also to make sure that children avoid wrong company and select good company, as friends easily influence them. Peer pressure is very strong for teenagers. Research has shown that drug addiction, juvenile delinquency, gang fighting and other criminal activities among the youth are augmented by peer pressure. Young people are generally prone to the so-called 'youth culture' of the day, in reality a 'culture' created by quite aged marketing forces for their own profit. Muslim youth, because of their ethnic and religious backgrounds, may be at the receiving end of hostility outside their homes and in their schools. Many become disaffected and disgruntled by the prejudice, discrimination and inequalities surrounding them. This can be the breeding ground for a hate mentality leading to extremism or even anti-social activities. The 2001 summer race riots in the north of England should be eye-openers to all. Parents need to be aware of this and provide young children with positive environments where they can spend their time with good Muslim friends. The Prophet Muhammad ﷺ has warned:

> A person is upon the deen of his friend, so see whom you take as a friend. (*Abu-Dawud, at-Tirmidhi* and *Ahmad*)

The best way to harness the potential of Muslim children is to involve them in Islamic circles from an early age, where they can be engaged in a host of activities. The Prophet Muhammad ﷺ revived and initiated social welfare work through an association called *Hilf al-Fudul*, in his youth. Parents should encourage their children to join good groups related to mosques or reputable Muslim organisations. There are now many groups to cater for children in their teens, but children need to start their communal responsibilities earlier, even from the age of seven or eight. Junior groups, like the Junior Muslim Circle (JMC) based in London, can engage very young children in challenging activities and create motivation in them to grow in Islam when they are still completely innocent.

A distinct Muslim youth culture is essential in the West. Muslim youth organisations have a historic responsibility in this. They have the monumental task of creating a sound Islamic environment within their organisations. They should focus on self-propelled *khidmah* (service) to youth through:

- organising social events.
- organising classes on Qur'an, Islamic knowledge, the Arabic language and spiritual development.
- organising sports, leisure and Islamically approved entertainment activities.
- organising campaigns against anti-social activities.
- advising and helping in homework, and career guidance, etc.
- organising training programmes to build Islamic character in them.

The world is now very small. Societies in the East and the West are gradually becoming pluralistic. Muslims, in the past, coexisted with other communities amicably. In many Western countries they are now living peacefully with others. Young Muslims need exposure to the wider society. That is the spirit of Islam. They need friends from all sections of the community, but they should be guided in finding close friends whose values of life are similar to their own or at least not antagonistic. There are non-Muslims who possess similar values to ours, and children should be made aware at an early age of our responsibility to invite them to Islam, and not merely take them as friends.

Muslim Celebrations

Every community has annual occasions to celebrate. Religious or cultural celebrations have their distinct characteristics. In Western countries children come across various kinds of celebrations, such as Halloween, Thanksgiving, Christmas, birthdays, New Year's day, Valentine's day, Labour day, Mothers day and so on. In some pluralist societies, major celebrations of important faith communities are also recognised. Muslims have two such celebrations: one, after the month-long fasting and the other to commemorate the sacrifice of the prophet Ibrahim ﷺ. The Prophet Muhammad ﷺ said that Allah has replaced the Eids (celebrations) of Jahiliyyah (days of ignorance) with these two Eids. Both these social occasions are meant to make an imprint on Muslim children of remembrance and worship of Allah with the wider Muslim community, and clean and innocent recreation. As Islamic recreation has a unique moral and spiritual dimension, Muslim parents should provide their children with the opportunity to enjoy it fully.

These two celebrations are meant to create a feeling of togetherness among Muslims all over the world. As the Muslim ummah, according to a hadith, is like a human body, Muslim communities around the world feel the pain of Muslim problems in other parts of the world.

Muslims children should be made to feel the joy of these celebrations through gifts, good food and clean clothing so that they proudly remember the occasions. The emphasis on the two

Eid is for men, women and children to go to a big open place to show gratitude to Allah in prayer and remembrance of Allah and meet other Muslims in the locality. As in Muslim countries, Muslims in some Western countries arrange their Eid congregation in open public places, when weather conditions are good.

HOLIDAYS

Schools in Western countries have long holidays in the summer. There are also shorter ones during the Christmas and Easter. Holidays are essential for education so that children can find relief from the pressure of work and get extra time if they are behind in their studies or if they need to do some course work. But these holidays can be daunting for parents, if they are not sure what to do with them during that period. In families where both parents have to work this can be a nightmare. As a result, many parents grumble during holidays, which are supposed to be a nice time for them and the young ones.

Holidays need to be planned with innovative thinking if parents want to keep children happy and busy. People in the West generally save money in the whole year for exotic holidays, which has become a part of their culture. Affluent Muslims, including converts, try to follow the trend. Others save money to visit their relatives, in their countries of origin. Some of them go for 'Umrah (lesser pilgrimage) to Makkah in Saudi Arabia. 'Umrah and visiting a Muslim country are important for the children to learn more about Islam and about their own historical past. Many children have re-invented their roots through these visits. To make holidays more effective, young Muslims can spend some time in learning Arabic from Arabic-speaking teachers in the West or even by going to a Middle Eastern country.

It is important that we parents arrange our holidays in planned ways. If we cannot take our children to distant places we should plan within our means to visit relatives and friends and create opportunities for our own children to mix with as many Muslim children as possible. Many Islamic organisations and mosques run good courses on Islam and the Arabic language. Major Muslim events are also organised during holidays in which children can play an active part. Authorities in many countries arrange summer programmes involving fun and education. In any case, there are a lot of opportunities for young people to engage themselves in recreation and meaningful learning during holidays.

Useful Tips

Muslim parents should use the following tips conscientiously and sensitively. We should:

- inculcate pride in Islam in children. As inheritors of the earth, believers are neither conceited nor over-meek. Young Muslims should grow as strong Muslims with balance and humility.
- follow Allah's guidance and the Sunnah of the Prophet ﷺ ourselves in our daily activities so that this creates love for them in the children. This includes the main Islamic rites, much remembrance of Allah, supplication and the *Masnoon Du'a* (supplications from the Sunnah) for any event or incident, as taught by the Prophet ﷺ.
- refer to Qur'an and Sunnah when talking about any issue. These two central sources should always be the reference points for Muslims.
- establish prayer on time. If the mosque is near, we fathers should take our children who are performing the prayer or beginning to learn it to the congregational prayers, or else we should make congregation at home at the prescribed times.
- make a practice of recitation of the Qur'an everyday. Children will also make a practice of doing that. Devoted and correct recitation of Qur'an has a moving effect on reciters and others.
- encourage children to reflect on the miracles of creation. Our whole existence and surroundings testify to the miracles of Allah. The more children are guided to think on these, the more they will be attached to Allah.

- socialise with Muslim families so that children can pick their closest friends from within the Muslim community. This is important for their confidence as young Muslims. Their ability to interact with the wider society will thus be enhanced.

- inculcate the spirit of *shahadah* (witnessing Islam) in the children. Exemplifying Islam in word and action is the essence of being a Muslim. This urge for *shahadah* should be embedded at a young age.

- maintain a cordial relationship with neighbours. This will create socialisation skills in the child and a tendency to help others in their need. This *khidmah* aspect of Islam is in the heart of the Prophetic Sunnah and a major ingredient of a happy community.

- arrange regular family sessions. They help bonding among family members and increase knowledge of and conviction in Islam. Parents can encourage their children in the affairs of the family through engagement in discussion of family issues.

- arrange healthy competition among the siblings on Islamic and general knowledge. Competition on knowledge and taqwa is encouraged in Islam and it pushes young people forward.

- educate children about the Muslim world and its history in order to create a sense of urgency in them for engaging in the intellectual, sociopolitical and financial upliftment of the ummah.

- provide Islamically approved recreation so that children do not have to follow others in indecent and sensual pleasures.

- enjoy the company of the child(ren). Young people are inherently innocent and instinctively happy. Their company transmits liveliness and innocence to elders who are sometimes overburdened with the affairs of the world.

NOTES

1 *The National Curriculum: Handbook for Primary Teachers in England*, DfEE, 1999.

2 *Achievement for All, A Practical Handbook for Teachers and Lecturers*, ATL Publication, London 1998

3 *Twelve Tips for childrearing*, Ibrahim Bowers, Q News: The Muslim Magazine, London, No.311, September, 1999 and *29 Tips on Raising Children*, Al Jumua: Your Guide to an Islamic Life, London, Vol.12, Issue 8, November 2000

4 *The Muslim Parents handbook: What every Muslim Parent should know*, Shabbir Akhtar, Ta-Ha Publishers, London, 1993. *Muslim Demands for Their Own Denominational Schools in the UK*, M. A. Bari, Muslim Education Quarterly, The Islamic Academy, Cambridge, Vol. 10, No. 2, 1993.

5 *The National curriculum: Handbook for Secondary Teachers in England*, DfEE, 1999.

6 Ibid.

7 *Post-modern Education and the Missing Dimension*, M. A. Bari, Muslim Education Quarterly, The Islamic Academy, Cambridge, Vol. 17, No. 2, 2000.

8 *Bullying - don't suffer in silence: An anti-bullying pack for schools*, p10, DfEE 2000

9 *Head Start - How to develop your child's mind*, Robert Fisher, Souvenir Press Ltd, London, 1999

10 *Head Start - How to develop your child's mind*, Robert Fisher, Souvenir Press Ltd, London, 1999

11 *De-schooling Society*, Ivan Illich.

12 *The Muslim Home - Forty Recommendations*, Sheikh Muhammad Salih al-Munajjid, www2.fwi.com/aliasidiqui/ sub/house.html

The Challenge of Adolescence

Executive Summary

- Adolescence is a period of commotion and great change. It can be a nightmare or a chivalric and knightly opening. Muslim parents have to accept that their children are growing up. They should understand the issues relevant to adolescence and be ready to change themselves.

- Puberty is the basic condition from the onset of which the Islamic Shari'ah is implemented in one's life. Fathers and mothers should take responsibility in guiding their adolescent boys and girls, respectively, so that they learn to become adult Muslim men and women.

- We Muslim parents should tirelessly try to equip our adolescent child to sail through the social waves that influence them, especially in the West. Muslim adolescents should be prepared to overcome the materialistic influences on their personal lives.

- We Muslim parents should be accommodative, pro-active and assertive, instead of being authoritarian or too liberal, in guiding our adolescents. We should keep on supplicating for them so that they come out in life better than we have. In any difficulties with our children, we must adopt Islamic procedures.

- To help adolescents becoming responsible adults, we should involve them fully in family and social affairs. We should give them freedom and personal space as well as confidence in decision making.

- We should help our children to find appropriate Islamic

groups so that they can take an active part in the process of bringing back Islam. This will also help them in developing their personal and social qualities.

- As Muslim adolescents are growing up in the midst of the numerous social ills of our time, such as, drugs, sex abuse, violence, and crime, etc., we should equip them well to come unscathed through the onslaught.
- Motivation is essential for self-esteem and success in life. Muslims draw motivation from the love and fear of Allah. We Muslim parents need to provide leadership in motivation through our exemplary behaviour, so that out children do not fall through the net.
- We should educate our children with the Prophet's model character ﷺ and the examples of right-acting Muslims so that the influence of contemporary negative role models cannot endanger their lives.
- We should be able to identify the potential and positive aspects of our children so that we can encourage them to take up proper careers. Some careers are more needed for the ummah. Children should be given opportunities to succeed, as success breeds success.
- Our responsibilities as parents towards our children ceases with adulthood, for then the young person has his or her own unique accounting with Allah. However, at that point we must make the transition to taking them as friends, as is recommended in the Sunnah, and then we owe them the counsel owed to other Muslims,but even more so because of their close relationship to us.

13. Adolescence

A Nightmare or Knightly Power?

Like every caring father, Tony Blair, the Prime Minister of Britain, found out in the early morning of 6th July 2000 that parenting in modern days is extremely difficult. 'Being Prime Minister was a tough job, but being a parent was tougher,' he lamented. The fact that his eldest son Euan's carefree fun after the pressure of GCSE exam ended up in 'drunkenness' and 'loutish' behaviour in Leicester Square, London and his subsequently lying at the police station to conceal his identity caused him disbelief and dismay as a parent. The experts and social pundits would, of course, take this as a natural adolescent expression and advise parents not to worry too much, but the fact of the matter remains, which few people now dare acknowledge, that in the sea of permissive and promiscuous modern life adolescents are at the receiving end and under tremendous social pressure to conform. Few are able to swim to the shore.

Adolescence has always attracted criticism from elders for its restlessness, and rash and impulsive outbursts. On the other hand, it draws attention for its creative enterprise. It is the period when human beings discover their energy and potential and want to do something special. If driven by high spiritual, social and moral values and positive social norms, its creative and dynamic power can lift a nation to the heights, but misguided adolescence is like untapped or misused energy that can let a society down or even create havoc. During the first few generations of Islam, and in other cyclical moments of expansion and renewal, some adolescents or post-adolescents even took the lead in enduring great sacrifice and expanding the frontiers of Islam by their zeal and vigour. Later on, in moments of cyclical decline when the Muslim ummah became too complacent with its past glory, the energy of youth was misused in vain pursuits.

There are both ups and downs, nasty shocks and pleasant surprises in a family raising adolescents. As long as parents understand that an unpredictable change in their children's behaviour is on the way, the 'horrors' of adolescence can be overcome with patience and understanding. Sometimes children may be charming and wonderful and on occasions they can be moody or even insolent. Rigid and dominating parents will have lot of problems with their children, especially in the West. If not dealt with properly, some parents will lose their loved ones.

THE GREAT CHANGE

Parents worry more about their children in adolescence because of the fact that this is a period of abrupt transition in their lives. Small children normally mirror what their parents have taught them. They easily conform to their parents' wishes, but, in adolescence, things can be different. Parents must learn to change their attitudes to young ones. They need to consider them as individuals in their own right. Their distinctive features should not only be tolerated, but wholeheartedly encouraged. The skills parents have learnt to deal with their young ones in their childhood are likely to be put to the test and many parents feel stretched and stressed with these 'new' children. Conscientious parents adjust quickly to this reality and engage with their children in a reassuring manner.

Adolescence is a stage that has unique features. As children cross the threshold from childhood and begin their exciting trek into young adulthood, they undergo extraordinary changes in their bodies as well as in their feelings and emotions. Growing up is an exhilarating and once-in-a-life-time experience. It is also painful for some, as they find difficulties in adjusting to the sudden change in life. It is a time when their personalities as new adults is manifest to themselves and others around them.

It is difficult to pinpoint with accuracy when exactly adolescence starts for individuals. It can start at the age of ten, sixteen or even eighteen. Generally, it spans the teenage period. By the time they leave school, fully-fledged adults have joined the family.

So, what happens at this stage? What is the myth and what is the reality surrounding adolescence?

Adolescence is a period of transformation that involves physical as well as social, intellectual, spiritual and emotional metamorphosis in one's life. Adolescence is the beginning of the end of childhood and it throws human beings into the world of responsibility. As it is a period of internal commotion in young people's lives, parents need to monitor them closely and guide them in this period of need. The changes that children undergo as well as being intellectual and spiritual can be classified as physical, social and emotional.

• Physical

The physical change, known as puberty, activates the body clock of children to function in a different mode, i.e. their bodies prepare themselves to make them physically capable of reproduction. Puberty brings more visible change in girls than in boys. Their body shapes suddenly become womanly and they start to menstruate once a month. Their physical changes involve the production of increasing amount of the female sex hormone, oestrogen, and the characteristic external and internal features of female bodies. However, boys grow more rapidly than do girls', within about two years, and this additional height and weight are maintained for the rest of their lives. In boys, puberty brings masculine features in their body, such as, the breaking of the voice. Allah has blessed girls with tender physical and psychological features, which are enhanced during their puberty. Energetic as they are, adolescent boys and girls need more nutrition for their growth and spiritual and intellectual nourishment for their self-control.

Parents should not only be aware of these changes in their children, but should acquire the basic tools to deal with them. Knowledge and awareness help them to keep close watch on their young ones. As puberty descends upon children, mothers should open up further to their daughters and discuss, as frankly as possible, important issues with their pubescent girls, e.g., on their metabolism, cleanliness during menstruation, cutting of unwanted hairs from their body and the fiqh (Islamic Jurisprudence) regarding basic Islamic rites. In the same way, fathers should be more open in discussing the bodily aspects with their sons, such as cleanliness after wet dreams and cutting unwanted pubic and armpit hair. While sensitivity is the guiding principle, embarrassment should not prevent parents teaching their children the necessities of adult life. The Qur'an itself discusses sensitive issues in a decent manner. Needless to say that a worthy child-parent relationship is essential for a successful dialogue in this period and a fruitful outcome.

Adolescence is the period from when the Shari'ah is enforceable on a Muslim. Boys and girls are then accepted as men and women in Islam, although they may still be teenagers. Islamic rulings on the man-woman relationship are at the core of maintaining a healthy society. Qur'an (4:23) has mentioned a list of close people (*mahram*), such as mothers and fathers, brothers and sisters, those whom they are unable to marry and beyond whom pubescent Muslim boys or girls are not allowed to spend time secluded with members of the opposite sex. They should never allow themselves to be intimate with members of the opposite sex in secluded places and should maintain conscious awareness of the presence and knowledge of Allah whenever they encounter one another in public places. Girls should maintain *hijab*, i.e. dressing modestly with covering of their limbs and hair, and both boys and girls should be modest in their dress and attitude. These wonderful injunctions are at the heart of virtuous relationships between men and women in Muslim societies and have, over the centuries, prevented the sexual permissiveness that has led to sexual promiscuity in modern societies.

• Social

Then, there are social changes when adolescents move from childhood, in which they are dependent on their families, towards being independent adults. With the newly understood independence they might be tempted to disrupt household routines, such as, meal-times and bedtimes etc. Children may resent participating in family activities, be discourteous to younger siblings and rude to elders, including parents. They may be interested in reading books or magazines, listening to music and watching TV programmes which parents do not like. They may sometimes come home late and refuse to go with their parents for shopping or visit family friends. They may pester their parents to buy certain expensive designer clothes or games. They know that they are still dependent on the parents, yet they are aware that they must become self-reliant and assert their independence. They are under pressure to conform to the youth culture of the wider society.

How far parents are prepared to put up with all this depends on what sorts of parents they are. The best way is the middle of the road, neither autocracy nor over permissiveness. Parents are neither friends nor bosses; they should be, or at least be seen to be, their children's best confidants. A right balance and sense of proportion, though difficult to maintain, are the way forward. Children should neither feel that they are ignored, nor should they get away with unacceptable behaviour. Properly trained and guided children understand their boundaries and the Islamic requirements of behaviour. They are aware of the dynamics in the family and in the Muslim community. They gradually learn to be responsible social human beings and make their place in the community.

• Emotional

Physical development brings natural shyness and embarrassment in adolescents. These and other emotional changes come as a result of the chemical changes in their bodies and from their growing experience of shouldering more and more responsibilities. Adolescents do not have any control over their physical growth. This change imposed on their bodies creates uncertain and confused feelings in them. As they are perceived differently by people around them, the ensuing psychological and emotional changes can make them unreasonable and unpredictable. They themselves cannot decide whether they are still children or adults. This uncertainty and these complex feeling perplex them for a certain period. Others cannot straight away guide them. This difficulty in fitting with others haunts them for some time in the early days of puberty. Conscientious parents do not press too hard on their adolescents to fit into their adult world. Rather, they give them space and time to settle.

THE ISSUES

Adolescence brings children and their parents to a new reality of life. Life never remains the same. New challenges, worries and threats change the dynamics in the family. Sensitive parents quickly learn to adjust and accommodate, and they adopt a different strategy to deal with the situation and harness the youthful energy of their adolescents. A number of issues arise and the parents need to tackle them before it is too late.

• The Issue of Sex

Puberty changes people's attitudes towards the opposite sex, as attraction grows stronger. Sexual libido becomes a dominant feature. The feeling of love and liking for someone in the opposite sex takes a new dimension. This is a time when passion and emotion run high. In promiscuous societies many simply give in to their base desires and feel free to satisfy their urges in Islamically illegal and wrongdoing ways.

In societies based on high moral and spiritual standards young people's energies are spent on creative and meaningful pursuits. Islam has specific requirements (*adab*) for the man-woman relationship. The Shari'ah provides young Muslim men and women the opportunity to develop their full potential and marry as soon as possible to start families and, most importantly, to channel their sex-drives for the pleasure of Allah. Uncontrolled mixing of the sexes, especially in youth, is detrimental for them and has negative emotional and social consequences. As such, Muslims are asked to lower their gaze and avoid physical proximity and seclusion with the opposite sex (Qur'an 24:30-31). Muslim adolescents who practise Islam and maintain *hijab* may unfortunately be treated in a negative manner in modern societies, but, this should not bother them, as they know that controlling the desire for the opposite sex is vital for the purity of their character. In order to achieve this character, self-discipline, good company and strong family anchorage are vital.

• School and Career

The period is also extremely important for building their future careers. By the time they enter adolescence they are already in secondary schools. Choosing a good school is thus very important. Their future career depends to some extent on their schooling.

As discussed earlier, Muslim parents should look for the best school they can afford. A good Islamic school should of course be the priority, if that is available and affordable. Mixed state schools should be the last option. Despite the argument by some educationalists that mixed education helps young people to know the opposite gender and is important for life skills, mixed schools provide a distasteful environment from an Islamic point of view. Even on educational terms there is no proof that they are better than single-sex schools. At the same time, Muslim parents should also avoid such schools that do not have enough credibility in terms of educational standards and their tackling bullying, racism, and Islamophobia.

Parents with gifted and talented children or children who underachieve for cognitive, physical or other reason should make sure that necessary provisions are available for their needs. Muslim parents should ensure that their chosen schools encourage and help their children in careers in which they can succeed and thrive.

• Friendship and Company

Good company is an essential ingredient for maintaining character in youth, especially in permissive societies. It helps adolescents protect themselves from social diseases and relate to other adolescents of similar thinking and liking. However, finding genuine friends is not always easy. Parents should be alert during this period and lend their support in finding friends from similar backgrounds. It does not matter whether the friend is of the same ethnic or linguistic origin. Islam transcends boundaries of race and language. Needless to say, bad company can ruin an adolescent's life, as young people tend to conform to peer pressure, the surrounding youth culture and the dominant social trends.

• The *hijab*

No issue has raised such controversy in the West's perception of Muslims as the issue of women in Islam, with *hijab* taking centre stage in any discussion of the topic. Many 'experts' have contributed to this debate for centuries, especially since the hey-days of European colonialism. The 'liberal' voice of the West has best been portrayed by Polly Toynbee, a columnist for the *Guardian* in London, on 29/10/99, in the following words:

> ... Islam is often a feared faith, whether it's mullahs in North London calling for holy war against all infidels, or the distressing spectacle of Muslim women shrouded in the most extreme form of mask and veil: Islam, extreme or moderate, does teach that women are always one step behind men in the divine order.

The fear of the *hijab* is definitely a myth; it is a fear in the Western and secular Muslim psyche and an embarrassment to apologetic Muslims. In Turkey, a Muslim majority country, an elected Member of Parliament (MP) was disbarred from her elective position for daring to wear a scarf. The country that saw a revolution on the basis of 'liberty, equality and fraternity' over two hundred years ago, France, is so fearful of the *hijab* that they adopted a heavy-handed approach against Muslim girls wearing decent clothes and headscarves in their schools.

In a world of the provocative display of women's bodies, the *hijab*, of course, looks odd. As a result, liberal bigots take this modest dress covering women's bodies from the lustful eyes of men and protecting their dignity, as a symbol of oppression. To them, the *hijab* is a chain that imprisons women in men's world.

Why is the *hijab* so important in Islam? The answer to this is simple. The command concerning the *hijab* is from Allah, the Almighty, Who alone knows wherein lies the dignity of human beings. There are excellent reasons behind His commands and they are for human benefit. Women are blessed with physical beauty and soft and gentle natures to complement men's masculine nature. Men are naturally sexually pro-active. The *hijab* works as a protection for women and their feminine features. Also, women's beauty can easily seduce men, and so the *hijab* is also a protection for men. 'Liberating' women from the *hijab* - something usually done by 'liberals' violently and at the point of a gun - means reducing them to sex objects, who are vulnerable to abuse. The sufferings of women in so-called 'liberated' societies have already created anguish among victims and social thinkers.

In contrast, imagine the position of women in Islam! As a daughter she is a blessing for her father, as a wife she is half the deen of her husband and as a mother she has the highest position for her children, their Garden under her feet. The reason why many educated young women from middle class family backgrounds in the West are joining the fold of Islam in droves is the desire for this dignity. In spite of the negative media image, they realise that Islam is the sanctuary for women. Muslims of today may have failed to live up to Islam, but Islam has not failed them. The fact that some Muslim societies marginalise their women has nothing to do with Islam, but to do with ignorance and decadence in all aspects of the life of those societies.

Dress, of course, is an essential ingredient of the *hijab*, but the spirit and attitude are fundamentally important. When the external symbol of purity and modesty match with internal submission to the will of Allah, the *hijab* elevates women to social and spiritual heights. Here are a few comments from those who have tested the pleasure of the *hijab*.

> The *hijab* is the most wonderful dress for women in the world. It gives women a sense of security in the world of prying eyes. (A young Muslim revert)

> Many non-Muslim women might think of such dress as restrictive or even oppressive, a sign of submission to men. But those who have adopted the *hijab* find it nothing less than liberating. (A Muslim convert)

> It's the total opposite of subordination. We wear it because we choose to; we refuse to let ourselves be sex objects. We're saying: 'Value us for what we are, our character, not how we look. We're not going to play the game of trying to look good for you. We won't let you hire us because you like our legs, or we'll look good around the office.' (A Muslim scholar)

> The religious mandate of modest dress is hardly limited to Islam. Observant Jewish women, for example, are urged to cover their hair and bodies to hide their beauty in public. Nuns' habits are rooted in a religious call for modesty, as well. (A Muslim activist)

Adolescent Muslim girls in the West face a big challenge in wearing the *hijab*. The social pressure on them to imitate so-called 'mainstream' culture is enormous. Thus, the *hijab* represents courage and the empowerment of women, which gives them a solid identity as Muslims. It is encouraging to see many Muslim girls, probably more in the West in proportion to some Muslim countries, consciously wearing the *hijab*.

• Money Matters

Adolescents gradually become independent as they grow. Should they earn money for themselves, and when? Should they spend money on themselves, and how? There is no blanket answer to these questions, which should be decided by parents and adolescents, keeping in view family and social conditions. A genuinely needy family has no recourse but to involve an adolescent in earning for their minimum sustenance. In fact, it is a duty to help the family keep up a decent living. But, whatever the situation, adolescents should not be denied their basic deen and worldly education. A proper understanding on how and when adolescents would earn and spend is essential. There are 'penny wise, pound foolish' parents who spoil the careers of their children in pursuit of earning immediate money. They can destroy their children's lives and the ummah's future. There are others who do not care about the job environment or whether the job involves dealing with halal or haram.

It is important that parents remember adolescents are young adults, not big babies. They should know how to handle money. Whether for money or experience, adolescent may need to work in real life situations. A part-time job in the holidays that does not hamper their education or compromise their deen may prove useful.

Personal Flaws to Watch out for

Adolescents generally like to stay on their own or hang around with their peers and friends. In the absence of any sensitive mentoring and guidelines from parents or responsible adults they are likely to be heavily influenced by the dominant youth culture. They could develop habits and features of the materialistic lifestyle, many of which might have nothing to do with Islam. Parents who ignore or procrastinate and fail to assert in guiding their young ones, could find them overwhelmed with problems, such as:

• Egocentrism

Children may acquire two opposing features in adolescence - one, outward looking and the other inward looking. Embarrassment related to their bodily growth and other factors can overtake them and develop in them an individualistic and self-centred attitude. Under the powerful influences of TV, video- and computer-games, they may find excuses to withdraw from the family and social affairs. In the absence of any brothers or sisters, they may find themselves solitary. Parental incompetence or indifference can further this problem. If children fail to relate to the family and the wider society, all sorts of psychological inadequacies can find a home in them and throw them into personal bad habits and social evils.

• Rudeness, Ill-manners

A Persian mystic said (sic) long ago, 'what a dichotomy, the softest part of our body can inflict the hardest pain!' The tongue, one of the soft parts of our body, has the ability to hit hard. Rude words and bad language, and even body language, are the source of enmity, hatred and anger that can turn into a war of words, and into stress and depression and be the cause of fights. The gifts of Allah can easily turn sour if children are not trained on how to use their tongues. The balanced development of a human being is enhanced in the sound environment of love, compassion, with smiles and good words. On the other hand, children can grow to be unpleasant and hurtful adults in an unhealthy environment of rudeness, ill manners, anger and frustration. Parents who practice gentleness in their talking with children and avoid rudeness, however provoked they may be, get positive results. Rudeness and ill-manners need to be dealt with strongly, but with sensitivity. Even if punishment is to be delivered for some reason, that should be done without being rude to them.

• Distasteful Styles and Fashions

The *Metro* of London reported on 5th April 2000 that:

The craze for body piercing is spreading. Noses, navels, eyebrows and nipples are the most popular places to sport a stud, bar or ring. Royal college of Nurses voted to lobby the government to regulate the practice to try to stem the rising number of potentially fatal infections caused by rogue piercers.

What is the reason for this craze?

Everyone is important in this world and feels themselves to be so. This feeling of self-worth and self-esteem is an element among those things that keep human beings going, although the muminun are kept going by their overwhelming appreciation of the high and exalted worth of Allah. However, for the muminun self-appreciation stems from their knowledge of Allah since their good opinion of themselves stems from their knowledge that they themselves are only Allah's creations. Without this awareness of Allah and high opinion of oneself simply because one is Allah's creation they would fall flat on their faces and lead meaningless lives. The common occurrence of suicide in the developed world is often traced to a feeling of worthlessness at some stage in the individual's life.

This feeling is influenced by social norms. The attitude of adolescents toward dress, hairstyle, make-up or jewellery is influenced by many factors. Even tattoos and body piercing that cause discomfort become a part of a social trend. Expensive garments, toys, games and gadgets become indispensable parts of social status. Girls want to use such make-up as is often treated as provocative. They want to look good to others and in this pursuit often lose a sense of decency. As a result they are treated as sex objects. They lose their dignity.

Not everyone among young Muslims can strike the right balance between this sense of worth and its external manifestation. As a result, some go beyond the limits of what Allah has allowed. They give in to showing-off and pride, which Allah does not like. Any quality that a man or woman has is from Allah, but pride is trespassing upon Allah's territory.

Pride is my cloak and greatness My robe, and he who competes with Me in respect of either of them I shall cast into the Fire. (*Abu Dawud* and *Ibn Majah*)

• Lying and Cheating

People lie because they fear that the truth will bring negative consequences. Fear of punishment may lead children to lie to their parents. At the same time, they tend to cover up their embarrassment or inadequacies. As many adolescents are confused in their transition this may develop in them the attitude to conceal, leading to the habit of lying or cheating. Lying is a serious human defect. It is a grave wrong action in Islam, as it is known as the 'mother of all wrong actions'. It is also known as the strongest sign of *nifaq* (hypocrisy).

> The signs of a hypocrite are three - when speaks he tells a lie, when he promises he breaks it and when he is entrusted with anything he deceives. (*Sahih al-Bukhari*)

In open, transparent and healthy family environments lying does not find any place. However, children's world is different. They may imagine, dream, visualise or fantasise something and tell others. They may lie or exaggerate in order to:

- make fun, play with others or manipulate, confuse or control
- present a better image of themselves
- extract something from their parents or get their attention
- get out of trouble or avoid someone's anger
- avoid facing an unpleasant truth
- maintain a fantasy they have developed

They may resort to cheating in order to

- maintain self-esteem through success, as they cannot accept failure
- avoid the consequences of their behaviour
- make themselves acceptable to others
- get a better reward

All these should be taken into consideration in tackling the problem. However, too much harshness or leniency on this can have grave psychological and moral consequences. We must make sure that our behaviour does not make our children compulsive liars. The best way is to teach them the unacceptability of lying so that they confess and apologise, rather than lie. Once they do so, they should not be pursued. Parents should encourage them to think of the danger of lying in this world and in the Hereafter and give them a chance to come clean. Any symptom of lying, especially in adolescence, should be carefully nipped in the bud.

• Defiance and Rebellion

Muslim parents should make sure that they never create an environment or excuse for their children to rebel. Allah, the Almighty, keeps on tolerating the worst wrongdoers on earth and leaves them alone without stopping their provision. Whatever the offence, children should not be dealt with so hard that the relationship is severed or they feel compelled to rebel. Parents should have the basic training of patience, anger management and stress control. We must not lose their tempers easily. We should try our best to keep the dialogue going, in spite of all provocation. We should try to see the context in which our children behave the way they are behaving. What are the positive elements in our children? Do we ourselves need to revise our strategy? Conscious parents realise that, with strong negative pulls from everywhere, our children could have become much worse than they are.

The best way to avoid this scenario is to prepare our children from their early childhood, give them limitless unconditional love and let them know the broader boundaries. Once again we should spend quality time with them - talking, laughing, touching and hugging. These are important for children's emotional needs. There should not be any barrier between children and parents. We should keep in mind that supplication for our offspring from the heart can work miracles.

Taking the 'Adolescent Bull' by the Horn

The physical changes in adolescence are obviously a natural progression in the human life-cycle. Any change in human life is delicate and should be treated with sensitivity. Adolescence is an adventurous journey for young people and a reminder of the past to parents. Unfortunate personal flaws can also creep in during adolescence, if not addressed in time. As boys and girls grow in their distinctive ways, fathers and mothers, respectively, should make sure their children can comfortably:

- adjust themselves as individual men and women,
- conform with their family and with the people close to them,
- find their position among others in the wider world .

Not every child grows in the same way. Some pass through their adolescence peacefully and smoothly, others have a turbulent time. Young people in their mid-teens can present a battlefield to their parents in a number of areas, such as untidiness, unpredictable moods, depression, lack of concentration, lethargy and staying out late. A stable family environment, an Islamic ethos at home and in the community, good and reliable friends and high expectation from parents and teachers are ingredients for winning this battle. We should show no let up in their efforts until our children settle as mature adults. At the same time we should give the necessary space and freedom depending on their age and intellectual maturity. To counter the dangers in a liberal and libertine society many parents tend to become over-protective. This temptation should be avoided, as it generally brings negative results.

• Show Extra Sympathy and Empathy

Children in the West are under all sorts of pressure. Boys and girls are expected to follow the trends, admire celebrity role models and conform to the new wave of youth culture. These have an impact on their dress, appearance and manners. Girls want to become slim to such an extent that many of them suffer from malnutrition. In this situation, boys and girls need someone to empathise with them. We need to understand what goes on in our children's world and positively show our interest. Children need guidance and help from someone close to them in looking after their health, watching their friendships and guiding them in life. Parental empathy and sympathy in this period are vital. Young people's health, education and friendship are important.

• Give Privacy and Personal Space

Adolescents suddenly become self-conscious especially about their bodies. They need privacy and, often, time of their own to reflect, to think. Ideally, they should be provided their own room, if parents can afford it. If not, brothers and sisters should at least be separated before the signs of adolescence. However, we should watch out what fills their rooms. There are Islamic requirements of behaving at home. Greeting with peace - *as-salamu 'alaikum* - showing respect to each other, such as, knocking before entering someone's room - all these are part and parcel of Islamic *adab*, especially from the period of adolescence. The culture of respect to each other in the family gives them a strong signal to follow suit in the wider society. The prophetic example on this is exemplary. He ﷺ used to follow decent practices in the house. On greeting his married daughter, Fatima, may Allah be pleased with her, later in life, he used to stand up and spread his garment for her.

• Use Moderation

Authoritarian parents make things worse for their children by trying to impose their opinions and will on them. Their patronising attitude kills off dynamism and creativity and creates simmering discontent, which, at a later stage, can give rise to rebellion. On the contrary, easy-going parents callously ignore their children by not interfering, even in times of necessity. They are either too liberal or are indifferent to their children and consider them adults when they are not. This leads young people to lose the basic discipline in life. In a society ridden with loose moral values, this liberalism can be fatal for children.

Being 'tough and tender' or using a 'carrot and stick' policy is the most sensible one that educationalists and psychologists generally advocate nowadays to teach children. Islam also tells about moderation, the best way of dealing with everything. The Prophet Muhammad ﷺ always adopted moderation and opted for the middle path. This is essential in dealing with children. Parental success depends on firmness and fairness.

• Ignore Sibling Arguments

Sibling rivalry is common in a family where there are brothers and sisters of similar ages. It is part of their development. This is how they spend their time, enjoy and relax. They learn from each other through argument, loud talk and heated debate. They enrich the family by talking, laughing, complaining and even crying. This may be stressful to parents, but, unless it is essential to interfere, we should keep away from it, or else, the children can outplay us. However, when we decide to get involved, we should not be biased or even look biased. We should not automatically blame the elder one for any quarrel, although it is natural to show sympathy with younger ones. We should use the occasion to teach them respect for elders and affection for the younger ones. Sibling rivalry phases out with time.

• Involvement in the Meaningful Pursuits of Life

There are now Islamic groups, clubs and associations in the major cities of the West. There are also Muslim groups pursuing positive and comprehensive changes in society. Muslim teenagers should be encouraged to become actively involved in some of those. Parents should help them in finding a reliable group with balanced social, moral and spiritual dimensions where they will thrive as practising and active Muslims. Unfortunately, there are groups that are bent on emotionalism or known to have only partial or one-sided views of Islam. Unwitting association with such groups can impede the development of character among young Muslims today.

We need to educate their young people on how to maintain a proper balance between their education, family responsibilities, and Islamic activities and acts of service. An unbalanced life during this period can hamper their futures. Parents must keep an eye on those with whom their children hang around, and positively guide them to take an active interest in the affairs of the Muslims. In a pleasant home atmosphere all children would know their boundaries.

• Provide with Islamic Recreation

Recreation is essential for renewal of energy. Human beings cannot work like machines. We are more than that. Our bodies and minds need relaxation in order to perform better. Recreation in vain pursuit hampers our minds and spirits. Recreation with intoxicants damages the body, and sensual pleasures damage spirituality. The Prophet Muhammad ﷺ recommended teaching young people horse riding, archery and swimming. Innocent games and exercises are a means for physical fitness and joy. They are strongly recommended in Islam. They are sources of self-confidence and physical strength, which are essential for helping the community.

• Involvement in the Family

Muslim adolescents should gradually become responsible members of their families. Only then can they genuinely become part of the Muslim community and the wider society. They should become involved in household work and keep themselves busy with creative and meaningful pursuits that please Allah. They should not let their brain wander around in the idle pastimes of the modern permissive life. 'An idle brain is the devil's work-shop'. The world-renowned Muslim leaders rose to the height of their achievement with their knowledge and hard work at younger ages. Muhammad ibn Qasim liberated the people of Sind, in present-day Pakistan, while he was only a teenager. 'Morning shows the day'. The early years of human beings show their po-tential in life. As children grow, their playful mentality should be replaced by the mature and responsible pursuit of life and a sense of urgency to work for the ummah and beyond. Life is a serious business that needs a serious approach.

The feeling of family loyalty and togetherness is also impor-tant for a lasting impact on the Muslim family ethos among chil-dren. Children should gradually be involved in the affairs of their families, starting with minor household chores. Regular family sessions create opportunities for free discussion of issues of im-portance and concern. They create cohesion and homogeneity in the family. Adolescents should be encouraged to talk and speak their minds so that they feel confident and learn from every-body, including their own contributions on a topic. It gives them a sense of responsibility and ownership.

WHAT IF THERE IS A CRISIS?[2]

Adolescence is a challenge. Big or small, this challenge has to be faced by all parents. In spite of good planning, continuous effort and supplication for children from birth, they can create prob-lems for the family, especially during their adolescence. How we parents tackle it depends on the preparation which in turn is based on our understanding and effort. It is, of course, really hard and emotionally disturbing for parents to deal with chil-dren who are bent on creating problems.

Children grow in the laps of their parents, so any symptom of a problem should be diagnosed well in time. If parents find it difficult to mould their characters in the colour of Islam they should consult with friends, imams and experts, rather than giv-ing up or procrastinating in the hope that one day they will come to their senses. This is dangerous. Procrastination is the enemy. Only, knowledgeable, caring and timely intervention can bring a remedy in this situation, but, like most things in this world, there is no quick fix or hasty solution to any problem. Unfortunately, 'human beings are ever hasty' (Qur'an 17:11).

Children who rebel or run away, register their complaint in that fashion. 'They vote with their feet', against their family, the society and often against themselves. In Western countries, thousands of young people between the ages of fourteen and sixteen run away from home. As the family bond is weakening and marriages breaking down, young children become the victims of family squabbles, lose patience with their parents and take their own decisions. The prevalent promiscuous consumer culture, violence on the screen and the easy availability of drugs augment this crisis. Added to them, are widespread ignorance, indifference and complacency among some parents.

What if a serious crisis really occurs in a family with an adolescent? The most important thing to remember in that situation is to keep one's nerve and resort to an Islamic solution, even in extreme situations. Some years ago, a Muslim father in Britain resorted to physical violence against his own daughter out of anger because she had an affair with a non-Muslim man. His rage only put him in prison, while he should have been careful from the beginning.

Many parents think about their dignity and family pride before basic Islamic demands. Out of love for their children or fear of being termed backward by others many Muslim parents forget their fundamental task of giving their young people Islamic nourishment. As a result, when their spiritually-impoverished children follow the footsteps of other slaves of the world, they suddenly wake up and try to impose their decisions on them, but that proves too late. No amount of anger can bring their children back from the path to destruction. Human beings are not robots that can suddenly be programmed to behave with piety.

Frustration and anger have never helped. They work like a fire, ignite emotion and create havoc. The Prophetic traditions on anger management are illuminating:

Anger is from the shaytan, and the shaytan is created from fire, and fire is extinguished by water. So, if one of you becomes angry let him perform wudu. (*Abu Dawud*)

If one of you becomes angry let him be silent. (*Ahmad*)

If one of you becomes angry while he is standing let him sit down, and if he is still angry let him lie down. (*Ahmad*)

The one who swallows his anger will be called out by Allah, the Exalted, to the forefront of the creatures on the Day of Rising and will be offered any pure-eyed virgin he would like. (*Abu Dawud*, and *at-Tirmidhi*)

Muslim parents need to learn from their historical roots and from contemporary social changes, before it is too late.

TOWARD RESPONSIBLE MEN AND WOMEN

Adolescence is the ladder to an adult life. It is forced upon every human being without any choice, but it is full of potential. Conscientious Muslim parents make sure that the transition becomes smooth and Islamically sound for their children. We should invest in them day-in-and-day-out so that one day, when we are not there, our children replace us with full responsibility and, in the cycle of life, take over with more responsibility. As the Islamic world is undergoing an intellectual and social transformation, we should try hard to raise our future generation in a way that they can genuinely claim to be the 'best of nations' in real sense of the term, i.e., through words and actions.

LEARNING THE 'TOOLS OF THE TRADE'

Experienced and hard-working parents are aware that there are positive techniques in managing teenage children. The widely accepted policy of reward and sanction, if used in the proper context and with clarity, leads to the successful upbringing of children and also solves many problems. There are no rules-of-thumb in this. However, the following guidelines have proven to be fruitful in dealing with adolescent children:

- Share decision-making: Teenagers often come up with clever ideas that can help in decision-making. At the same time, inclusion in decision-making helps them feel part of the decision.
- Be consistent: Parents should not go into frequent mood swings for any reason. Teenagers may start to feel confused, or they might start thinking that they are part of normal life.
- Confess mistakes: It needs extra courage to accept one's own mistakes and we parents should show this if we make any mistake at any time with our children.
- Be principled: Success in coping with adolescence depends on a family environment based on discipline, flexibility and freedom. Muslim life is guided by the principles and fundamental tenets of Islam.
- Talk and explain: Parents must not be bossy, especially with their teenagers. We should take extra pains in talking to them and explaining things. If the young people feel they are pushed hard there will be a distance between parents and them. This can prove disastrous in future.
- Negotiate and bargain: There might arise some situation when parents have to negotiate with their teenagers for a better outcome. Just because parents are parents, does not mean that they are always right.
- Ignore their mistakes and give them space: Adolescents make mistakes, but, they need space to get rid of their embarrassment, anger, depression and frustration. Parents must not always bother them. They should leave them alone on occasions.
- Supplication: Muslims always rely on Allah for their actions and outcomes. Guidance is from Allah alone. Continuous *du'a* (supplication) for the guidance of children is essential for believing parents.

14. The Onslaught of Social Ills

Evil enters like a needle and spreads like an oak tree. (A West African proverb).

SICKNESS PROLIFERATES FASTER THAN DOES GOOD HEALTH

Sickness, not health, spreads easily. Germs and bacteria multiply in congenial conditions. Like infectious diseases, social ills also spread quickly in a permissive environment. In a society where *nafsaniat* (sensuality and promiscuity) are encouraged to proliferate, the pressure on individuals is very high indeed. This is all the more serious for young people, especially during puberty.

Adolescents generally lack stability and maturity. They are not yet prepared to face the challenges of life. Human being is neither angel, nor devil. Allah, in His wisdom, has instilled in man the dual nature of evil and piety (Qur'an 91:8). In a healthy society piety is encouraged and promoted to flourish and evil suppressed. Piety needs nourishment and proper environment, not only for its growth but also for survival. But this is not the case with permissive societies, where children pick up materialistic ideas from their early age. Ask the young people of those societies about their ambition in life. The general answers would be - 'to have fun', 'to earn money' or 'I don't know'.

Throughout human history schools and institutions had been established to create good human beings. No school was ever established to train rapists, paedophiles, prostitutes, gang fighters, drug users and people of evil nature. They grow and multiply when a society loses its anchor, the direction. In the beginning, a few perverts take lead in promoting vices. If not vehemently opposed, the society gradually accommodates with them and slides into degeneration. Young people become the vulnerable targets and find themselves struggling to cope. The fall of all the world powers is inherently linked to their internal decay and social ills. As epidemics, like plague, wipe out communities from earth, widespread social ills also bring down empires from their material height.

Human race has made celebrating intellectual and technological achievements. Standard of life in the developed world has risen and diseases are being fought effectively. But, there are reasons to be appalled by the present degeneration of human beings, disintegration of family and dehumanisation of women. In the days of globalisation, vulgarity and other evils have also become global. The rest in the poor world is not sharing the wealth of the richer nations, but tragically sharing their social ills. Some of them directly affect children in the educational institutions and some influence them from around the society. The following are a few major social ills relevant to the young people in a modern society.

• Bullying and Intimidation

Bullying is a major and common problem, not only in schools but in work places and in the wider society. The bullying in schools has been discussed in the previous section. It destroys the self-image of the victim and leaves a long-term scar on him. Both the bully and the victim lack self-esteem and some might have undergone abuse in their lives. Bullies compensate for it through bullying, but the victims generally fail to put up with it. A bully is most often an unhappy person who is eager to transfer his anger, and bitter and defeatist attitude to life on to his victims. People of minority groups, especially religious and ethnic groups, can easily become targets of bullying. A loner or socially passive person has more chance of being bullied.

Bullying and teasing cause psychological damage to the victims. Muslims can be the targets of teasing because of their race, deen, dress, attitude and culture. We should prepare our children to be assertive and instil confidence in them to face this challenge. We should make sure that a trust is built with our children during their early years so that they do not fail to inform us about bullying, if it ever occurs to them. Muslim children should be taught that Muslims are all worthy, and that we are required to invite all non-Muslims both by our behaviour and in words to Islam, and there is no room in either case for teasing or bullying anyone (Qur'an 49:11).

• Gangsterism

Delinquency is considered a symptom of adolescent rebelliousness against family and society. It can be a sign of emotional or moral disturbance. With increasing family problems and numerous other social ills, discipline among adolescents has become a serious issue. Youth's tendency to rebel against the status quo and follow their role models has a tremendous influence on their behaviour and thus many turn to anti-social activities. Some have a tendency to get into trouble with teachers and police for petty reasons. It is feared that in some Western countries about fifty percent of youth, both boys and girls, break the law in their early teens.

Many schools are struggling to put the genie of delinquency back in the bottle. Gangsterism in the vicinity of secondary schools and around pubs is worrying to parents, police, youth service and social thinkers.

Gang violence among Muslim adolescents in some areas of Britain has become a phenomenon over the years. Like black-on-black violence in some parts of Britain, gang fighting among some Muslim boys has increased in some inner city areas. Young people who are disaffected or disenfranchised are sometimes bullied into gang conflicts. Others become entangled because they feel they would lose their street credibility if they kept away. Many are influenced by drugs and the street culture.

This is symptomatic of a disease that is spreading among the younger generation. Sociologists and community leaders are of the opinion that social deprivation, massive unemployment and under-achievement in schools are linked to this problem. In spite of some positive attempts at the establishment of social inclusion, Muslim communities are still excluded from mainstream society in a real sense of the term. The rhetoric of urban regeneration among faith communities hardly affects the Muslims. In some cases they do not have the capacity to tap government resources and in others they face too many obstacles.

This has put heavy pressure on Muslim youth groups with their limited resources, as secular politicians and youth leaders in the Muslim community have little clue about or intention of addressing it. Muslim parents need to be aware of what is going on in the wider community and discuss the issue with their children so that they understand the context and keep away from the anti-social youth culture.

GANGFIGHTING: TACKLING THE MENACE

If it were not because of some hard-working young Muslim activists, two gangs of Bangladeshi youth in two neighbourhoods of East London would have caused bloodshed among themselves a few years ago. Nobody knew exactly what prompted these youth, having the same language and religious backgrounds, to come to that stage of taking revenge on each other with sophisticated weapons. The way they organised their groups was laudable, but it was a suicidal attempt and it tarnished the image of the community and destabilised it.

Fortunately, before anyone was killed, Muslim activists successfully intervened. They belonged to the grassroots and had influence over the leaders of both the camps. That brought about three hundred of the young warriors to the local mosque. Of course, a lot of background work was done beforehand and the choice of the mosque was also deliberate. When an emotional talk was delivered by a respected youth leader about the futility of their action and the responsibility of Muslim youth in building the ummah, very few could control their tears. They promised, one by one, that they would never again start a war against their own people. I still vividly remember the faces of the youth from both camps when they hugged each other after the speech.

• Drug Abuse

> O you who believe! wine and gambling, stone altars and divining arrows are filth from the handiwork of shaytan. Avoid them completely so that hopefully you will be successful. Shaytan wants to stir up enmity and hatred between you by means of wine and gambling and to debar you from remembrance of Allah and prayer. Will you not then give up? (Qur'an 5:90-91)

Drug abuse has increased to a frightening degree in many Western countries. Drugs, sex and violence are intertwined. Unfortunately, the problem with drugs is not an easy one; it has backing from powerful people, often with international links, in the underground. Only a decade ago, the Muslim community, for example in Britain, could proudly shrug off any complaint of Muslim involvement in these vices, but things have changed. Adolescents of Muslim background are now catching up, and in some places are leading the drugs business. Many inner-city Muslim adolescents are gradually being sucked into the problem.

Drugs create addiction. In the beginning adolescents may be curious about them or they may be persuaded by someone to experiment with them. The drug dealers may offer them for free at first, as they know that once their target is addicted he cannot help using them.

The effect of alcohol is no less physically devastating, and even more devastating socially, than drugs. The Royal College of Physicians in Britain, in a finding published in January 2000, reported that alcohol abuse costs Britain £6bn a year! Then there are the detrimental physical effects of smoking. Many adolescents drink and smoke in imitation of others or in defiance of their elders. As a result, their health is ruined. This affects the national economy and our social life. Peer pressure in schools works as catalysts for adolescents to take up smoking and drinking. Drinking alcohol and taking drugs can lead to liver, heart and stomach problems, as smoking can lead to serious lung complaints. Parents need to be conscious about who their child is hanging around with. We need to talk to our children about drugs and related issues, give them the Islamic viewpoint on them and the danger that they bring to people in terms of health and morality. Young people should be warned that their safety and wellbeing are at stake with the drug abuse.

Fortunately, Muslims in many places have woken up and are now trying to create a defensive shield against drugs and intoxicants. Many mosques and Islamic organisations are trying hard to educate the community in the strong Islamic views on intoxicant and their inevitable implications. Some voluntary organisations are now in place to combat this evil. Some Muslim groups in different parts of the world have succeeded in creating drug-free zones in their areas. Their success could be shared with others, even though the danger is widespread in many inner cities.

• Racism and Xenophobia

The Lawrence Report on Britain has highlighted how endemic racism is in Western countries. It is now an open secret that institutionalised racism is embedded in Western establishments. The extent and depth of the problem is being acknowledged by many. Many are worried by the fact that the economic and social costs of racism are enormous.

Racism and xenophobia are inhuman and abhorrent social diseases that have brought catastrophic human losses in history. Their products are slavery, colonialism, ruthless wars and killings. Nations were wiped out in the past because of their perceived racial inferiority. The two catastrophic World Wars were also rooted in the arrogance of racial superiority. Recent ethnic cleansing in the Balkans and some other parts of the world that has so horrified the world has its root in naked racism. In day-to-day life, in schools and workplaces, racism creates fear and distrust. It kills decent human behaviour and makes society loathsome.

We Muslim parents should, on one hand, equip our children to defend themselves and fight against these diseases and on the

other, educate them with the Qur'anic teaching on human beings' diversity which is for a divine purpose (Qur'an 49:13). Young
Muslims should be the carriers of the message that taqwa, not
race, is the criterion of superiority in the eyes of Allah. They
should be reminded that the battle against racism cannot be won
with counter racism or hatred, as some tend to advocate. No
matter how much Muslims suffer from racist bigots, we should
fight back with dignity, not revenge.

• Religious Discrimination

As secularism and materialism have taken a dominant role in the
modern West, the Christian religion has become irrelevant or is
regarded as merely rituals by most people. The Christian ethos is
ostensibly looked down upon in society. Nevertheless, non-Chris-
tians and even minority denominations within Christianity face
visible religious discrimination. Islam, because of its uncompromising stand on tawhid, its morality and values, suffers most in
terms of its image and treatment. Muslims have a bad image in
the press. The Muslim freedom movements across the world are
deliberately coloured as separatism or terrorism. The inhuman
sufferings of Muslims in Palestine, Kashmir, Chechnya and elsewhere are sidelined and equated with 'violence'. This distortion
of fact and unjust portrayal of Islam is deep in the Western psyche for historical reasons and is a source of frustration for Muslims in the West.

Many Muslim children also experience prejudice and discrimination for their Islamic and cultural backgrounds. The issue was
discussed in depth and highlighted in Britain by a well-docu-
mented report, *Islamophobia: A Challenge for us all* by an independent research and policy agency, The Runnymede Trust, in 1997.
Islamophobia, like anti-Semitism in the past, has now become a
widespread phenomenon. Like racism, it has its root in ignorance
about Islam that creates hatred, prejudice, discrimination and
violence against Islam as a deen and Muslims as a nation. Social

exclusion, in all its forms, envelops the Muslim community. The situation becomes worse when some un-Islamic cultural practices among some Muslims, e.g., poor treatment of women, are projected as Islamic. At the same time, cheap simplistic rhetoric by some Muslim leaders or groups offers further ammunition to the media.

Muslim adolescents in schools face the brunt of Islamophobic prejudice because of an insensitive and Euro-centric curriculum or because of the prevailing ethos. Their pastoral, Islamic and cultural needs may remain unattended to. In some schools young Muslims may even encounter outright opposition to their growing a beard or wearing the *hijab*. This may have negative effects on their academic achievement and social performance. In actual fact, this is happening to Muslim communities in many Western countries. Muslim adolescents need to be prepared to face this challenge in order to make an impact on the others.

• Sexual Mayhem

The three-letter word, sex, is now a determining factor in the lifestyles of modern permissive societies. The media world is awash with this subject. It has become the world's hottest commodity and its trade has become globalised. It is disgraceful that the sex industry has become a source of national income in some countries.

Adultery and fornication are some of the gravest wrong actions in human society. Allah, the Almighty, has not only prohibited adultery, but commanded people not to go near it (Qur'an 17:32). As the sexual urge is wild, Muslims are asked to tame it. It should only be unleashed where and when appropriate.

Sexual promiscuity is endangering the human species and, in addition to spreading social chaos, giving rise to sexually transmitted diseases (STD) like HIV, gonorrhoea and syphilis, especially among young people. Public Health in the developed countries is experiencing a traumatic rise of STD and the so-called 'safe sex' message there is giving the wrong signal to people. In a conservative country like Britain, 'up to 295,000 women are raped or suffer other forms of sexual assault every year', according to Home Office sources published in February 2000. This is an astonishing figure in a country where sexual relationships are so liberal that women, on average, have had eight to nine sexual partners by the time they are twenty-five. Needless to say that men generally go further women in this competition!

Young girls are under tremendous pressure to conform to the sexual desires of their male partners. A whole life pattern has been changed dramatically within generations. The *Guardian* of London published a research report on the trend among teenage girls of Britain on 22nd June 2000:

"Girls are reaching puberty younger, according to the study by Bristol University's Institute of Child Health - terrifying one in six by the age of eight, compared with one in 100 just a generation ago. Linked to that is the research showing that one in four girls has under-age sex according to the latest edition of Population Trends; they are five times more likely than their mothers and 24 times more likely than their grandmothers to have sex before the age of 16. In a summit of 40 magazine editors in Downing Street on 21 June one pointed out that 90% of girls and women across all social and ethnic groupings restrain their appetite because of anxiety about their body shape, a pervasive culture promoting one image of female beauty." (The *Guardian* of London 22nd June 2000)

Already a high proportion of children in the West are born outside wedlock. Many of them do not know their fathers, grow in single families and end up becoming problem children. This is a major social problem in modern industrialised societies. If the present trend continues unabated, there will come a time when marriage as an institution may be regarded as irrelevant and the human species may go further astray in sexual behaviour.

On top of this frightening picture, the issue of homosexuality, meaning same-sex relationships, is gaining momentum in the name of equality and freedom. Laws that have governed human beings since the beginning of history are being re-written in many countries on the basis of the indifference of the sexual orientation of a man or woman. The aggressive campaign by a small but powerful lobby under the pretext of civil liberty or human rights and the apologetic response from the religious establishment have forced many Western governments to accept this distasteful practice as normal human behaviour. On 28th October 1999 the House of Lords in Britain ruled that a homosexual couple in a stable relationship can be defined as a 'family' and, on the basis of this, a former Royal Navy serviceman was entitled to inherit the tenancy of his late partner's flat. The British Labour government also tried hard to repeal its Section 28 of the Local Government Act, mentioned below, that protected young children from the onslaught of homosexual education in their schools:

A local authority shall not -

a) intentionally promote homosexuality or publish material with the intention of promoting homosexuality;

b) promote the teaching in any maintained school of the acceptability of homosexuality as a pretended family relationship.

The outcry from Muslims and other faith communities merely thwarted it for the time being. Other Western governments, e.g., the former Clinton administration in the US, have been making many concessions to the homosexual lobby.

Homosexual practice is unnatural and morally wrong. Individuals might have desire a wrong act, but that does not make it acceptable by law. Wrong needs correction, not approval. The people engaged in homosexual practice during the time of the prophet Lut ﷺ made a show of their obscenity and transgression, for which they were given an exemplary punishment by Allah (Qur'an 7:80-84, 11:77-83, 27:54-56, 29:28-34, 37:133-137). The wrong action is considered so grave that the Prophet Muhammad ﷺ commanded:

The one who you find doing the action of the people of Lut then kill both of them and the one who you find doing that with an animal kill him and kill the animal. (*An-Nasa'i* and *Abu Dawud*).

Promotion of this practice in the wider society exposes adolescents, and school children, to libertine attitudes. It adds fuel to the fire of existing teenage promiscuity. It makes them vulnerable, undermines the institution of the family and damages the fabric of a decent society. It carries higher health risks, exposing people to HIV, Hepatitis B and other diseases.

Homosexual proselytes are trying to impose their concept that same-sex relationships are equivalent to marriage. They are on the propaganda offensive to recruit more people to their fold and give them confidence in their perverted sexuality. They claim that homosexuality is normal and not incompatible with religion. The question is, which religion? Adulterated religions may give in to the pressure from this lobby, but Islam's position is clear. If our future generations are not educated on the Islamic stand on this, they might fall into the pitfalls of others. If the family, as a primary carrier of values, is undermined the whole basis of human civilisation will collapse.

• Commercialisation of Eroticism

The exploitation of eroticism, capitalising mainly on young and attractive women's bodies, has probably become one of the worst weapons in the debasement of women-folk. The deliberate public display of their bodies is not only dehumanising to them and to women in general but deeply offensive to anyone who has any sense of value as well. Unfortunately, many women do not realise that the commercialisation eroticism simply feeds on men's lusts for women's body and the greed of advertisers and capitalists for money. Some who sell their bodies, prostitutes, might take this 'job' for mere 'survival', forgetting utterly that their provider is Allah, but, what about those who find pleasure in displaying their bodies and regard modelling as a glamorous profession? The

Prophet Muhammad ﷺ has warned us of the danger of infatuating and seductive women. Men are not tempted by anything as they are tempted by women (see the hadith in this sense in *Sahih al-Bukhari, Muslim, at-Tirmidhi*).

In many parts of the world, even today, women are traded as sex slaves. Women's beauty, the gift of Allah, has been made a commodity with which to earn money and cause people to deviate from the path. The multi-billion dollar pornography and modelling businesses are a curse that aids in the proliferation of wrong action in the world and lowers human beings to levels worse than the animals. The use of eroticism in adverts, TV films and pornographic print media are provocative to the adolescent mind. Many tabloids and magazines publish nude pictures of women and compete with each other in doing that in order to increase their circulation. Millions of copies of those obscene publications around the world are costing millions of trees every year, as one tree can only produce about four hundred average-size newspapers. This additional deforestation, caused just by this most high-profile example of pointless publishing, is probably speeding up ecological disaster in the world, and it is only a tiny fraction of the repugnant waste and destruction caused by modern society.

At the same time, beauty contests, which have been rightly termed 'cattle markets' by women's rights movements, and fashion shows continue unabated in some cities of the world. Airlines and numerous other organisations generally recruit good-looking young girls to run the show. With seductive dresses they are often coerced to remain thin in order to look good to the customers. This has psychological and sometimes physical implications for their self-images. The way that uniquely masculine and feminine features are now contested by both sexes gives the impression that neither men nor women are happy about their own sex roles.

Extreme feminism sees woman's role in society as being competitive with man's, rather than complementary. Christian and

Jewish women, of course, suffered in the past and still suffer in many cultures today, but by pulling them away from their designated roles as respected mothers and home-makers modern feminism has put a heavy burden on them. Girls in school are at the receiving end of this burden.

It is an irony that societies, such as the Christian West where women did not receive basic rights for centuries, have gone to the other extreme by attempting to play with the gender balance in the name of equality. The consequences have already proved fatal in many cases and costly.

Allah has given man and woman dignity, dignity in their characteristic features. The pernicious attack on women by exposing their bodies to satisfy the whims of those in the commercial sector by stimulating the lusts of men is an affront to their respect and honour. This false eroticism creates an atmosphere that opens the floodgates for other vices and crimes in society. It is a shame that this obscenity has become a flourishing industry in almost every country in the world. And now newer technologies, such as the Internet, are being used to spread this pseudo-eroticism globally.

• Prostitution

Prostitution, especially child prostitution, is spreading rapidly in many parts of the world. A new form of slave trade is on the rise where young girls are enticed, sold like cattle and used for prostitution. In recent decades, the poorer countries in Asia and post-Communist East European countries have been targeted by criminal gangs who allure young women for a better life in the West. Most of them end up doing sex work for others.

Women from poorer countries, recently from Eastern European countries, are sometimes enticed by slave traffickers and end up in prostitution in other countries. As some teenagers in the contemporary promiscuous environment do not want to miss the fun of sex, their temptation for first time sex ends up in prostitution. Pimps in society prey on vulnerable young girls and through treachery or force take control of their lives.

The proliferation of prostitution is linked partially to modern promiscuity which has thrown women on the receiving end of ignominy, but at its root promiscuity is an economic issue. Some countries in the world consider prostitution a social need and reap financial benefit from the thriving business originating from this immoral practice. Influential people, often with government approval, generally run the red-light areas. As a result, prostitution has become an essential part of the sex industry in those countries. This has created shockwaves in the inner cities where prostitutes, on occasion, are a public nuisance on the streets. Outcry from decent people and vigilante groups has driven the evil from some areas, but, the problem is too big and deep-rooted to weed out, largely because it is wrongly regarded as a moral issue and not the economic issue which it is in reality.

• Domestic Violence and the Family problem

From a report by 'Family Policy Studies Centre' in Britain a frightful picture was published in the *Guardian* of London (27 March 2000) under the title, 'Are we turning into a nation of loners?' about family issues in Britain. It is disturbing that 38% of babies are born outside marriage (compared to only 7.2% in 1964), the number of lone parents has trebled from 7% in 1972 to 21% and more British people are becoming used to living alone.

With the sexual mayhem leading to increasing teenage pregnancies in many Western countries, we are living in an era of social disintegration in danger of a potentially disastrous future. But the solution is being sought in superficial measures, such as free distribution of 'morning after pills' for girls and condoms for boys. There is a rigid unwillingness to 'catch the bull by the horn', i.e., address the deep roots of the problem. As a result, boys and girls are becoming parents without acquiring a sense of responsibility and accountability. Their relationship is only skin deep, and there is little plan for a long-term family bond. Materialism has given rise to egocentrism and the desire selfishly to enjoy no matter what the consequences, which makes it hard for people to live under the same roof for a length of time. Marriage is losing its importance as the source of permanent relationship between man and woman, and divorce is increasing at an alarming rate and living together without any formal arrangement is becoming the norm.

The TV, computer and other gadgets are keeping people away from one-to-one and social relationships. While ostentatious love-making in public places is ample, husbands and wives or unmarried partners argue, fight and abuse each other at home. This public lovey-dovey behaviour and private squabbling is on the increase. Once again, women are the ones who suffer the most. It has been reported that, in Britain, more and more men are beating women at home. The result is distraught children caught in the crossfire of family squabbles, becoming pawns in the family disintegration and creating problems in schools and on the streets.

As an integral part of the society, there is no reason why Muslims in the West will not be gradually sucked into this social black hole. Muslim family help-lines in recent years have recorded that verbal and physical abuse within Muslim families is increasing. The causes of abuse are linked to drug- and substance-abuse, extra-marital affairs, unemployment-related frustration, media influence, free-mixing of the sexes outside the home, interference of in-laws, etc.

• Paedophilia

Young people are like plants that need nurturing, not misuse or abuse. Unfortunately, every community has its share of criminals who abuse these vulnerable children when they deserve nothing but love and affection. Paedophilia is not only inhuman, but also a crime that destroys the innocence of children at a tender age.

Some paedophiles are even bent on taking the precious lives of young children. The killing of eight year old Sarah Payne of Britain in the summer of 2000 highlighted the scourge of paedophilia in Western society where sadly it is on the rise. In civilised societies the agencies of law and order rely on the civic responsibility of people. It is a trust among members of the society. Paedophiles are criminals who take advantage of this social trust. We Muslim parents need to take a leading role in rooting out the scourge of paedophilia from the societies in which we live.

• Laissez-faire Morality

Over the centuries, materialism has pushed aside Christianity from its position of moral influence in the West and society has given in to amorality. The post-modern West has seen the rise of moral relativism in which there is little room for clear values in life. The result is confusion and uncertainty. In this moral maze, universal values, such as, honesty, integrity, fidelity, fairness and a sense of justice are now selectively used, especially by people in authority. Scientific theories, such as, Heisenberg's 'Uncertainty Principle' and Einstein's 'Theory of Relativity' at the beginning of the last century have been falsely used to influence the changing views on morality. The absence of transcendental values has unfortunately given rise to double standards in significant areas of life such as, education and employment, law and order, politics and media. Young Muslims growing in this environment risk becoming confused. They may find it difficult to cope with the dichotomy in real life - a value-rich upbringing at home and value-less social norms outside.

• Secular Inroads in Muslim Activism!

The pervading culture of the materialist secular lifestyle has its influence on Muslim youth. The lack of Islamic etiquette in relationships is apparent among many young Muslims in the West, even among youth engaged in Islamic activities. Caring and responsible behaviour is the essence of social life. Muslims, throughout history, emulated the model character of the Prophet Muhammad ﷺ and created societies full of love, compassion and concern for others, but, it seems that egotism and self-centred individualism, the products of modern materialism, are penetrating into the behaviour of many supposed torchbearers of Islam. Young Muslims are failing to maintain the right balance in their Islam and prioritise their works. Parents of some of those Muslim activists grumble about their own children.

The egocentric attitude among these young Muslims is proving disastrous, particularly in their own married lives. Some of them, for no apparent reason, marry late. Some of those who decide, even on their own choice, to marry each other find difficulties in staying together. A very conscientious and learned imam of a big mosque in the heart of a Muslim community in England was once on the verge of tears, because of the growing commotion among this group of young Muslim couples. Personally, I know some young couples with good Islamic commitment separating from each other within years of their marriage. Although the problem is not yet widespread, it has deeper implications unless addressed properly.

We live in societies where the importance of marriage is under threat, as more and more men and women live together out of wedlock. Even terms like husband and wife are now being replaced by terms such as 'partners'. This wholesale disintegration of the social fabric is having its impact on the attitudes, approaches, verbal communications, body language and even the thinking of many Muslim activists. The influence of materialism on Muslims in general is understandable, but secularism within Muslim activism is sad indeed.

FIGHTING THE ILLS

The challenge of fighting social ills is enormous, especially in the context of the present weak position of Muslims in the West. However, these are not only Muslim issues. They are common among many other people, in fact all human beings. As such, the Muslim attempt to challenge and minimise these ills should include concerned people from across the wider community. Muslims should co-operate and forge links with any effort that wants to eradicate violence and obscenity in the media and the entertainment industry as well as other social ills in the lands in which live. Of course, as an important line of defence, we should try to create a protective shield around our own children by various means, but for an effective challenge, we need to widen our struggle and fight for spiritual regeneration in all communities.

A small island in a sea of social ills can easily be washed away in time. An epidemic cannot be fought either by running away from it or through selfish attempt at individual or group protection. This is neither effective nor Islamically acceptable. The sooner we understand the better.

15. Motivating to Excel

People are like mines: The best of them in Jahiliyyah (the period of ignorance) will be the best of them in Islam, so long as they attain a proper understanding of Islam. (*Sahih al-Bukhari* and *Muslim*)

The creation of each human being by Allah is unique. They have the edge over angels in terms of knowledge and free will. Yet these two things put the first two people in trouble before they arrived on earth. However, their repentance saved them from the ultimate downfall. There is a lesson for all of us in this story. Human beings are fortunate that Allah has created the world full of challenges. Without challenges the human mind would become static, despondent at the monotony. In an easy life there is little to think about and the human being is in a state of lethargic self-centredness. Challenges motivate people to think and lead them forward for change.

So, what is motivation then and what does it do? Broadly speaking, motivation is:

- the ability to drive and inspire.
- the strong will or stamina, i.e., a real determination to see things through.
- a passion to make a difference.
- a vision of success.
- the capacity to implement the vision in a manner that is manageable.
- the commitment to continuous monitoring and evaluation.

Thus, motivation is at the heart of human success. It is the inner urge, enthusiasm, passion and fire that sustain commitment. Motivation is central to commitment, but, by nature, it is intangible and cannot be measured. In school, in sport or in the workplace motivation brings success. The fire of motivation needs fuel, which parents, elders and teachers need to provide at the beginning of children's lives. What makes young people tick or motivated to do something? Is human behaviour driven by the urge of physiological or physical safety, social, egoistic or self-actualisation needs, as Maslow and his co-thinkers put it? Are human beings inherently positive or negative toward doing something? Are they intrinsically good or bad in life?

These questions may seem philosophical, but are very important in our personal and social lives. From the dawn of civilisation these questions have haunted human beings, but outside of revelation they only receive partial or biased answers. A balanced and holistic answer is available in Islam, dealt with mainly in Part One of this book. The human being is a complex creation of Allah, Who has given us tremendous potential. All human beings have characteristic features of their own and there are many variables that affect our lives. The environment causes our potential to flower or remain dormant and unfulfilled. The Arabs, after the advent of Islam, and many other nations in their heydays, had displayed monumental human qualities that helped shape the world in the way it is today. They were then highly motivated. Later on, many of them became fossilised in their thinking and passive.

Why? The reason is their loss of direction that paved the way for a lack of motivation. Incompetent, complacent and idle people replaced dynamic and forward-looking leaders who used to trigger motivation in their people. The Muslim case is not that different. With the passage of time, as we were losing the spirit of Islam as well as power of motivation, our competence, pride, self-determination, sense of responsibility, creativity, innovation, initiative and confidence gradually evaporated.

How can young people be motivated to do what they are supposed to do? How could Muslim adolescents be made more creative, positive and motivated in their thinking and action so that they can play the required civilisational role for the future?

DEJECTION IN CHILDREN

Children are generally idealistic and impulsive, as they have not yet come to terms with the reality and complexity of life. They need continuous encouragement, appreciation and recognition from elders. If this is missing, they can get lost in their motivational journey. Labelling them with words, such as, 'useless', 'loser', 'hopeless', 'idiot' and 'dumb' can paralyse them. Comparing them with more able children can create an inferiority complex and frustration, which have a negative impact on their characters. Performance in their school or exam results can be a cause of friction, especially with parents of Asian origin. Gifted or talented children may also lose motivation if they are inadequately challenged or put down for being 'too clever', 'boffins', or for holding unconventional ideas.

Vulnerable and de-motivated children lose confidence in themselves. If this deepens, they may even go in for self-denigration and rejection in preference to praise. As we parents feel impotent to tackle this issue, we might resort to insensitive remarks or arguments with our children, which only makes things worse.

Dejected children need careful handling. Words, body postures and the whole approach have to be carefully chosen so that they feel positive about them and are able to rediscover their self-worth. They need reminding that all human beings have tremendous potential, as mentioned in the hadith at the beginning of this chapter.

POSITIVE ROLE MODELLING

Here comes the issue of positive role modelling which provides invisible psychological leadership to the young people. Islamic history is full of people, including male and female youth, who were role models in the past. The Prophet Muhammad ﷺ is the finest role model for people of all ages

> You have an excellent model in the Messenger of Allah, for all who put their hope in Allah and the Last Day and remember Allah much. (Qur'an 33:21).

Where are the role models today? Muslim adolescents in the West, and for that matter anywhere in the world now, open their eyes and step into a world full of disappointment. The environment around them is ripe with the failure and impotence of the ummah and its marginalisation in the world arena. There is little confidence in the present Muslim leadership and the number of role models is frustratingly minimal. This vacuum has been filled with role models stooped in materialism and the commercialisation of sensuality. Most celebrities that young people now idolise have a singular philosophy of life, 'eat, drink, fornicate and be merry'. They are the products of consumer culture and the materialistic view of life.

The absence of positive role models around young people, in the community and in the broader society, has been a destabilising factor among Muslim youth. It is a great distress for Muslim parents and social thinkers. Achieving success is important for children, but they have to know what they should achieve, and understand what success means. They have to gain confidence to plan and competence to achieve. At the same time, they have to know the benchmarks for success.

Given their age and maturity they need help in setting their own targets, with the help of people they trust. The targets have to be high, but not so high as to be off-putting. They need to be at ease with their parents who should help them in clarifying goals with manageable time-frames.

Allah has instilled in human hearts a perpetual quest for pleasure and tranquillity that can only be achieved through meaningful work. The Prophet of Islam ﷺ, with his captivating character, and as 'a witness and a conveyer of good tidings and a warner' (Qur'an 33:45) revealed a sky-high vision among his companions, the first generation Muslims. They, in turn, became role models for the rest of humanity. In addition, both the substance and style of Islam's message created self-motivation in the thirsty hearts of Arabia. Thus, deep understanding of Islam motivates a Muslim to move ahead.

The struggle for good and the welfare of others need to be guided by selfless motivation, not by the urge for self-fulfilment. There must be a vision and hope, without which human beings are doomed to passivity and lethargy. The glad tidings of the Garden and the warning of the Fire are the motivating factors for Muslims in the world. The Qur'an has mentioned the multiplicity of rewards (Qur'an 48:29) which catapult Muslims toward making more efforts. The ultimate motivation derives from the fact that Allah, the Creator, will reveal Himself to His obedient slaves in the Garden. That is the pinnacle of success for a human being.

As emissaries of Allah, human beings have an inherent urge towards a higher goal, although that is often marred by the effects of the surroundings. The highest motivation leads to laying down one's earthly life for Allah, (Qur'an 6:162, 9:111), His deen and upholding the honour of human beings. The essence of Muslim life is to work for the service of Allah, not to live for selfish goals.

The hard facts that haunt Muslims in most Western countries are the prejudice, discrimination and inequalities they face. Even second or third generation children of minority ethnic background need to work twice as hard and be encouraged twice as much by their teachers, if they are to be successful. Given the wider Islamophobic environment, Muslim children need more motivation to work harder. Needless to say, parents have to be extra inspiring and caring in motivating their children.

SELF-ESTEEM

Self-esteem is a positive life-view that reflects one's self-image, self-awareness and self-confidence. In believers self-esteem is indicative of esteem for Allah, since being Allah's creations we must have the highest opinion of ourselves. This is contrary to the usage in popular secular psychology, in which it is a term of no interest whatsoever. How do parents measure their child's self-esteem? The following personal qualities are useful indicators and parents can grade them, if they are serious about it.[3]

adaptable	adventurous	ambitious	cheerful	confident
conscientious	considerate	dependable	determined	energetic
enthusiastic	friendly	helpful	honest	loyal
lively	neat	patient	polite	popular
punctual	responsible	thoughtful	trustworthy	virtuous

Keeping the above in mind, we should build on the positive aspects of our children. They need to be noticed, recognised and respected. Whether infant or adolescent, they need this from their near ones, parents, teachers and other elders close to them. All children think of themselves as special. They expect their parents to treat them specially. This is in human nature. The Messenger of Allah ﷺ understood this perfectly and, as such, gave every companion full attention to such an extent that every one of them considered themselves to be closest to the Prophet ﷺ.

Praise encourages young people, but this has to be genuine. Indiscriminate praise or flattery is detrimental in the long run, as it can make them complacent. Parents often tend to compare their children with others, but insensitive comparison can undermine their confidence. Islam encourages Muslims to reflect on their spiritual shortcomings and compare themselves with people of taqwa to improve themselves.

Children are learners and making mistakes is all too natural. Good parents make no bones about this. However, they do not overlook intentional or major mistakes. Even then they deal with them in the proper context and with mercy. At any cost, children must not be let down. This can be the recipe for failure in future. As they gradually enter into the world of responsibility, they learn from their own mistakes. Understanding and self-correction by people themselves is better than forced correction.

Parental expectation is also an important factor in motivating children and creating self-confidence in them. A low expectation, especially from parents, can shatter their self-image and pride. On the other hand, too high an expectation can confuse them and ruin their chances of success. It is Allah's blessings that most children are resilient and have the instinct to survive in difficult situations.

A BALANCED GROWTH

Children are raw material. In order to groom them to succeed in life parents need to deal with the whole child. Love of Allah and His Messenger ﷺ and pride in Islam and a wider vision of life are the best things that parents can impart to them. At the same time, a broad and balanced education, which effectively deals with both the world and Hereafter, is important for their identity as Muslims. This is only possible if children are given a holistic education, not the rote learning that has crippled the creativity of some Muslims.

Maintaining a healthy balance in one's life is always a difficult task and it is easier said than done. As adolescent children often tend to follow their role models, parents need to link them with such people who have positive and balanced views on life. As such, they should be encouraged to study great figures in the world. There should be in-depth study of the Prophet's *Seerah* so that young Muslims can come to love him and draw inspiration from his history, and emulate his blessed life to some degree.

'Nothing Succeeds Like Success'

Children who feel successful develop a positive self-image. Allah quotes Shu'ayb ﷺ as saying, 'My success is with Allah alone' (Surah Hud: 88). This is the great knowledge of the Muslims: success is only by and from Allah, and that real success lies with Allah. Conscientious parents recognise and encourage the positive aspects of their children and build upon them. They encourage their self-appraisal and let them feel proud that Allah granted them their successes. Where a family provides a stable and trusting environment and free space for the children and the deep insights of tawhid they themselves then take responsibility for their efforts and realise that their achievements are purely gifts from Allah. Every parent likes a successful child, but, the concept of success varies. For a Muslim real success lies in achieving 'the good of the world and the Hereafter' (Qur'an 2:201).

Parents with high achieving children should closely watch their physical and mental development. Fast-track children need fast-track challenges so that they can engage themselves without being bored. They definitely need more attention than children of average ability. On the other hand, parents with under-achieving children, need to make sure they get proper care and the necessary educational support. Phenomenal work has already been done in the West in the field of Special Educational Needs (SEN). In recent years inclusive education and social inclusion have become widely discussed issues in Britain. Inclusive education creates an inclusive society, in which everybody contributes and nobody becomes a burden on others. If children display learning, behavioural or other difficulties, physical or mental handicaps, or special talents they should not be stigmatised. What they need is professional support and special care. Many children with special needs have turned out to be highly gifted children who later contributed to human civilisation.

STEP BY STEP DEVELOPMENT[4]

Human qualities like willpower, perseverance, fortitude and self-discipline are the ingredients of success in life. They do not come suddenly or by chance, they need nourishment and step-by-step development. Not all human beings possess these qualities to the same degree and indeed some can lack one or several of these qualities from birth. However, a positive environment at home and surroundings can compensate for such inadequacies to some extent. Parents have a major role to play in inculcating these qualities in their children.

Children need encouragement to explore and feel relaxed. They need recognition, reassurance and quality time from their parents. If parents can genuinely instil trust in Allah and in His Messenger ﷺ, self-belief, self-efficacy and self-direction in their character will follow and will be the driving forces for a confident life. Parents cannot be with their children forever, but they can sow the seeds of success in their lives by:

- showing interest, but not becoming intrusive,
- offering direction, but not being directive,
- encouraging talents, yet keeping them in control,
- containing, but not confining them,
- establishing routines, but by building flexibility,
- supporting and encouraging, but not controlling and pushing,
- offering choice, but avoiding manipulation.

Parents should not demand too much from their children, but they need to be stretched in their work. For steady progress this is important. The world can be a tough and competitive place, and the path through life can be thorny. This makes life challenging, adventurous and enjoyable. Life means hard work and one must have a determination to succeed, in the sense of success which we outlined above. The torchbearers of Islam in the past could only achieve their goals by their sweat, blood and tears. They put aside the comforts of this world in order to bring human beings into servitude to Allah, i.e., liberating them from slavery to mini-gods, whims and desires. This raised them to unparalleled spiritual and civilisational heights. Muslim parents have a duty to educate and train their children to follow in the footsteps of those pious predecessors.

MANAGING FAILURE

Human beings experience failure. Some success can even lead to failure, in particular where the successful person forgets that his or her success is by Allah. Failure teaches us to understand ourselves. In some cases, failure can be a pillar of success. For a Muslim there is no failure, even if it apparently seems to be so. Whatever we do in our lives with the intention of pleasing our Lord we are rewarded on the basis of our intentions and our efforts. However, human beings always look for immediate gain (Qur'an 61:13), for we were ever hasty (Qur'an 17:11). If children fail for some reason, parents should be able to separate failure from them. One cannot be good at everything, so failure in one area is not the end of the world. For children with positive outlooks on life, failure can sharpen their determination to win over a problem and this increases their motivation. Through failure they learn new skills and techniques. It increases their self-awareness. However, parents need to bail out their children in cases where there is fear that their failure is going to ruin their lives.

Children are human beings, not puppets or dolls. They are creative and talented and have hopes, fears and feelings. Parents are there to nurture the whole child. If they want their children to be self-starters they have to guide them positively, supplicate for them and refrain from being negative.

ENTHUSING THE YOUNG MIND

Parents need neither a high degree nor wealth to help their children flourish. They may be added advantages, but are not essential for motivating young people. What we need is passion and quality time to make sure that both home and school environments push them towards being self-motivating.

• At School

As mentioned earlier, children need a good school where they get continuous encouragement through its:

- learning culture
- positive ethos
- high expectation
- set of goals in curriculum areas
- recognition of rights and responsibilities
- clear, consistent and fair discipline
- relationship based on respect and trust
- positive competition
- involvement in creative activities

• At Home

We parents should make sure that our young ones feel loved and wanted at all times. They should experience that the ownership of success is entirely Allah's. They should be constructively reminded or sensitively criticised for any mistakes. Childhood is a time of exploration, discovery and experiment. To err is human. In Islam, there is single reward for effort and double reward for success. If they know the framework of discipline and Islamic boundaries of behaviour they will feel at ease with everything. To motivate children at home, the following are important.

We should:

- not put a barrier between us and our children.
- have a sense of humour so that children get along with us. People without humour are dull.
- trust our children to do things.
- encourage children to take responsibility for a task.
- empower them and delegate them some jobs.

- teach through example, not by words only.
- make choices visible and available to them.
- observe their level of maturity before asking them to do a job.
- break the goal in to bite-size, achievable targets. Small wins provide a sense of achievement, give self-confidence and have a multiplier effect.
- introduce them to new ideas. We should see the merit in their ideas, even if it contradicts ours.
- accept their mistakes. They should start from what they are and not what we want them to be.
- be available to talk to them, even when under pressure.
- praise and recognise the children.

While praising, we should be

- specific
- straightforward and honest. We should not use conditional words, like 'if' and 'but'
- spontaneous
- overt in physical expression, such as smiles, hugs and kisses
- generous in giving them credit, even if they got help from us
- measured. We should not spoil them with too much praise.

IGNITING THE FIRE OF MOTIVATION

While drugs and other social ills were making inroads in the Muslim community, some young professionals, themselves devoted Muslims, foresaw the dangers. They realised that social diseases need social doctors and in their opinion drugs were not the only factor causing young people to drift from their deen. The challenges lie within - the crisis in their knowledge of tawhid and of Islam. They realised that traditional Muslims would never go near pork or alcohol, yet they had little idea when it came to drugs. With a view to combating the evil they trained themselves to tackle the problems head on. This is how one of them encountered a group of 'young Muslims'. Let us call the young professional, 'Mahmud'. His encounter with the street boys was not a planned one, but he relied on Allah when it came. He believed that every disease has a cure, one just has to try, and to pray to Allah.

Half a dozen of them. Young Muslims of Asian and Afro-Caribbean origin, in their teens, in an inner-city estate of Britain. They miss school, hang around the streets or parks and do nothing. Sometimes they gather outside a secondary school and tease girls. Yet in their early teens they were not like they are today. Their first-generation parents had high hopes for them. They were all brought up like other children in the community. Now, they are avoided by their school-mates, feared by teachers and despised by their community. Most of them are permanently excluded from their schools. They have started experimenting with drugs. They are now in search of the ultimate 'trip' or 'buzz'. They are not criminals as such, but some of them have already had encounters with the local police. They are occasional offenders in the locality. Their parents do not have any clue as to why their nice young boys have turned into 'monsters' and are trying to put them to shame.

What happened in their upper secondary school when they are supposed to prepare for their GCSE, the gateway to their future careers? Who is at fault - parents, teachers, community elders, imams, society at large or they themselves? There is no single answer. Many factors added to their disenchantment. Continuous neglect from families, low expectations from teachers and prospects of certain unemployment or an uncertain future may have pushed them toward their anti-social behaviour. They have now rebelled against everybody, including themselves. They have rebelled against the system and now they want to run away from the reality of life. They are at the receiving end of the system, people for whom unemployment is over four times the national average. They are in the front line of social disadvantage, prejudice and discrimination. They are the victims of social exclusion and are now falling through the nets of the so-called 'Inclusive Education'. Few bother about them, as they are known as 'problem children'.

But something happened to them one day that changed their life once again and gave them a new hope for the future. And with

Allah's grace Mahmud was instrumental in this.

Mahmud was in a hurry and passing through an alleyway after the congregational prayer in the local mosque. Suddenly the group appeared before him and asked whether he had any drugs to sell. He was taken aback for a while. He was also surprised at their blunt question, as he knew one of them. But he kept his nerve. He thought this might be an opportunity to talk to them and help them in their difficulties.

With a smile in his face he replied, 'Looking for drugs? Come on, let's talk.' The one who knew him lowered his head and mumbled to others, 'No, let's go.' The others did not hear it, they ignored. By that time Mahmud had already sat on a dry patch of land. The boys did not have any time to think, they just followed one by one.

'What sort of drugs are you looking for?', Mahmud asked them in a confident manner.

All of them were silent. They realised that they had targeted the wrong person. One of them said, 'Sorry, we didn't mean it. Can we go?'

'Don' worry. We can talk. Can't we?' Mahmud had a comforting voice.

They were again silent, looking downward. Mahmud looked intently at each of them.

'They could have been my own brothers', he thought. He realised that these young men had not yet lost respect for their elders. He silently prayed to Allah for guidance and decided to say a few words to them. He took a breath and started:

'Young brothers, I've got something else with me, which is better than the drugs you're looking for. Shall I tell you what that is?' He asked rhetorically.

All were silent. Mahmud continued, 'I'll tell you about it. Brothers, we are the sons of Islam and you know our predecessors were engrossed in more vices than we are today. Alcohol was their life. They were people despised by each other, but Allah decided to raise their status and they raised themselves to such a height that history looks back in surprise. Do you know how?' Mahmud asked.

One of them looked up and asked in a creaky voice, 'by accepting Islam?'

'Excellent', said Mahmud. 'You're right'.

With a pause Mahmud started again, 'Yes, Allah decided to bless them with Islam. He sent His Prophet ﷺ with a book, the Qur'an. And that was it. Islam's golden touch was enough for them. Human history changed its course. The Prophet ﷺ is gone, but has left the Qur'an and his exemplary life for us. They can change our fate again, can't they?' he stopped for a while.

'But, we can never be like his followers. We don't see any hope in our lives,' another boy said.

'We're so bad, nobody likes us any more,' Added the third boy.

Mahmud realised that the boys were opening up. He said, 'No brothers, its not true. If the worst people in history can transform themselves into teachers of humanity, why couldn't we? What we need is pride in ourselves. The pride that will motivate us as Muslims and give us confidence to succeed. You are the young soldiers of Islam today. Please don't kill yourselves, my young brothers.' Mahmud's voice was heavy. He instinctively put his hands out to the boys.

There was a long silence. Nobody dared look at Mahmud's face. What was he thinking? Was he weeping? One of them could not control himself. He burst into tears and said, 'I'm sorry, brother. I'm sorry.'

It was a spark, the others could not take it any more. One by one, they raised their heads and said, 'I'm sorry.'

Mahmud controlled his tears so far. This time he could not. In a sobbing voice he said, 'Alhamdulillah. Let's go somewhere and talk further'.

16. Into the World of Responsibility

PARENTS ARE ALWAYS PARENTS

Prophets and sages of the past not only advised their children in their childhood and adolescence, but reminded and guided them when they became adults. They did not shy away from their responsibilities thinking that their children had grown up and can be left on their own. Of course, in adult life, people take responsibility for what they do, but as Muslims we owe each other counsel as long as we are alive. This has bonded the Muslim family and made it unimaginably humane. Unlike some societies where old people are left alone to be looked after by social services, even when they have children or grandchildren, Islam has made it compulsory for people to look after their parents, value them and supplicate for them. In the Muslim family environment parents feel confident to counsel their children without any hesitation. Luqman, a sage of pre-Islamic times, counselled his son regarding pure tawhid and about his duties (Qur'an 31:13-19). His advice was the essence of the Islam that later came and showered blessings on humanity.

In the same manner, Ibrahim ﷺ in his old age performed his role as a father. When he found that the wife of his beloved son Isma'il ﷺ failed to pass the test of loyalty to her husband, he advised Isma'il to get rid of the ungrateful wife and find a better one, which Isma'il dutifully carried out. This is narrated by 'Abdullah ibn 'Abbas î in a long hadith in *Sahih al-Bukhari*.

History has also recorded the motherly counsel of Asma bint Abi Bakr, may Allah be pleased with her, who, in her old age, encouraged her son, the famous 'Abdullah ibn az-Zubayr î not to waver in his fight against the notorious Hajjaj ibn Yusuf. When she heard that 'Abdullah was a bit distressed about the possible mutilation of his body after his imminent martyrdom, she tenderly rebuked him not to worry so much about what would happen to his dead body.

These stories carry a significant message about Muslim parents' role in Islam. A parent's duty never terminates, although it transforms in nature since we are counselled in the noble hadith to begin to take our young ones as friends when they come into adulthood, and thus we owe them the duty of good counsel. We never wash our hands of our job. Allah has elevated parents in the eyes of children. However, this distinct position of parents is not for arbitrary use or abuse. This is in line with the spirit of the family institution as indicated by Allah, u, in His Qur'an. It is natural, if not always the case, that Muslim parents be generally wiser because of their maturity and experience.

GUIDANCE IN CHOICE OF CAREER

Education in Western countries offers wide options to students, but are the young people bright enough academically to go to university? If so, what career are they going to choose and what are their professions going to be? Informed parents can guide their children directly in these crucial decisions and help other parents with their children. However, the academic brightness of children should not be seen as the only ladder of success in life. Professional and social skills, self-discipline, and organisational qualities are all important. Halal (Islamically permitted) earnings and dignified living are elementary requirements for Muslims. Successful parents are those who infuse in their children the strength of Iman that makes no compromise with forbidden modes of earning, no matter what the temptation. They guide their children in self-exploration so that their potential is harnessed to the full. Young Muslims may choose to be business people, teachers, doctors, and social workers or may choose any profession that suits them, but their focus in serving Allah by serving the ummah ought never to be missed. Whatever they do in their lives is for Islam, meaning for their success in the *Akhirah* (life after death).

It is also important not to force children into occupations they do not like. Parents may have had life-long ambitions for their children, but they should not expect them to fulfil them unless the children really want. After all, it is their lives, not their parents'. We parents should discuss the career choices openly in the light of our knowledge and past experiences.

UNIVERSITY: THE FRONTIER OF CHALLENGE

Education, when properly understood, can be the backbone of a people. University education can open the frontiers of knowledge in a challenging world. Muslim youth should be encouraged to take up the challenge if they have the ability and means to do so. The outward intention is that universities should be unique places where lecturers try to disseminate open-ended knowledge in a free environment, although they rarely live up to these high ideals. There are clubs and societies - political, religious and others. Muslim students can form Islamic Societies in which they have the opportunity to get involved in a variety of activities, but they should steer clear of extremist groups and ideas, which go beyond the clear path of the Book and the Sunnah, and should tread the middle path, if they want to serve the ummah in its regeneration. It is important for young Muslims to maintain the right balance between their Islamic, social and academic activities in order to prepare themselves for a greater role in society. They should never ignore their personal development.

Higher education provides the opportunity to gain skills in public relations, media relations, research and development, public outreach, government relations, and in defending civil and legal rights. It also facilitates young people to embark on some of the subjects, the physical and biological sciences, that are a part of the foundation of contemporary culture. As the future of the ummah, young Muslims must equip themselves with the practical knowledge relevant to bringing about a civilisational change on the basis of revealed knowledge.

Unfortunately, in an atmosphere of ignorance about Islam, some Muslim youth may be tempted to hide their deen. This comes from their lack of knowledge and self-respect. This is sad but understandable to a certain extent, given the negative media image of Muslims today. However, it is vital that young Muslims in university feel proud of being Muslims, yet without indulging in empty rhetoric. Islam is a gift for humanity, not something to be embarrassed about. It is the latest edition of divine guidance comprehensibly delivered by the last Prophet, Muhammad ﷺ, which has remained free of human adulteration. Muslims built dazzling civilisations with leading political, scientific and intellectual thinkers, which has endured for over a thousand years. It was instrumental in ushering in the European Renaissance by providing its intellectual foundations, although understandably at that time European scholars only took what suited them.

DA'WAH OPPORTUNITIES EVERYWHERE

If atheistic and promiscuous people can display pride and promote their ideologies with confidence, why should Muslim youth not be proud of that with which Allah has favoured them? Nothing should bar us from letting people know about tawhid - the unitary knowledge of Allah, and the Messenger ﷺ - the deen of Islam and about our heritage and culture, witnessing to the truth of Islam. What we say, wear, eat or spend their time on carries a message. We can use every little opportunity in our daily lives to bear witness to the message of Islam in word and deed. Our personal appearance, the beard, the *hijab*, our humility, positive behaviour and strong character are all important signposts of Islam. We could easily use occasions such as the Eid to inform others about the cultural dimension of Islam. In fact, we can attract human hearts by being living examples of Islam. For example, when we go for prayer during the lunch hour we should be open and frank by speaking the truth that we are going for prayer, instead of showing unease about this. In modern pluralist societies, there is nothing to be embarrassed about in practising one's deen. Islam demands transparency in action and integrity of character. This open practice of Islam could be beneficial in many ways. It encourages and emboldens fellow Muslims. It also evokes curiosity about and interest in Islam in other people's minds, an influential tool that could open restless hearts to the divine Truth.

The opportunities to create interest in Islam in educational institutions or in work places are numerous. Overt attempts to invite people are generally counter-productive, but, natural exposure of Islam through one's personality, e.g., integrity of character, honesty, hard work and openness, on the one hand, and avoidance of forbidden (*haram*) things, on the other, create a very positive image of the Islamic way of life. Those who have open hearts may be blessed by seeing the truth.

CHOOSING PROFESSIONS THAT HELP THE UMMAH

The Muslim ummah needs quality people in all areas of life, from Astronomy to Zoology. Unfortunately, education has been probably the least priority area in many Muslim countries, spending insignificant fractions of national budgets compared to other developing countries. Even among educated sections of the ummah there is an imbalance in subject choice and there is less interest in creative and social sciences. At the same time, education in general is more or less based on rote-learning, with little scope or encouragement for creativity and innovation.

Education is not just about gaining university degrees. It is about effective building of a life in service of Allah and His Messenger ﷺ and one that promotes the well-being of society. If young people cannot quite manage to go on for higher education, they should not be looked down upon. There are numerous ways of educating oneself. Instead of giving up they should confidently look for such a job or profession that will educate them throughout their lives. Earning a halal (Islamically acceptable) livelihood and at the same time working for the benefit of the community should be high on everybody's agenda. Muslim youth should strive for sufficient earning so that they do not have to depend on others in the family or on state benefits. In order to choose a career and enhance skills they should take advice from career specialists and experts in the community. There are many opportunities for work in Western countries. It would be a shame if young Muslims ended up becoming burden to themselves, their family and the community by allowing themselves to fall through the net. Muslim parents need to have a wide outlook upon advising their children for a good career.

IN THE CYCLE OF LIFE

As adolescents grow to adulthood, they take on board the role their parents took or should have taken. It may occur that some parents have failed in their responsibilities or could not quite make it in their roles as parents. The new generation should not waste their time blaming their predecessors. They have an Islamic obligation to respect their parents and make up for their weaknesses.

Muslims are never complacent, even for a single moment. We attempt to improve upon our shortcomings and that continues unabated until our last breath. All parents have a stake in their children. To Muslim parents time is important and, as such, every moment has to be productive, whether that is in the sense of being a moment of deep reflection on the meaning of our existence, a moment in prayer or remembrance of Allah, or those moments given to earning a livelihood, and the moments given to one's family. We may not achieve immediate or tangible results in what we do, but we know our actions are being continuously recorded by the 'Noble Recorders' (Qur'an 82:11). We also know the numerous Prophetic traditions on how human beings can lose out if we lead a carefree and flippant life. Life is too serious to play around.

> He whose two days are equal (in accomplishments) is a sure loser.
> (*Sunan ad-Daylami*)

THE UMMAH'S NEED AND MUSLIM YOUTH

Success in parenting comes about when children grow with their natural qualities into responsible adults. Muslim adults have a responsibility not only toward themselves, their families and community, but toward the ummah and humanity at large. Parents who dedicate their efforts to educating their children and creating in them a wider vision of humanity are blessed with Allah's favour.

Guiding young people to become self-motivating human beings in the modern West is definitely a major challenge. In the world of apathy towards deen and craving for self-fulfilment and egocentrism, communal feelings or working together for a common purpose are generally missing, but, the success of Islam lies in the unity of the ummah and we are commanded to 'Hold fast to the rope of Allah all together, and do not separate'. (Qur'an 3:103). Parents should be instrumental in bringing their children to feel sympathy and work for the community. When we ourselves are actively involved in such works, children easily fit in them.

The Muslim ummah is huge in numbers, but, how many Muslims were there in the beginning when they ventured to shape the world in the mould of Islam? While number is important, Islam's strength is always derived from the quality of its people. What is most needed today is Muslims who possess honesty, integrity, commitment and a passion to transform the ummah once again to be the 'best nation' on earth. Humanity today needs the type of Muslims - those who have intentionally surrendered to Allah - who have the sense of urgency and vision to re-establish the *Khilafah 'ala Minhaj an-Nubuwwah* (khalifate based on the Prophetic model). Their number may be small, but they would be the people who can move the world and usher in an era of human liberation from slavery to whims and desires.

In spite of hostility from its adversaries, Islam is now universally acknowledged as the only unadulterated deen. But what Islam has sometimes missed in recent centuries are Muslims, the Muslims who have in their hearts the depth of iman and conviction, and the limit of commitment and action. The lack of great numbers of these Muslims has deprived the world of justice, balance and order, reducing human beings to servility to their own ignorance. In spite of material prosperity, the modern world is now undergoing a period of Jahiliyyah, with arrogance and deep social and intellectual crises. On the other hand, the present ruling Muslim elite have dismally failed the ummah and dis-empowered them from their natural rights. The world is waiting for a change.

Like a derelict palace, the Muslim ummah has undergone external onslaught and internal intellectual and social stagnation over the last few centuries. The reconstruction of the ummah thus requires an all-out effort on all fronts. It is a gigantic task that needs dynamism, maturity and vision. Can the new generation of Muslims wake up to the call to the ummah's regeneration?

NOTES

1   Abu Omar, Courtesy Witness-Pioneer

2   *Adolescence - the survival guide for Parents and Teenagers,* Elizabeth Fenwick and Dr. Tony Smith, London 1994

3   *From Disaffection to Social Inclusion: A Social Skills Preparation for Active Citizenship and Employment* - John Huskins, p50, 2000, UK

4   *Motivating Your Child: Tools and Tactics to Help Your Child be a Self-starter,* Elizabeth Hartley-Brewer, pp2-5, 1998, London)

5   *Training Guide for Islamic Workers,* Hisham Altalib, IIIT, p105, 1991, US

6   *Helping Children with Reading and Spelling: A Special Needs Manual,* Rea Reason and Rene Boote, pp20,21, 1994, UK)

The Prize and the Price

Executive Summary

- Ignorance, apathy, sluggishness and complacency have unfortunately become the present-day impediments of some of the Muslim ummah. We need to shun them for our own sakes. We must try to equip ourselves with the basic understanding of Islam and the modern world so that the new generation of Muslim youth get inspiration from us.
- We Muslim parents should have the sense of urgency to put quality time and wholehearted efforts into raising our children as 'sons or daughters of Islam' of the present era. We should never be 'too busy' with our careers or professions, at the cost of raising our children in Islam.
- We should rediscover the Prophetic way of dealing with our children and undertake parenting as an Islamic obligation, instead of using an inherited or cultural method. Knowing 'the tools of the trade' is essential in raising children in the West.
- Positive parenting has become a civilisational task for Muslim parents, given the predicament of the ummah in the last few centuries. We should always be conscious about the holistic development of our children in order to achieve the pleasure of Allah.
- Parenting is an immense job in the present world. It is joyful as well. The prize of positive parenting is great and the price of poor parenting is dreadful. We should not lose our *Dunya* (this world) and *Akhirah* (Hereafter) because of our blessed children.

257

- Islam has so much to give humanity, as it is in tune with the physical and biological world as well as human *fitrah* (nature). Islam is a joy to follow as it addresses all the issues in the world with moderation and justice. We Muslim parents should find pleasure in rearing our children in this universal way of life.

17. Reap As You Sow

Allah does not impose on any self any more than it can stand. (Qur'an 2: 286)

... man will have nothing but what he strives for. (Qur'an 53: 39)

Parents and families have the primary responsibility for nurturing children and preparing them in such a way that they develop the basic social skills necessary for success in life and for the smooth running of society. Communities and schools have the responsibility for providing the social, health and educational services necessary to complement the role of families in promoting the development of the future generation.

Social factors such as unemployment, poverty, inadequate housing, single parenthood, racism, and social exclusion make parenting more difficult. Factors such as family dysfunction, the demise of the extended family, changed gender roles and technological change exacerbate the difficulties of parenting. The development of the whole child with sound physical, emotional, social and spiritual qualities depends on the triangle of responsibilities of: the family, community and school. A sound partnership between these agencies creates and sustains civilisation.[1]

Parenting is a challenge; it is a joy as well. The joy depends on preparation, skill, dedication and above all *Tawakkul* (reliance) on Allah. If the wider community is in harmony with Islam, parenting becomes easier. If not, parents have to work harder. As discussed earlier, the wider community and schools in the West often clash with the values and ethos of Islam. This puts an extra burden on Muslim families and communities to work out their responsibilities for their children. Muslim parents in their heyday left better children after their deaths who carried on the message of Islam. What are we doing now? The answer is mixed. Among 'census' Muslims in the world today there are even those, although very few, who find pleasure in mocking the very root of Islam. On the other hand, there are encouraging signs of Muslims coming back to Islam everywhere. A flurry of activities to rejuvenate Muslim youth has started.

POOR PARENTING

The overall situation needs massive improvement. The disease of degeneration needs to be cured and many problems need to be solved. Muslims have to address them with a holistic approach. Any attempt to regenerate the ummah must involve well-thought-out plans to prepare future generations. It is encouraging to find that the present generation of Muslim parents do realise that they are ill equipped to face the challenges of the time and they want a change. That is a good beginning. But, we need to understand what constitutes positive parenting so that we can play a catalytic role in building our next generation who would be better equipped to shoulder greater responsibilities. Mere love and enthusiasm are not enough to raise children in Islam. Parenting skills are of vital importance, as are passion and vision.

What are the reasons behind poor or ineffective parenting? The following are some of the reasons parents or aspiring parents should be wary of when about to embark on this rough journey.

• Ignorance

Ignorance is never bliss; it is a curse. The deen that swept the world with its knowledge and scholarly excellence has lost its impetus because of the ignorance and incompetence of some of its adherents. Parenting in the modern complex world needs knowledge, understanding, creativity and assertive management qualities. It needs positive efforts and plans, skills and professionalism, enthusiasm and passion, without which parents cannot feel confident in dealing with their children. Some in the Muslim community probably assume that biological fatherhood or motherhood is all that matters; the child will, by default, follow in their footsteps. This is not only wrong, but also dangerous.

How can a Muslim remain ignorant? Ignorance is multidimensional and against the very purpose of human creation. Ignorance about our own selves will fail us, ignorance about the environment will put us at the receiving end of all sorts of disasters and ignorance of how to cope in varying situations will put us in danger. The parable of ignorance is darkness, and that of knowledge light. Lighted darkness cannot exist. Ignorance about human beings' divine purpose on earth will lead us astray, meaning eternal failure. As rearing children in the Islamic way is an Islamic requirement, parents need knowledge and understanding of their job of parenting. Ignorance is an enemy in this trade.

• Complacency

Some Muslims may hold very simplistic views on parenting. They love their children and possess strong emotional attachments to them. They do not fail in working hard in order to bring smiles to the faces of their loved ones. That is excellent. However, in doing so, they forget to look beyond and fail to comprehend the consequences. Some of them have blind trust in their children and display the 'ostrich syndrome', as if no trouble could ever touch their trusted ones. Some in the beginning even dislike constructive criticism from friends and well-wishers, as if their children were immune to temptations and social diseases. They simply cannot conceive that their beloved ones could, one day, lose their and hurt them in any way. Unfortunately, they only realise when the young ones are finally spoilt.

• Indifference

There is no dearth of Muslim parents, even among the educated, who are indifferent to the educational and spiritual needs of their children. They shy away from their responsibilities on parenting and disregard the needs of their young ones. Apathy rules their lives. Sometimes they ignore and often they procrastinate, probably thinking that their children are growing naturally and they need not contribute much to build their characters. They may love their children more than anybody else, but their concept of love is one-sided and blind. As discussed elsewhere, even plants need a minimum of nurturing for their survival, let alone growth. A human being is a complex creature. Young children, especially, need delicate nursing. Children are keen observers of people and events. The message they pick up from their parents' indifference can lead to disaster. Once children get used to untimely and uncontrolled 'freedom' or apathy from their parents they can easily fall prey to a host of social ills.

• Lack of Experience

Many parents, especially those new to parenthood, lack experience. This can be forgiven to a certain extent in the beginning of parenting, but experience is something that is gained through effort and a sincere desire to learn. One cannot make excuses of inexperience forever. Human beings gain life-experience every moment. We do not live in an isolated world, we should learn from others or from our surroundings, and the sooner the better.

We live in societies where information is abundant. There are opportunities to learn from people. Age is not a barrier. What is required is serious observation and conscious follow-up. Parents are dealing with live and complex human beings with tremendous creativity and vigour. Thus, parenting has to be a creative endeavour. Lethargic, reactive and rigid approaches simply do not work. If we Muslim parents really want to raise their children in the way of Islam, we must grab every opportunity to learn the 'tools of the trade', in order to be effective in parenting. As stake holders in our children's success and the ummah's future we cannot afford to make excuses.

• Inherited Methods of Parenting

Society changes. While the target of parenting and vision of Muslim life remains the same throughout ages and all over the world, the techniques and approaches have to be changed. They cannot remain the same, especially when we are confronted with such a radically different society as we are here in the West. As human information expands, it is become even clearer that the Prophetic model of rearing children is the best and most scientific. Instead, many Muslim parents resort to culturally inherited methods or pseudo-modern techniques in raising their children. This either creates a sense of fear and control or a laissez-faire environment at home, leading to undesirable consequences in future. Rigidity and control kill off creativity and innovation in the children, and make them timid and docile. On the other hand, too much liberalism spoils the children. With the open social environment prevailing in the West both techniques are dangerous. They can push children to permissiveness or rebellion against their family, religion and community.

• Family Misfortune

Accidents, mishaps and misfortune can strike without warning and leave a legacy of distress or long-term hardship. Parents can divorce for both genuine and egotistical reasons. In any event, a domestic problem puts extreme pressure on the single parent, who finds it incredibly hard to carry out the job of parenting. Children suffer and in some cases their lives can be ruined, although it can happen that out of the constriction and difficulty good and healthy young people can emerge, just as out of the healthy, trouble-free, bourgeois family egotistical monsters can be produced. Although most Western countries have social and financial support systems to fall back upon, it is not easy to rear children, especially in their teens, without active support from a vital member of the family.

• Pressures of Life

Modern human beings are under heavy pressure. Survival itself can seem to be a struggle. To many, there may appear to be no breathing space for days or weeks. Even those of us who manage to do some work for Islam often forget to balance our various roles, and neglect the vital job of looking after our children properly, especially in their formative period. As a result, the danger of losing the future generation has become acute.

Passive people might give in. In their ignorance they blame the 'lack of time' and their destinies, and forget that parenting is a primordial task. Parenting needs to be taken with zeal to make it effective and joyful. Everything in our life is destined by Allah, and none of us know what is ahead. We can only work hard to fulfil our destinies for without making effort one should not complain. The Prophet Nuh ï tried his best to save his son. He failed in that, but succeeded in pleasing Allah. Allah asks human beings to work with sincerity and to the best of their abilities. The result is by Allah. This unique concept of hard work and *Tawakkul* makes Muslim individuals ever dynamic. Life is a matter of balance and priority. The busiest people are generally balanced if they are serious and well-planned. The complaint of 'lack of time' comes from unbalanced people. Who else was busier than the last Prophet ﷺ? And yet he was the most perfectly balanced man on earth.

THE PRIZE AND THE PRICE

What is the price of poor parenting? What is the price of the ignorance, indifference, lethargy, complacency, arrogance or ill-planning in raising the future generation, in this world and in the Hereafter? What price for turning away from the gift of Allah, which He sent to two responsible and mature adults? The crime of poor parenting is serious, as it has a lasting impact on human civilisation. The crime becomes more grievous when the environment is ripe with Jahiliyyah.

Young people at the receiving end of Jahiliyyah lack vision, clarity of thought and focus in their lives. Under an overpowering materialistic and hedonistic culture, Muslim youth are experiencing breakdown of values, ethos, and Islamic character. Except for a small section of youth, who are trying hard to uphold their identities as balanced Muslims, many are lapsing into the post-modern Jahiliyyah. They suffer from identity crisis, confusion and inferiority complex. As a result, their confidence is shattered and their future becomes uncertain. Many are now living in two worlds. In the absence of role-models and tangible hope for the future, many of them lack aspiration and ambition. Some will end up in the world of vice and crime. Muslim youth are as susceptible to all these social pitfalls as others. If this trend is not challenged, Muslims from immigrant backgrounds can be reduced to a disadvantaged ghettoised community on the periphery of mainstream society, which will further add to the civilisational crisis of human beings we have been experiencing over the past few hundred years.

This prospect of an impending nightmare scenario may sound pessimistic, but it is better that we prepare than suffer. Parents who fail to plan and prepare, cannot prioritise their acts. Once they let their children down for whatever reasons, they have the unfortunate likelihood of seeing their beloved ones bring tears, sufferings and even ignominy to their families. The rudeness, rebellion, delinquency and lack of values that we see today among young people can engulf us all if parenting is not given due importance. The vicious circle of poor parenting marginalises communities and nations. It is a terrible loss in this transient world, but the loss on the Day of Judgement is eternal. The cost of poor parenting is thus too high indeed.

In contrast, positive parenting produces generations, which keep on benefiting humanity. The cycle becomes a virtuous one that transcends generations. Good children give worth to their parents. They become successful inheritors on earth. There are of course some pains in positive parenting, for as the maxim goes - 'no pain, no gain'. Definitely, there are difficulties, challenges and sacrifices in the process of raising children, but they are pleasurable. There are also physical, financial, psychological costs in the pursuit of positive parenting, but, there are joy, happiness and a sense of achievement that outweighs everything. The worldly reward of rearing successful children is happiness and success. The ultimate reward is with Allah, Who will elevate good parents who have acted purely for the sake of Allah and in accordance with the Sunnah of the Messenger of Allah ﷺ to the Garden.

18. Conclusion

When the child of Adam dies, all his or her deeds are cut off except three. These are: continuous sadaqah, useful knowledge that benefits others, and a right-acting child who prays for him or her. (*Sahih Muslim*)

I have attempted to discuss parenting as an obligatory task which is linked with the mission and purpose of human life. To Muslims, parenting is ever important for our *Dunya* and *Akhirah*. The Qur'an tells us that children are a 'test' and 'trust' for Muslim parents. It is an immense responsibility entrusted by Allah to us. The purpose of parenting is to develop effective emissaries of Allah on earth through love, care and proper education and training. Allah wants us to strive as best as we can to keep this earth as His well-managed 'garden'. Effective parenting means passing on values, ethos and a sense of responsibility to children. The family as an institution in which fathers and mothers create a happy, joyful and learning atmosphere is central. A loving and caring family environment anchors young people with their parents and family members, through which they learn to love their community, and other human beings. This is embedded in Muslim nature and is the essence of Islamic social life.

I have also attempted to bring home the fact that parenting is fundamentally an assertive and interactive endeavour that needs strategies, forward planning, continuous vigilance, pro-active enterprise and undiluted commitment. Parenting starts from the moment a baby is conceived in the mother's womb and is a life-long process. It involves physical sustenance, emotional support, social upbringing and spiritual nourishment of the young from their earliest years. The sacrifice involved in parenting at different stages of a child's life brings new challenges, adventure, joy and happiness. The reward is enormous - a sense of achievement in this world and *Ridwanullah* (the pleasure of Allah) in the Hereafter. On the other hand, ineffective parenting can bring unhappiness in the world and sad consequences in the Hereafter.

Unfortunately, the modern world is steeped in Jahiliyyah. Owing to technological achievements, this Jahiliyyah has unfortunately deepened, broadened and now become global. It has many dimensions - political, social, moral and spiritual. On the political and social front the modern West has made some apparent efforts towards bringing equality and justice in societies, but these are often selective and unfortunately do not include all. As a result, not all human beings are equal, but 'some are more equal than others'. The overall political and socioeconomic condition of the world was objectively described by a demonstrator during the World Trade Organisation (WTO) meeting in Seattle a few years ago, when he mentioned that the planet earth has been 'privatised by a few'!

On the moral and spiritual fronts too many human beings have become confused and restless, because they have lost or are not aware of the meaning of life. Many are roaming in the wilderness of atheism, materialism and a laissez-faire lifestyle. In this predicament some Muslims are also giving in to the existing social trends, their whims and desires. As a result, the Muslim community in the West is also experiencing an erosion of values and breakdown of discipline among the younger generation. The situation is already worrying in many inner cities of Western countries, where Muslims constitute a good percentage of the population. It seems that some Muslims are going to follow the footsteps of the derailed people of the past, as prophesied in the hadith, '… even if they manage to get themselves into a lizard's hole, the Muslims will follow irrationally' (*Sahih Muslim*).

While this is the bleak side of modern human life, there are many positive aspects. The world is still full of hope and optimism, something to celebrate. In spite of social ills in many places, the spirit of love, compassion, mercy and sacrifice is everywhere flowing in human hearts. In spite of all the chaos, instability and insecurity, there is still some discipline and order. The inherent piety (*taqwa*) in human nature overrides evil (*fujur*), if the environment is even a little bit positive. The physical and biological worlds follow the discipline ordered by Allah, the Creator. There is harmony in the natural world. What we need is to attune ourselves, human beings, with this harmony.

Human beings are naturally prone to follow the commands of Allah alone. It is the vested interest of Jahiliyyah that tempts us to disobey our Lord. However, behind all the arrogance and rebellion we cry for solace, peace and justice. Not everybody has the ability to fight for this. There are many who need help and support to earn this enduring quality. There is always the necessity of a group of people who, with their sweat and blood, contribute to the peace and happiness of others. That is the purpose of the emergence of that group among the Muslim community who struggle in the way of Allah, as mentioned in the Qur'an and in the noble hadith. It is in this context that a new generation of Muslims, with a confident worldview and balanced life, need to emerge.

The challenge of replacing the established Jahiliyyah with the Prophetic way of life is obviously enormous. The need is for a group of people with Sahabah-type features and qualities, who would strive to liberate human beings from the clutches of this Jahiliyyah. This is a divine task for the slave of Allah, a civilisational task. In order to embark on this historic role Muslim parents in the West have to undergo an internal psychological shift and external metamorphosis. We need to mobilise our full potential with a view to training, educating, and leading our children effectively so that the younger ones can take on this responsibility when they grow into adults. A renewed paradigm on the basis of transcendental values of life is now the only guarantee for human beings to remain as emissaries on earth and Muslim parents can play their part in setting the milestones for it.

All human beings are created with a prescribed time to live on earth, which we do not know. This makes it all the more important that we act with a sense of urgency in order to carry out, at least, the basic tasks of life. Islam has taught Muslims to prioritise between compulsory, preferred and recommended acts. It is essential that we prioritise our personal, professional, family and social works in emulation of the life of the Prophet Muhammad ﷺ. There should be no doubt that parenting must be one of the top items on this priority list, especially in the West.

Life has only one chance and no sensible parent can afford to gamble on this. Poor parenting is a disaster - for parents, children and society. In the family, it brings destruction and, in a nation, it invites calamity. In the West, it can be the recipe for total disorientation of the ummah and its assimilation into the materialistic culture within a few generations. That is what happened with weaker nations in the past in various parts of the world. It is true that an uphill journey or swimming upstream is always difficult, but not un-achievable. For those who have courage it is rather adventurous and enjoyable.

Muslims at their best have always been adventurous, enterprising, focused and decisive. Allah demands such from Islam's adherents at this present juncture of time. Those who easily give in, then failure is their destiny. Those who remain steadfast and tough, victory is their lot. The world is not for the coward, as 'The brave die once but cowards die many times before their death'. It is definitely for the brave. Islam is such a deen that gives courage to individuals and pride to peoples. Islam changes peoples from within. It gives hope to those who willingly surrender to Allah. Muslims never lose hope in their future, as despondency is a major wrong action (Qur'an 12:87). Islam is ever positive.

Once again, parenting is an assertive, positive and innovative endeavour. It needs creative thinking, strategic planning and full commitment for success. As leaders, mentors and teachers of their children we parents have the ultimate responsibility for our children's futures, in this world and in the Hereafter. Can Muslim parents of our generation make an impact on the ummah's destiny by changing the greatest gifts to the greatest assets of Islam?

Do not give up and do not be downhearted. You shall be uppermost if you are believers. (Qur'an 3:139)

NOTES

[1] *From Disaffection to Social Inclusion: A Social Skills Preparation for Active Citizenship and Employment* – John Huskins, p50, 2000, UK

Bibliography

Abdalhaqq and Aisha Bewley (1999). *The Noble Qur'an: A New rendering of its Meaning in English*, Bookwork, Norwich.

Akhtar, Shabbir (1993). *The Muslim Parents Handbook: What Every Muslim Parent Should Know*, Ta-Ha Publishers, London.

Al-Affendi, M H and Baloch, N A (1980). *Curriculum and Teaching Education* (Ed)., Hodder and Stoughton.

Al-Albani, Muhammad Naasir-ud-deen (1998). *The Etiquettes of Marriage: In the Pure Tradition of the Prophet*, Ihyaa' Minhaaj Al-Sunnah, UK.

Al-Areefee, Yoosuf ibn Abdullah (1996). *Manners of Welcoming the NewBorn Child in Islam*, Maktaba Darus Salaam, UK.

Al-Bukhari, *Sahih al-Bukhari*, Translated by Dr. Muhammad Muhsin Khan (1997). Darussalam, Riyadh.

Alghazali, M (1989). *Muslim Character*, IIFSO.

Al-Kaysi, Marwan I (1994). *Morals and Manners in Islam: A Guide to Islamic Adab*, The Islamic Foundation, UK.

Altalib, Hisham, (1993). *Training Guide for Islamic Workers*. Herndon, VA: IIIT and IIFSO.

Ali Nadwi, Abul Hasan (1983). *Islam and the World*, IIFSO.

Anwar, Muhammad (1994) *Young Muslims in Britain: Attitudes, Educational Needs and Policy Implications*, The Islamic Foundation, Leicester.

Asad, Muhammad ((1980). *The Message of the Qur'an*, Dar al-Andalus Limited, Gibraltar.

ATL, (1998). *Achievement for All, A Practical handbook for Teachers and Lecturers*, ATL Publication, London.

Azami, Iqbal A (1990). *Muslim Manners*, UK Islamic Academy, UK.

Badri, Malik B, (1979). *The Dilemma of Muslim Psychologists*, MWH London Publishers, 1979.

Bashier, Zakaria (1991). *Makkan Crucible*, The Islamic Foundation, Leicester.

Bashier, Zakaria (1998). *Sunshine at Madinah*, The Islamic Foundation, Leicester.

Beshir, Ekram and Mohamed Rida, (1998). *Meeting the Challenge of Parenting in the West: An Islamic Perspective*. Amanah Publications, USA.

Beekun, R I and Badawi, J (1999). *Leadership: An Islamic Perspective*, Amana Publications, USA.

Campion, Mukti J (1993). *The Good Parent Guide*, Element, UK.

DfEE, (1999). *The National Curriculum: Handbook for Primary Teachers in England*, DfEE, UK.

DfEE, (1999). *The National Curriculum: Handbook for Secondary Teachers in England*, DfEE, UK.

Doi, Abdur Rahman I, (1989) *Woman in Shariah*, Ta-Ha, London.

D'Oyen, Fatima M (1996). *The Miracle of Life: A Guide on Islamic Family Life and Sex Education for Young People*, The Islamic Foundation, Leicester.

Eyre, Linda and Richard, (1980). *Teaching Your Children Joy*, Fireside, New York.

Eyre, Linda and Richard, (1993). *Teaching Your Children Values*, Fireside, New York.

Eyre, Linda and Richard, (1994). *Teaching Your Children Responsibility*, Fireside, New York.

Fenwick, Elizabeth and Smith, Dr. Tony, (1994). *Adolescence – The Survival Guide for Parents and Teenagers*, London.

Fisher, Robert, (1999). *Head Start – How to Develop Your Child's Mind*, Souvenir Press Ltd, London.

Gaffney, Maureen, et. al, (1991). *Parenting: A Handbook for Parents*, Town House, UK.

Hamid, AbdulWahid (1995). *Companions of the Prophet*, MELS, Leicester.

Haralambos and Holborn Sociology, (1995, 4th Ed). *Sociology: Themes and Perspectives*, Harper Collins, London.

Hammudah Abd al-Ati, (1977). *The Family Structure in Islam*, American Trust Publication.

Hartley-Brewer, Elizabeth (1998). *Motivating Your Child: Tools and Tactics to Help Your Child be a Self-starter*, Vermilion, London.

Hasan, Suhaib (1998). *Raising Children in Islam*, Al-Qur'an Society, London.

Haykal, M. H. (1976). *The Life of Muhammad* ﷺ, American Trust Publication, Indianapolis, USA.

Hofmann, Murad Wilfried (2001). *Journey to Islam: Diary of a German Diplomat (19501-2000)*, The Islamic Foundation, Leicester.

Huda-al-Khattab, (1997). *Bent Rib: A Journey Through Women's Issue in Islam*, Ta-Ha Publishers, London.

Huntington, Samuel P (1997). *The Clash of Civilisations and the Remaking of World Order*, Touchstone, New York.

Huskins, John, (2000). *From Disaffection to Social Inclusion: A Social Skills Preparation for Active Citizenship and Employment*, UK.

Imam Ghazzali, (1991). *Ihya Ulum-id-din*, Book II, New Delhi.

Joslin, Karen R, (1994). *The Parent's Problem Solver: Practical Solutions to over 140 Childhood problems*, Vermilion, London.

Klein Mavis and Piatkus Judy, (1991). *Understanding Your Child: An A-Z for Parents*, Piatkus Ltd, London.

Lang, Jeffrey (1997). *Even Angels Ask – A Journey to Islam in America*,

Lang, Jeffrey (1994). *Struggling to Surrender*, Amana Publications, USA.

Lemu, Aisha and Hereen, Fatima (1978). *Women in Islam*, The Islamic Foundation, Leicester.

Maqsood, Ruqaiyyah Waris (1995). *Living with Teenagers: A Guide for Muslim Parents*, Ta-Ha Publishers, London.

Maudoodi, Sayyid, Abul A'la (1982). *Let us be Muslims*, Edited by Khurram Murad, The Islamic Foundation, Leicester.

Bibliography

Maudoodi, Sayyid, Abul A'la (1995). *Towards Understanding Islam,* The Islamic Foundation, Leicester.

Maudoodi, Sayyid, Abul A'la (1991). *The Islamic Movement: Dynamics of Values, Power and Change,* Edited by Khurram Murad, The Islamic Foundation, Leicester.

Murad, Khurram (1986). *Da'wah among Non-Muslims in the West,* The Islamic Foundation, Leicester.

Murad, Khurram (2000). *In the Early Hours: Reflections on Spiritual and Self Development,* Revival Publications, the UK.

Muslim, Imam, *Sahih Muslim,* Translated by Abdul Hamid Siddiqi (1990). Ashraf Islamic Publishers, Lahore.

Muslim Students' Association, (1976). *Parents' manual: A Guide for Muslim parents Living in North America,* American Trust Publications, USA.

An-Nawawi, Imam (1998). *Riyad-us-Saleheen,* Islamic Book Service, Delhi.

Pickthall, Muhammad Marmaduke, *The Meaning of the Glorious Qur'an: Text and Explanatory Translation,* New American Library.

Policy Studies Institute, (1997). *Ethnic Minorities in Britain: Diversity and Disadvantage,* (The Fourth National survey of Ethnic Minorities), London.

Rahman, Afzalur (1986). *Role of Muslim Woman in Society,* Seerah Foundation, London.

Ramadan, Tariq (1999). *To be a European Muslim,* The Islamic Foundation, Leicester.

Reason, Rea and Boote, Rene (1994). *Helping Children with Reading and Spelling: A Special Needs Manual,* Routledge, London.

Sabiq, As-Sayyid (1404AH). *Fiqh-us-Sunnah,* Dar El Fateh for Arab Information, Plainfield, Indiana.

Sarwar, G (1996). *Sex Education: The Muslim Perspective,* The Muslim Educational Trust, London.

Sarwar, G (2001). *Islamic Education: Its Meaning, Problems and Prospects,* The Muslim Educational Trust, London.

At-Tirmidhi, Imam. *Shamaa-il Tirmidhi* (2001). Darul Ishaat, Karachi.

Wali Muhammad, Matina (1994). *Stories: Good and True for Children* (translated), Ta-Ha Publishers, London.

West, Sylvia (1993). *Educational Values for School Leadership*, Kogan Page.

Yusuf Ali, Abdullah (1997) *The Holy Qur'an*, Islamic Book Service, Delhi.

Glossary of Islamic Terms

Adab	Good manners, etiquette, custom. In Islam it has ethical and social implications. It includes the meaning of civility, courtesy and refinement.
Adhan	Call to prayer uttered loudly summoning Muslims to pray together behind the imam in the mosque.
'Adl	Justice, fairness, equilibrium and equity. A fundamental value governing social behaviour, dealings and the legal framework.
Allah	Creator and Sustainer of all. This Arabic word is unique. It has no feminine and no plural. No other word, in any language, carries the meaning of 'Allah'.
Ahl al-Kitab	People of the Book, i.e. those people who received an authentic revelation before Islam, meaning the Jews and Christians. The judgement has been extended to some degree to other religions. People of the Book may live under the governance of Islam by their own revelations and laws, under certain conditions.
Akhirah	Hereafter. The Day of Judgement and the life after death. One of the articles of faith in Islam.
ﷺ 'alaihi's-s-salam	May Allah's peace be upon him.
Amanah	Trust. Something given to someone for safekeeping. The human being undertook The Trust offered by Allah, and if true to that trust he is said to have *iman*.
Amir	Leader, lit.: 'commander'. A term applied both to the Caliph and to subsidiary and other leaders in general.

Ansar	Lit.: helpers. In specific meaning, companions of Prophet Muhammad ﷺ in Madinah who helped the Prophet ﷺ and his companions when they migrated from Makkah to Madinah.
'Aqiqah	Sacrifice of an animal and feeding people from its meat out of joy and gratitude at the birth of a baby.
'Asabiyyah	Tribal loyalty and the whole complex of relationships to be found in natural peoples because of their kin structures. Where people put it and the needs of their group or clan ahead of the deen of Allah and the needs of the whole community it becomes a blameworthy concept.
As-salamu 'alaikum	The Islamic greeting, 'Peace be upon you'.
Awqaf (sing. Waqf)	A trusteeship. Endowment. An inalienable property whose ownership is returned to Allah and whose use is dedicated to some purpose usually of a charitable nature. Most of the social welfare of the Muslims was taken care of by means of *awqaf*, and in the nineteenth century as much as two-thirds of Ottoman land and property was in the form of such charitable endowments.
Ayat (sing. ayah)	Verses of the Qur'an. It literally means a sign or an indication, and also means a miracle.
Caliph/Khalifah	The leader of the Muslim ummah.
Da'wah	Invitation, call. Refers to the duty of Muslims to invite others to submission to Allah and the natural path of Islam.
Deen	The life-transaction. More than 'religion' since it encompasses all aspects of life including buying and selling, and the governance of the Muslims.
Du'a	Supplication to Allah.
Dunya	The present world. It stems from a root which means *lower* or *nearer*.
'Eid	Celebration. Eid al-Fitr is the celebration upon con-

clusion of the month of fasting and 'Eid al-Adha is the celebration of sacrifice upon conclusion of the Hajj.

Fajr   Dawn. The very first light at the end of the night.

Fiqh   Islamic jurisprudence, from a verb which means 'to understand'.

Fitrah   Nature, natural condition of the human being.

Hadith (pl. Ahadith) Literally, an account. Accounts of the sayings, deeds and tacit approvals of the Messenger of Allah ﷺ.

Hadith Qudsi   Sayings of Prophet Muhammad ﷺ in which he quotes the words of Allah, when he mentioned 'Allah has said ...'. It is distinct from the Qur'an which is the words of Allah sent by the medium of the angel Jibril ﷿.

Hafidh (pl. Huffadh) A Muslim who memorises the whole Qur'an by heart. Among Muslim scholars it is furthermore taken to refer to someone who having memorised the Qur'an has also committed to memory substantial numbers of ahadith.

Hajj   Pilgrimage. Once in a lifetime journey of a physically and economically capable adult Muslim to Makkah. Elements in it stem from the time of Adam ﷿, and from the sacrifice of the prophet Ibrahim ﷿.

Halal   Permissible. Lawful. Anything permitted by Islamic Shari'ah.

Haram   Unlawful. Anything prohibited by the Shari'ah.

Hayah   Modesty, shame.

Hijab   Modest dress worn by a Muslim woman, and in particular that which covers her hair.

Hilf al-Fudhul   A welfare organisation during the youth and pre-prophetic period of the life of the Prophet Muhammad ﷺ to serve people in need, and to see that justice was done in the society.

'Ibadah   Worship, obedience to Allah.

Iblis	A member of the unseen Jinn, who fell from grace and became cursed because of his refusal to submit to Adam, and because of his disobedience and arrogance. From him have come many *shayatin* (pl. of *shaytan*) among both the Jinn and mankind.
Ijtihad	Exertion of independent judgement in light of Islamic guidance and authentic knowledge. It is the disciplined use of reasoning to draw a necessary conclusion in accordance with both the law and the spirit of Islam. It may only be exercised by a competent exponent of Fiqh whose excellence is universally acknowledged by other scholars and who, some hold, is authorised by the Caliph or a Sultan to do so.
'Ilm	Knowledge. In Islam this includes empirical as well as legal knowledge of the Shari'ah and transcendental knowledge, and in fact means unqualified knowledge.
Imam	Today it means a person who leads congregational prayers. Also a reputable scholar but, in its original meaning, the leader of the Muslim community.
Iman	Belief in and affirmation of the articles of iman enunciated in the Qur'an and the Sunnah: i.e. belief in Allah, His Messengers, His Books, His angels, the Last Day and that the Decree of good and evil is from Him. Iman, which can increase or decrease, is the doorway to Islam.
Islam	Literally to submit and to offer peace. Life-transaction (see Deen) of submission to the will of Allah, expounded by all the prophets.
Istikharah	Special prayer intended to ask for an indication or guidance from Allah when taking a difficult decision as to which choice is likely to be of benefit.
Jahiliyyah	Ignorance (of divine guidance). Refers to the later part of the period between prophet 'Isa (Jesus) ﷺ and the Messenger of Allah ﷺ when people forgot the teachings of the prophets.

Jihad	Literally, to struggle, to make effort. Striving to create a just society which worships Allah. It also means armed struggle. It must be for the sake of Allah. It also includes one's continuous effort to shun one's selfish whims, desires and appetites.
Ka'bah	Literally, cube. The cube-shaped building in Makkah built by the prophet Ibrahim ﷺ and his son Isma'il ﷺ, as the first house for the worship of Allah. Said to have been originally built at the time of Adam ﷺ. The direction all Muslims face when praying, and the locus to which they gravitate when performing the 'Umrah or Hajj.
Kalimah	Literally, word, and sometimes intending the phrase, "There is no god but Allah, Muhammad is Allah's Messenger", the conscious uttering of which makes someone a Muslim.
Khidmah	Service, working for the welfare of human beings.
Khul'	The process through which a Muslim woman obtains a divorce from her husband through an Islamic court. If a Muslim woman finds that she is simply incompatible with her husband, she may offer to return some or all of her dowry or in some other manner to compensate him, and thus obtain a divorce.
Madrasah	School, but traditionally a school for study of the deen.
Mahr	Dower, a compulsory due (cash or kind) to a bride from the groom according to his financial ability.
Mahram	Blood relation with whom marriage is forbidden. *Ghair Mahram* is someone who does not fall into the category of Mahram.
Masnun	From the Sunnah. There are specific *Masnun Du'a* for specific occasions.
Muhajir (pl. Muhajirun)	Literally, an emigrant. The early Muslims who migrated to Madinah from Makkah with the

Prophet ﷺ in order to be able to practise the deen without fear, and to escape from persecution.

Mujahid	Related to the word Jihad. One who strives for the cause of Allah.
Murabbi	One who undertakes another's upbringing, whether as a parent or as teacher or instructor in later life.
Muslim	A believer who willingly submits to Allah alone and practises Islam.
Nafsaniat	Whims and desires of the *nafs*–self that lead a human being toward wrongdoing. Among the most obstinate and dangerous of such traits are the subtle desires of a person to be recognised and respected in the community.
Nasheed	Islamic song, meaningful and instructional in content and comprising *dhikr*-remembrance of Allah and asking blessings on the Messenger of Allah ﷺ.
Nifaq	Hypocrisy, two-facedness and double standards which are deplorable in Islam. Originally it signified in its major form someone who insincerely accepted Islam. According to a hadith, the signs of Nifaq are – lying, breaking promises, and abuse or misuse of trust.
Nikah	Marriage according to a simple Islamic contract.
Qist	Similar to 'Adl. Justice, fairness, equilibrium and equity. A fundamental value governing social behaviour, dealings and legal framework.
Qur'an	The final Book and revelation from Allah to mankind, revealed to the Prophet Muhammad ﷺ over a span of 23 years.
ؓ Radi'Allahu 'anhu (Fem. Radi'Allahu 'anha, pl. ؓ Radi'Allahu 'anhum). May Allah be pleased with him/her/them.	
Rahmah	Mercy.
Ramadan	The 9th month of the Islamic calendar during which Muslims fast from dawn to sunset.

Risalah	The Message, the revelation and the shari'ah itself, and the concept that Allah sent prophets to human beings to guide them. One of the articles of faith in Islam.
Ruh	Spirit.
Ruku'	Bowing. The specific physical posture during the daily prayers.
Sabr	Steadfastness. The word has a wider and more positive meaning in Islam than simple patient endurance of suffering.
Sahabah	Companions of the Prophet Muhammad ﷺ during his lifetime. There are many hadith that indicate they were the best of all generations of humanity.
Sahih	Literally 'sound'. A hadith whose chain of narrators are each authentic in their beliefs, characters, scholarship and memories and who each have received it directly from the previous such narrator in the chain of transmission which connects directly back to the Messenger of Allah ﷺ. Higher than it in status is the *Mutawatir* hadith which is transmitted by so many different chains of narration that there can be no possible doubt about its authenticity.
Sajdah	Prostration. The specific physical posture during the daily prayers.
Sakinah	Tranquillity of mind that comes due to the blessings of Allah
Sayyiduna	Our master. A term of respect.
Sirah	The biography of the Messenger of Allah ﷺ from authentic sources.
Shari'ah	Derived from a work meaning 'a road' particularly one leading to water in the desert. Used to mean Islam's legal system and the rules by which Muslims abide.
Shahadah	Literally, witnessing. Declaration of the acceptance of Islam.

Sunnah	pl. Sunan. Literally, a custom or practice. The body of practices of the Prophet Muhammad ﷺ. It also includes the practice established by the rightly guided first four Caliphs. It is sometimes mistakenly assumed to be synonymous with hadith.
Surah	Chapter of the Qur'an. There are 114 Surah, some of which are very long and others short.
Taharah	Cleanliness that entails bodily and ritual purity.
Tajdid	Revival, enlivening.
Talaq	Divorce initiated by men. There are Shari'ah requirements for it.
Taqwa	Fear or consciousness of Allah that leads to abandonment of wrong action and embodiment of right action. It is both an inner feeling of a human being towards the Creator and the effects of that upon his actions.
Tarbiyah	Nurturing, training. Physical, moral, intellectual and spiritual development. The modern Arabic term for education. The person who undertakes such instruction is a Murabbi.
Tawakkul	Reliance on Allah. It gives mental tranquillity.
Tawhid	The concept of the absolute Oneness of Allah. The fundamental article of faith in Islam.
Tazkiyah	Purification. Growth.
'Ulama (sing. 'Alim)	People of knowledge. The term has wrongly become confined to religious scholars.
Ummah	Community of believers worldwide, irrespective of race, colour, language or geographical boundary. The universal body of Muslims as a single community, properly when living by the Shari'ah and living under the governance of Islamic rulers.
Umm al-Mu'minin	Mother of the believers (a name for each of the Prophet Muhammad's wives)

'Umrah   Lesser pilgrimage to Makkah with specific rites.

Zakah   The compulsory yearly due payable by a wealthy Muslim, as a part of his obligation, mainly for the benefit of the poor and the needy. Its amount is 2.5% on his cash and on the proceeds of business, 10% or 20% of crops, and specific proportions of cattle, the cash to be paid in gold and silver, and the other categories to be paid in kind to the authorised zakat collectors of an Amir who may, if necessary, take it by force. This pillar is wrongly thought to be an act of personal charity left to the conscious of the individual Muslim.